Pens, Plows, & Gunpowder

The Collected Works of J.P. Irvine

Edited by Dustin Renwick

Copyright © 2017 Dustin Renwick.

All rights reserved. Printed in the United States.

ISBN: 0-9976265-2-6
ISBN-13: 978-0-9976265-2-0

Published by Fleetwing Books.
www.fleetwingbooks.com

Cover design by Cara Willenbrock.

Other Books By This Author

Beyond the Gray Leaf: The Life and Poems of J.P. Irvine

CONTENTS

Introduction 1

Notes 5

1855-1859 9

1860-1869 27

1870-1879 155

1880-1889 265

1890-1892 349

Index 407

ACKNOWLEDGMENTS

Thank you to:

Rick Sayre, Monmouth College Hewes Library; Lynne Devlin, Warren County Illinois Genealogical Society; Kathy Nichols, Western Illinois University Leslie F. Malpass Library; Zoe Norwood and Jean Lythgoe, Rockford Public Library.

The staffs at the Abraham Lincoln Presidential Library and Museum; American Antiquarian Society; District of Columbia Public Library Special Collections Department; Henderson County Public Library (IL); Indiana State Library; Library of Congress; Special Collections and College Archives at Gettysburg College; Special Collections Research Center at George Washington University; Warren County Public Library (IL); and Wisconsin Historical Society.

University of Illinois at Urbana-Champaign's Illinois Newspaper Project. This book would suffer from more holes without the team's work digitizing the historical newspapers in the state.

The Maple City Writers Retreat.

INTRODUCTION

"This I hold to be the chief office of history, to rescue virtuous actions from the oblivion to which the want of records would consign them..."
—Tacitus

J.P. Irvine earns the distinction of being the most forgotten Midwestern poet in the 19th century. He performed his noteworthy piece, "Unknown," at the 1873 Memorial Day ceremonies in front of President Ulysses S. Grant and a crowd of 10,000. Today, the few people who had heard of Irvine considered those words lost until I found, transcribed, and included them in *Beyond the Gray Leaf: The Life and Poems of J.P. Irvine*.

Born in 1835, Irvine published most of his work in Illinois newspapers, with a handful of exceptions in national literary magazines. His only book, *The Green Leaf and the Gray*, arrived in 1891. The author died the next year.

I left out nearly 100 poems and letters when I wrote his biography, and my transcriptions sat idle on my computer. His words had simply swapped hidden locations, from microfilm to my hard drive. This book changes that for the best. Every published piece by Irvine that I encountered in my research is printed in the following pages. Academics interested in 19th-century American poetry, particularly that of the Middle West, have everything they need regarding this writer. Plus, anyone who read my first book and wanted to witness Irvine's full range and repertoire will find it here, from the average to the incredible.

Originally, I'd planned to call this the "complete works," but that would not have portrayed this book with total accuracy. The Notes section details a handful of poems and speeches for which I have descriptions or titles but no text. Plus, gaps in newspaper microfilm records mean some of his pieces have almost certainly vanished forever. Even the poems and letters I collected aren't all whole. Irvine's words blurred into obscurity or were altogether absent due to the condition of the newspapers, some of which dated to more than 160 years ago. In these cases, you'll find [illegible] in place of text I couldn't decipher.

In the ideal scenario, his family would have cataloged his writings after his death and left a handy index and full transcripts. Those and any other personal papers, including his diary, have yet to turn up. I constructed five guesses as to their potential location in *Beyond the Gray Leaf*, but any family documents have likely disappeared into the dustbin history so faithfully keeps, as Tacitus reminds us.

A trove of personal papers could show Irvine's thought processes, revisions, and unpublished works.

Yet without such a record, we still have insights because of his published alterations. Several poems appeared in different versions with months and years between. His published changes appear in this book in <*italics*>. Irvine also pulled apart longer poems to create shorter, separate pieces or mixed stanzas of shorter poems into longer works. Additional information like this carries my [— Ed.] mark.

These attributable palimpsests catalog his approaches in a semblance of what we might find in a stack of papers on his desk. For now, such shadows are what's available.

— Dustin Renwick, editor

NOTES

No. 1
"Every element in a poem — every word, line break, stanza pattern, indentation, even all punctuation — potentially carries expressive meaning," wrote Dana Gioia, poet and former chair of the National Endowment for the Arts. I balanced Gioia's truth with the reality of physical page space. Irvine tended to separate his stanzas with Roman numerals, even in poems as short as two stanzas. I eliminated these in all but the longer works or complex pieces that benefit from such organization. I also corrected spelling errors, but I did not alter Irvine's use of dialects or British forms.

No. 2
This book presents Irvine's works in chronological order by first publication date and coded with the following abbreviations.

AD: The Advance
AX: The Annex

BF: Belford's
CA: The Capital
CH: Chicago Daily Tribune
CY: The Century
DG: The Daily Graphic
DR: The Daily Review
ES: The Evening Star
GL: The Green Leaf and the Gray
HH: Hearth and Home
HC: Henderson County Journal
HP: Harper's
MA: The Monmouth Atlas
MR: The Monmouth Review
PG: U.S. Pension Record and Departmental Gazette
RR: Rockford Register
SB: Scribner's
TR: The Travelers Record
WC: Winnebago County Chief
WO: Wild Oats

No. 3

I've found only mentions of the following works. Without full texts to verify, the unnamed pieces in the list might represent additions or, conversely, published writing already included in this book.

Untitled project about the editors and journalists of Washington, D.C.
Summer 1873

Poem read at Horatio King's Literary Reunion in

Washington, D.C.
Spring 1874

Poem read at Arlington National Cemetery
May 30, 1874

A series of "Street Ballads" published in New York City's *The Daily Graphic*
Spring 1875

A book of ballads illustrated by Eustace J. Collett and Alfred Downing
Fall 1875

"Plymouth by the Sea" read at a New England Society social event in Washington, D.C.
Dec. 21, 1876

Poem read at the 36th Illinois Infantry reunion in Chicago
September 1884

Speeches at the annual gatherings of the Old Settlers Association of Warren and Henderson Counties (IL)
Sept. 4, 1890 and Aug. 12, 1891

"Quatrains of the Months and Seasons"
Fall 1892

Long poem unfinished at his death
Fall 1892

1855-1859

AN ADDRESS TO RELIGION
MA Aug. 3, 1855

Oh, who can tell thy noble worth,
Or cast an eye of shame,
At thee, thou Angel of this Earth,
Whose laws in Heaven doth reign?

Thou rid'st upon the Cherub's wings,
Where holy angels stand,
And sends through Heaven's fleeting winds
The Almighty's strict command.

The smiles of holiness repose
With Truth, thy sister dear,
Upon thy brow, which doth disclose
The secrets of our fear.

Enwreathed upon thy beauteous breast,
And on thy head divine,
Are words of truth and righteousness,

Which guide the Christian mind.

Should man not go to thee and learn
How he his ways should guide?
Should he not learn how to discern
How thou on wings doth ride?

Teach me thy pure unblemished law,
Stamp wisdom on my heart,
And I will ne'er break nor flaw,
Nor from thy truths depart.

Linden [later Young America, later Kirkwood — Ed.]

Winter
MR Jan. 11, 1856

Dreary Winter's come at last,
From out the cold and northern blast,
Swaying a despotic reign
O'er nature's ever changing frame.
Ah! see that tall and sturdy oak,
Stripped of her green and verdured cloak.
Behold the grove that stood so proud,
Now mantled in a snowy shroud.
Review the place where once the bower
Displayed the loved and brilliant flower;
And where the weary maidens chose
The mossy seat for sweet repose.

But lo! the storm and wintry blast
Have left those beauties with the past,
And laid their spiral visage low,
Beneath a dim and dismal snow.
The merry songsters all have flown
To southern climes and parts unknown,
And left us in this wintry state,
Without one charm to celebrate.

Washington [Iowa — Ed.]

Twilight
MR July 4, 1856

Now the burning sun has gone,
His torrid rays have fled,
And gently o'er the wood and lawn,
Are robes of twilight spread.

All nature rests in sweet repose,
From one more toiling hour;
The dew-drops lightly tint the rose,
And tinge the woodland flower.

The modest moon, that floats on high,
Sends down a silvery ray —
The golden stars that gem the sky,
Smile on the leafy spray.

Day's sounds of toil are hushed and still,
Men wearied, calmly rest,
Whilst sweetly sings the whippoor-will,
The lone and nightly guest.

A zephyr floats in silence by,
But ripples not the stream,
Which mirrors true the azure sky,
And her nocturnal Queen.

How sweet the honey dew distills
Upon the leafy bower;
The clover bloom with nectar fills,
Amidst this silent hour.

Thus twilight brings an hour of rest,
And sheds her fragrance round,
And leaves a proof divinely blessed,
That heavenly gifts abound.

It proves His power and works divine,
Which cloud all human art,
And teaches poor and frail mankind,
Of love he doth impart.

Washington, Iowa

My Homestead
MR Oct. 22, 1858

My homestead, dear, thou art no more
To me as when in days of yore,
And sadness stealeth o'er my heart
To think that we are doomed to part,
O, let the silent tear but tell,
And breathe the word farewell, farewell!
Here perfumed rose and hawthorn sweet,
With dew drops trembled at my feet;
Then glimmering in the sunny ray,
Then pending drops soon passed away,
The woodbine clustered 'round the door,
With glittering gems all studded o'er,
Reflecting color from the sky,
Like Tibet's springs of varied dye.
'Twas here at morn and eve we knelt,
'Twas here a father's prayer was felt,
'Twas here the penitential tear
Was shed to feel a Saviour near.
'Twas here death's angel gloomed the morn —
We wept to feel our sire had gone.
Me thought bright seraphs hovered nigh
To bear his spirit to the sky,
Where the limpid waters flow
From the melting founts of snow.
Far in that realm of beauty bright
Methinks I see his form of light.
The many ties that bind me here
Are mirrored by affection's tear.

In memory's wreath thy name I'll trace,
Ne'er dimmed 'twill be by time or place —
One bright oasis thou will be
On life's cold dull monotony
And oft will childhood's happy day
Return to soothe life's weary way.

THE STORM OF ELLISON
MR JUNE 3, 1859

ONE YEAR AGO TO-DAY, MAY 30TH

In annual rounds the seasons call
Their past events to mind,
Though rolling on with innate speed,
A record's left behind.
Come read, come read the record of
One year ago to-day;
Go see the ruins of the storm
That passed in queenly May.

It came — and she was clad as now,
In robes of vernal fair,
As Sabbath crowned her regal crest,
And shed her lustre there.
It came amidst the peaceful hour,
Fleet as an angry foe,
Or swiftly as Aquila's dart
Upon her prey below.

The halo of the sun had fled,
And darkness veiled his form.
His crown was sable — King of death,
And death the king of storm.
His cloud was dark, and thunder charged,
And fraught with vengeful ire,
Whilst from its folds there issued forth
Eclectic streams of fire.

His chariot was the whirlwind fierce,
His steeds the lightning sharp;
His music was the thunder's voice,
His spear the thunder's dart.
He came swift as the lion's bound,
In horror, death, despair,
Then passed as doth the conqueror,
And left his carnage there.

The scenes, the scenes he left behind,
Might blush the battle-field;
It but portrays the wrath of man,
But this of God revealed.
Would the battle-field not blush,
To hear the little child
Call its dying mother home,
In wailings deep and wild?

It ne'er has seen the lover wail
The blasted marriage vow,
Nor wipe the damp of death from off
His dying maiden's brow;

While mother wraps the winding sheet
Around her pulseless form,
Then leaves to meet her child no more,
Until the judgment morn.

Should not it mourn for homeless ones,
Whose tattered garments lay
'Midst naked forms and shattered limbs,
All mixed with blood and clay.
Would not the warrior, stout and brave,
Throw off his waving plume,
And pour the tear of pity forth,
And sorrow o'er their tomb?

Will not the years in fleeting by
A cypress wreath entwine?
Will each returning spring not call
That sad event to mind?
Yes, each successive May will sigh
Thy ruins deeply o'er,
And mourn for thee, oh Ellison,
'Till seasons pass no more.

Monmouth

The Plow, the Anvil and Loom
MR June 10, 1859

You may sing of the honor and titles of fame

The sword, the sceptre and crown
You may talk of that phantom that spell all a name
Of wealth, of distinction, renown.
Why go to the field of the warrior to glean,
Why to the sceptre and plume?
Why not let us sing of a nobler theme
Of the Plow, the Anvil and Loom.

The sceptre of monarchy and warriors' swords
Are held by an absolute hand
But friends, industrious, honest, and true,
Our God and our country demand
Then hail to the weaver, the farmer, and smith
Let their toils produce [illegible]
Be the union of hearts and the union of hands
With the Plow, the Anvil and Loom.

Washington followed the rustic old Plow,
The Anvil knew Burritt, the learned;
The Loom was the seat of Simpson, I vow,
The shuttle spool often he turned
Then health to industry, the poor man's gold,
A wealth we all may assume,
If we roll up our sleeves and proudly lay hold
Of the Plow, the Anvil and Loom.

Let the Plow take the place of the cannon and shield,
The Anvil the throne of the king,
Let the Plow turn the sod on the battle's red field,
And strokes from the Anvil loud ring.
Let the pelth from the hand of the weaver be heard,

From night, from morning till noon;
May the heart of each one with industry be stirred,
By the Plow, the Anvil and Loom.

Monmouth

THE MANIAC'S GRAVE
MR Aug. 29, 1859; <MA July 27, 1860>

[The 1860 version contained enough changes to warrant a separate entry in full. It was published with Irvine's name, but the 1859 version only listed a printer's mark of three unfilled dots arranged in an inverted pyramid. Either he plagiarized the text, or the pyramid is something of a pseudonym for Irvine. The same mark appeared on three other pieces I have attributed to him, indicated by a + symbol in the index. — Ed.]

In the midst of a dense forest, in the southern portion of Oregon, there is a lone grave, situated near a beautiful little streamlet. This grave is supposed to be the resting place of a young lady who died from the effects of insanity occasioned by the death of her lover. The rippling of the streamlet is said to resemble the language of a human telling of her melancholy fate.

In a woodland, deep and darksome,
Sleeps a rustic, blue-eyed maid;
All is dreary, wild, and lonely —

All assumes a deathly shade.
Through this woodland flows a streamlet,
Flows a streamlet's silvery tide —
Babbling forth its murmuring language
To the great Pacific's side.

Always are its limpid wavelets
Rippling on through shade and sun;
Ceaseless — ceaseless, is its language,
Telling of this sleeping one.
"Time has fleeted swiftly onward,
Onward, with a fearless prow —
Since her face my waters mirrored,
Since they bathed her fevered brow.

'Twas then she told me of a river,
Colder than the Arctic's breath,
Calling it the stream of Jordan,
Calling it the tide of death."
O'er this river has crossed her lover —
Victor of her youthful heart —
He, in crossing, stole her reason,
She into this forest dark.

Ever constant were her wailings,
For this lover, kind and true —
Ever ceaseless were her murmurings,
Ever rolled her eyes of blue.
Ah! they wore a mournful sadness,
Like the dreary wild-wood deep,
Of, the fading day of autumn,

Sinking into languid sleep.

But there came a guardian Angel,
Borne on pinions decked with gold,
Fringed with blue and silvered plumage,
From beyond the starry hold;
Came he from the hand of promise,
From the hand that tints the bow,
Paints the modest blush of morning,
Paints the sun's meridian glow.

In his hand he held this maiden,
Held her spirit — held her breath;
Bore her spirit, o'er the river,
Left her in the shades of death,
Drops the foliage of the willow,
To return with vernal bloom,
But the cord that bound her reason,
Dropped to build a maniac's tomb.

Here the maiden sweetly slumbers,
Slumbers near the babbling stream,
Babbling forth its rippling language,
Ceaseless as the noon-tide's beam.
Here she rests from all her sorrow,
All that stings and throbs is o'er;
Here the sleep that knows no waking,
Bars the grave's eternal door.

Monmouth

<1860 version, same intro>

In a woodland, deep and darksome,
Sleeps a rustic, blue-eyed maid;
All is dreary, wild, and lonely —
All assumes a deathly shade.
Whilst the dove, a drear companion.
Pipes a sad and mournful sound,
Floating in a doleful murmur
On the dreary wildness round.

Through this woodland flows a streamlet,
With a clear and silver tide,
Babbling forth its murmuring language
To the great Pacific's side;
Always are its limpid wavelets
Rippling on through shade and sun;
Ceaseless its mysterious language,
Telling of this sleeping one.

"Time has wrought his magic changes
In the heart and on the brow,
Since along my banks she wandered
Murmuring just as I am now;
Then she told me of a river,
Colder than the Arctic's breath,
Calling it the stream of Jordan,
Calling it the tide of death."

O'er this river has crossed her lover
To the golden shores beyond,

Where the harps attuned in music
To his angel song respond;
But that crossing stole her reason,
As a chill autumnal day
Steals the fragrance of the lily
And assigns it to decay.

Long she wandered through this wild-wood,
Wailing for this lover true,
Ever ceaseless were her murmurings —
Ever rolled her eyes of blue;
Ah! they wore a dreamy sadness,
Mantled in a sorrow deep,
Like a drowsy day in summer
Sinking into languid sleep.

But there came a guardian Angel,
Borne on pinions decked with gold,
Fringed and tipped with silvered plumage,
From beyond the starry hold;
Came he from the land of promise,
From the hand that tints the bow,
Paints the modest blush of morning,
Paints the sun's meridian glow.

In his hand he held this maiden,
Held her spirit — held her breath,
Bore her gently o'er the river,
Left her in the shades of death;
Drops the foliage of the willow,
To return with vernal bloom,

But the cord that bound her reason,
Dropped to build a maniac's tomb.

And now this maiden sweetly slumbers,
Near this lone mysterious stream,
Babbling forth in rippling numbers,
Ceaseless as the noontide's beam;
Here she rests from all her sorrow,
All that stings and throbs is o'er,
Here the sleep that knows no waking,
Bars the grave's eternal door.

THE OFFICE CALENDAR
MR Sept. 6, 1859

Just seven, twelve, and thirty-one,
Are the figures and the cards of the Calendar,
To be shuffled — to be shuffled
At each returning sun,
To aggregate the days —
The flitting — flitting days,
By the score, by the ten, and by the integer.
And thus, another month has gone!
(Go change the Calendar.)
Go, change it for a shorter month,
By leaving out the integer.
Thus, for the year's division,
We'll sing a merry chime;
For the future make provision

By the shuffling — and the shuffling,
And the changing — and the changing
Of the Calendar — the Calendar,
The monitor of Time.

Yes, seven, twelve, and thirty-one,
Are the cards that compose the office Calendar;
And they are thus divided — thus divided
To mark the time we run,
So that each may understand —
May quickly understand —
How his days are fleeting by the shuffled monitor.
'Tis strange! yes, very strange,
That in the shuffling o'er this Calendar,
We never mark the change —
Minus just the integer.
Then, for this month's division
We'll sing no merry chime;
For the future make provision,
By the shuffling — by the shuffling
And the changing — and the changing
Of the Calendar — the Calendar,
The monitor of Time.

The seven, twelve, and thirty-one,
Are the days, the weeks, and months of the Calendar.
The seven make the weeks, make the weeks,
And seven times the round of the sun;
And the twelve are the moons —
The transient silver moons —
The twelve centre cards of the Calendar.

But hold! another year has passed!
Go, change the Calendar;
Time cannot always last —
Oh, had I but watched the monitor.
Then, for this year's division
We'll sing no merry chime;
For the future make provision,
By the shuffling — by the shuffling
And the changing — and the changing
Of the Calendar — the Calendar,
The monitor of Time.

Oh, the seven, twelve, and thirty-one,
Are the figures and the cards of the Calendar;
To be shuffled — to be shuffled
At each returning sun,
To aggregate the days —
The flitting, flitting days —
Which build a sable bier to bear us to the grave.
And thus our days are fleeting on,
And shuffling life away!
And thus we sigh for all that's past,
And strive to grasp the coming day.
Then for our life's division,
We'll sing no merry chime;
For the future make provision,
By the shuffling — by the shuffling
And the changing — and the changing
Of the Calendar — the Calendar,
The monitor of Time.

1860-1869

THE SLAVE'S LAMENTATION
MA APR. 6, 1860

An aged slave lamenting,
And crowned with locks of snow,
Came wandering from a planter's field
With palsied steps and slow;
And the sun was setting golden —
Setting golden in the west —
And the parent bird returning
To her offspring in the nest;
But the poor old man, so weary,
Sat down beneath a tree,
There standing lone and royal,
And wept for liberty.

Full well he spake the language
Of a tutored English tongue,
For long his Afric speech had ceased
Its native course to run;
But an Afric heart was beating —

Beating swiftly, beating time —
With a soul that stung with anguish,
As the conscience for a crime;
For the fetters — for the fetters —
Of a master's stern decree,
With the iron links of bondage
Had chained his liberty.

The soul, the throne of conscience
And the brain and heart akin,
Were the promptings of a [illegible]
That dwelt his frame within;
It told his ear to listen
To the freeman's joyous song,
And his eye to watch the banner
With the stars and stripes thereon;
To mark the independent,
The glorious and the free,
The heart and hand of union,
The strength of liberty.

How the eagle free on mountain
Unfurls his daring wing,
And soars to meet the thunder cloud
To bathe his plumage in;
How he darts along the valley
And around the woodland side,
And through the hazy distance
In all his kingly pride;
Through the hazy distance
And o'er the rolling sea,

Then upward wheeling greets the sun
In glorious liberty.

On the hill-side sport the lambkins,
And in the meadows play;
They're free — they bear no tyrant's chains,
They feel no master's sway;
Athletic bounds the timid roe
The verdant landscape o'er,
And through the forest broad and deep
That skirts the ocean's shore;
And there beyond the billows leap
And whirl to meet the lea,
And wildly lash the pebbled strand
In sportive liberty.

And while he thus was musing,
The wings of night unfurled,
And golden sank the setting sun
And pulseless lay the world;
But he was still and pulseless
And death's cold mantle wore,
For best it doth befit the one
[illegible]
No golden hue is worn by death
So dark and stern is he,
'Tis only for the king of day
And gems of liberty.

And thus his chains and fetters,
Which he from childhood wore,

Had purchased him a mantle
From the "night's Plutonian shore,"
Which he wears beside the waters
That lash the sable strand;
Now holding strange communion
With the pale and ghostly band;
And near the planter's field
Still remains the royal tree,
Where the aged slave lamenting,
Wept for liberty.

Monmouth, Ill.

Heaven
MA May 4, 1860

"And the gates of it shall not be shut at all by day for there shall be no night there." — Rev. xxi 25

Twelve gates swing on the jasper walls
That skirt the city round,
Twelve precious gates — twelve crystal gates —
Twelve open gates are found,
Three face the north — and three the south,
Beset with costly pearl,
And three the east — and three the west,
Of amethyst and beryl.
And by these flashing gates there stand.
Twelve angels pure and white

The guardians of these jasper walls
Which knoweth not the night,
For none can enter there.

For God, Jehovah, Lord of all!
The Father, Lamb, and Son
The holy King — the righteous King —
The self-omniscient One,
Lights up the streets — the golden streets —
In floods of endless day,
That wears a hue — a brilliant hue —
Which fleeteth not away.
For nothing in that city fades
Nor wears an earthly form
And bask her Angel citizens
In one eternal morn,
For night is never there.

The waters of a river flow
From underneath His throne
In limpid waves — in silver waves —
In crystal waves alone;
And on its shores — its garnished shores —
The tree of life doth stand,
That bears the fruits — the healing fruits —
Of God's almighty hand
The hand which laid the Corner stone
And furled the wings of night
And girdled his pavilion round
With bells of dazzling light
For night is never there.

But oh the turbid waters of
Death's dark and mystic stream
Roll with a tide — a ceaseless tide —
This earth and that between,
This side its shores — its murky shores —
Life's stormy clouds doth lower,
O'er wretched man — vain sinful man —
The insect of an hour;
Who cometh forth a tender plant
And grows in sorrow's vale
Then plunges in that tide of Death
And sinks beneath its gale,
Where night eternal reigns.

Then in the [illegible] and silent grave
He sleeps that last long sleep
That wondrous rest — mysterious rest —
That slumber strange and deep,
Until that morn — that dreadful morn —
That day of vengeful ire,
When shall the Judge in chariots come
Behind his steeds of fire.
Then shall the tomb become unlocked
Unbarred the gates of death
And hurled away the universe
At His almighty breath,
And night from off his throne.

Then countless myriads on his right
Shall plume their angel wings
And pass the gates — the crystal gates —

Beyond terrestrial things;
And walk the streets — the golden streets —
And play the golden harps,
And touch the cords — the silver cords —
That tune their grateful hearts,
For days of sorrow, nights of anguish
Months of mourning, years of pain
Shall have ceased and gone forever —
Gone — and peace and pleasure reign.

Monmouth

THE FARMER
MA May 25, 1860

Hail! Farmer, hail your station high,
I love the hand of honest toil,
Come, yoke the cattle — speed the plow
And turn the rich productive soil;
File the coulter sharp and keen,
Smoothly cut the stubble through,
Straightly guide the oaken beam,
Draw the furrow deep and true.
I love to watch your honest hand
Though clumsy, rough and weather-tanned,
Display its skillful art;
The master of a noble trade,
The highest in superior grade,
The index of the heart.

And now the fields in rustling corn,
In wheat and bearded rye,
In silken ears and yellow tops
Proclaim the harvest nigh;
Aurora peeps — the reaper's out,
The binder comes — they roll their sleeves
And soon their hands bestud the fields
With sturdy shocks of golden sheaves.
Come see, come see his honest hand
Though clumsy, rough and weather-tanned,
Display its skillful art;
The master of a noble trade,
The highest in superior grade,
The index of the heart.

The meadows now in wavy green
And velvet robes inviting, stand
And nod their plumage in the breeze,
Prepared to greet the farmer's hand;
He comes — he whets his glittering scythe,
In measured strokes he cuts his way,
And leaves behind a shaven lawn
And heavy swaths of scented hay.
From year to year his honest hand
Though clumsy, rough and weather-tanned,
Display its skillful art;
The master of a noble trade,
The highest in superior grade,
The index of the heart.
But then I knew a farmer old,
Whose name is Time — he farms the brow;

He draws his furrows down the cheeks
And deeply runs his constant plow;
He ceases not for Winter's storms,
Nor heeds its snows nor chilly breath,
But ceaseless works Old Farmer Time
To fit us for the reaper Death.
Then let us mark his ruthless hand
Though very old and weather-tanned,
Display its magic art;
And be prepared to run and meet
And bow beneath the reaper's feet,
And yield this mortal part.

Because his sickle's sharp and keen,
And daily reaps with giant sway;
It touches, and like withered leaves
We fall and pass unknown away;
If bound in sheaves, he does it not,
If garnered up, 'tis not by him,
He reaps the flowers and bearded grain
But ceases not to gather in.
Then let us mark Time's ruthless hand,
Though very old and weather-tanned,
Display its magic art;
And be prepared to run and meet
And bow beneath the reaper's feet,
And yield this mortal part.

Monmouth

FREEDOM'S EXCELSIOR
MA Aug. 10, 1860

Air — "A wet sheet and a flowing sea."

Throw up the flag of Freedom proud
Against the deep blue sky,
And there unfurl its stripes and stars
Aloft the breeze on high;
Within its folds an angel dwells,
The guardian of the free,
And there foretells the glorious news
Of "Right" and "Victory."

And so the name of Lincoln true,
Before November's by —
With that of noble Hamlin too,
Will be waving far on high.

Oh, see the eagle free and proud
Unfurl his daring wing —
And soar to meet the thunder cloud,
To bathe his plumage in
Oh, see, he knows no tyrant's sway,
Nor chains, nor fettered form,
But sports amid the thunder's home
The lightning — and the storm.

And so the name of Lincoln true,
Before November's by —
With that of noble Hamlin too,

Will be soaring far on high.

Then let the streams of Freedom swell,
And gushing downward flow,
Till all the valleys, hills and dales
Will smile and leap below;
"Free Labor's" name will still remain
Upon the mountain's brow;
Upon the fields of rustling corn,
The sickle, and the plow.

And so the name of Lincoln true,
Before November's by —
With that of noble Hamlin too,
Can be seen in the "Rails" thereby.

Then gird yourselves about with truth,
And arm yourselves with "Right,"
And proudly leave the battle ground,
Triumphant in the fight,
And write the name of "Honest Abe,"
Upon the banner's folds,
Amid the gleaming stripes and stars,
By marking to the "polls."

And so the name of Lincoln true,
Before November's by —
With that of noble Hamlin too,
Will be written far on high.

Monmouth

LOSS OF THE LADY ELGIN
MA SEPT. 28, 1860

In music and mirth she leaves the bright shore,
With the love-smitten hearts of the fair and the brave;
Ah! little reck they of the dangers before,
As boldly she plows through the wrath-hidden wave.
She goes out to meet the storm-monarch's career,
With a tempest-tried prow which has oft felt his breath,
But alas! she knows not how the shadows draw near
From the broad murky wings of the Angel of Death

In the darkness chaotic broods a spirit of ire;
The waters are troubled — Oh, God! from beneath
They rise into billows like mountains of fire
As the lightnings break forth from the cloud's sable wreath
Then the roar of the thunder in grandeur bursts down,
And rolls o'er the deep with a jar and a swell,
Till it shakes the big world from its centre all round,
Then rumbling sinks down to the caverns of hell.

Then a crash! and a shriek! oh, God! she is done,
All shattered she struggles a twain-riven form,
As high o'er her deck the bold white breakers run,
When, alas, she goes down 'mid the roar of the storm!
Why struggle in vain, thou ill-fated crew,
Whey cling to that splinter, why buffet the waves,
See! the deep has sent up its Death Angel for you,
And each must go down to his coral reef'd grave.

With the monarch of storm in his chariot of wrath
He has ridden and conquered, unarmed and alone,
And fleet as the wind o'er his billow-tossed path
He hath gathered them in to an absolute home,
Ye winds and ye waves, cease your stormy career,
Why longer should'st thou in thy fury thus rave,
'Neath your murmur far down in the tomb of the sea,
There you have garnered the fair and the brave.

Monmouth, Ill.

GRANDPA IN THE COTTAGE OF DEATH
MA Nov. 30, 1860

Ah! the letter of silver is broken
And shattered the vessel of gold,
The cedar has withered and fallen
And its years are numbered and told

Away for dominions ethereal —
Dominions celestial and bright,
A soul on the wings of an angel
Has taken its mystical flight

That mystical flight of the spirit,
That wonderful flight of the soul,
Is alone for the cherubs of Heaven,
Alone for the Lord to behold,

'Tis only a thought with the living —
A thought with the feeling sublime,
Which lifts up the heart of the mortal
As the tendril lifts up the vine

An idea linked with the feelings
Whose tendrils encircle the heart,
And realized only when dying,
When the soul is plumed to depart

But list, oh! list to the tempest
As it sweeps by the old cottage walls
Baptizing the ivy and cypress
With tears from the rain as it falls

But within is the wail of no tempest,
Not even a footfall or breath —
'Til changed from the cot of the living
To the sorrowful chamber of death

A heart with the stillness coeval
Is wrapped in an absolute sleep
And the pulse of its ventricle chamber
Has ceased and no longer shall beat

His beard is unshorn and silvered
Though once like the raven and sloe
And his hair disarranged on his temples
Resembles the frost and the snow

His face is pale and distorted

And changed from its manhood and prime,
And plowed into ridges and furrows
By the steady old farmer of time

His eyes are sunken and glassy,
And open half, vacant they stare
Through the lids and wild scattered lashes,
As familiar with sorrow and care.

Ah! the sea has been troubled and stormy,
And his ship by the hurricane's breath
Has been wrecked on the reef and the breakers
Which skirt the dark haven of death

Go make him a shroud of white cambric
Fold the poor withered hands on his breast
Straighten his limbs for the coffin
And lay him in gently to rest.

Come gather around in a circle,
In sorrow bow down the head
Near to the cold clammy features
And take the last look at the dead.

Close up the lids of the coffin,
Dry the tears as they flow like the rain,
Write the scene on the tablet of memory —
Tread away in the funeral train.

Away to the grave in the valley —
No sickness, no sorrow, no tears

Can enter the door of that dwelling
In the midst of the long evening years.

Monmouth, Ill.

THE BURIAL IN THE SNOW STORM
MA DEC. 14, 1860

'Twas after the noon of the Sabbath,
And stormy and dreary the day,
When I saw a solemn procession
Move silently over the way
When I saw the hearse and the mourners
As slowly they moved in a row,
Away to the grave-yard so quiet
Enwrapt in a mantel of snow.

And the poor old Sexton, I saw,
As he leaned on his spade to wait,
Wipes a tear from his care-worn cheek
As the train passed on through the gate
And I knew that his heart was tender,
And his thoughts told him he must go
Very soon, like the one in the coffin
To a grave down under the snow.

But passed has the funeral train,
With a slow and measured tread,
By the mansions and through the white alleys

To a home newly built for the dead,
When the coffin was lifted and lowered
To the vault, well fitted below
When the [illegible] and the tears of the mourners
Mutely fell as the flakes of the snow.

Mutely fell, till a mound was built up
Where memory untarnished will cling,
Though wrapped in a mantel of winter,
Or clothed with the verdure of spring;
Till the season comes round when the mourners,
Like her shall be summoned to go
To rest in the mansion of silence,
Like hers, now mantled in snow.

Fort Donelson
MA Mar. 21, 1861

Our poet fathers touched with skill
The magic lyre of plaintive rhyme,
In memory of the gallant slain
At Bunker Hill and Brandy-wine.
Then let my hand its cunning show,
By sounding every silver cord
For those who smite a Union foe
And fearless wield a loyal sword.

The bugle call — the clarion fife —
The rattling, rolling drums, to arms

Anew inspire the soldier's life
And fill the tented field with charms.
Then, bugle, blow, and fife and drums
Enchant their ranks with martial airs,
And when the gory conflict comes,
The field and vanquished foe are theirs.

And thou, my harp, all newly strung,
Play well for that heroic band
Who won the field of Donelson
Near by the deep blue Cumberland —
Where forth in silence grandeur rolls
Her flood along the rocky floors,
Where nature rears her wooded knolls
Upon the high defiant shores.

Those wooded knolls have sacred grown
Of late, from our boys' precious blood,
Those slopes and deep ravines have shown
From crimson foot-prints where they stood —
And where in "double quick" they flanked
And stormed rebellion left and right,
And who among the dead were ranked
As victims of the battles' might.

Heroic boys, how brave and true!
And how alike through weal and woe
They fought, determined to subdue,
Or, bleeding, die before the foe.
Their hearts were all aglow with zeal
And love for every stripe and star,

Their arms were nerved with trusty steel
And pregnant with the fire of war.

And now, my hand, a minor key
Strike thou in honor of the slain —
The valiant ones — whose memory
In living green will still remain.
Where hushed shall be the battles' din
Beneath the round of changing years,
When all their forms have scattered been
In dust throughout this vale of tears.

BOB WHITE
MA AUG. 2, 1861

Ay, ay, and what's up now, my little friend?
You are not angry, sure? God's little pets
Methinks are not ill-bred, for He who in
His tenderness first broke the tinny shell,
And gave they wee soft feet their light and fleet
Elastic step, to glide unharmed beneath
The bonnie green-woods' tangled copse, hath too
Much care for thee, and loves thee with that love
Divine too well, I ween, to teach thee wrong.
Pray then, kind sir, what mean those words of thine?
That nick-name of my friend poor Robert White?
Come tell me what has Robert done, that thou
Should spoil his pretty Christian name? Perhaps
You're just in fun, you little rogue? Come, come,

Keep down your fright, and sing away, I would
Not harm thee for the world, for I
No cruel sportsman am; I keep no pointer dog,
Quail net, nor fowling piece. 'Tis but
A rustic cane I hold, whereon you now
Might safely rest as when it stood
A harmless shrub o'er where thy mother brooded thee
When young — "Bob White" — yes, there it is again.
Well, well, mock on, and nick-name if you will,
It may be that's "your fort." I know
Sweet "Katie Did" and "Bob-o-Link," but who on earth's
"Bob White?" If 'tis not Robert, then "I'm sold."
But what's your name? — "Bob White" — Ha, ha, well done
For you — "I'll give up beat." I've heard thee called
By huntsmen oft, "Cock partridge," "quail"
But never learned before thy name in song.
So now for all my accusations false
'Galnat thee, I'll ask thy pardon, Bob,
And now let's talk on graver themes.
Lo, many circling years
Have swiftly wheeled away since in
My boyhoods' sunny days I heard
That pretty name sung from my father's gate
And wheat-field fence, and many a sweet, sweet
Song since then has timed the steps of marshalling
Changes to the lone dim world of shade.
And Oh, alas, they in their ceaseless march
Have borne away the many names I learned
To love. I know those lips can call them yet,
And calling weave a music plaintive as

Thine own sweet song of [illegible]
But no terrestrial sound can pierce
"The dull, cold ear of death," nor break
Their iron sleep.
Cease then my tongue to sing of them,
Thy music's lost. And thou my erring lips,
Be still, thy notes are borne away unheard
Upon the hollow wind, and like to those
On whom they call, return no more.
And oh sad heart be thou resigned
The [illegible] whirligig of time,
Is cutting swiftly, strange and quaint
Fantastic carvings on my cheek,
Whilst in his silent cave the magic Smith
Is forging chains to bind me captive in
The dungeon cells of death where I with [illegible]
Shall sleep away the years till sounds
The judgment trump, when tombs shall burst
And mountains fall, and worlds in fervent heat
Dissolve away, and music from the harps
Of angels welcome through the golden gates
The countless throng in snow-white robes
Cleansed from the blood of him who died
On Calvary.

Monmouth

HYMN FOR THE BATTLE YEAR
MA JAN. 3, 1862

Time, time,
Alas, thou ceaseless voyager!
We know not what thou art, nor yet
From whence you came, nor whither thou
Dost go; and yet, withal, we know
Thou'rt wondrous strong, mysterious
Unseen, fleet and real — strong and
Absolute as Death — mysterious
And unseen as immortality,
And fleet as veins of fiery
Lightnings darting through the clouds,
When angry tempests rise and shake
The rock-rib'd world.

Still, side by side with thee, the muse
Her chariot drives, with Jehu speed,
And chants a plaintive hymn, as o'er
The golden lyre her fingers sweep
With grace; in mournful strains the while
Her voice falls mingling with the
Tremulous notes from off its
Quivering cords, as sang the bards
Of classic Eld through years
And centuries gone.

How strange it seems!
Those bards grew old and died; and he
[illegible]

But in these modern days since Mars,
The god of War stalks rampant up
And down the earth, and walks it to
And fro, they say: "Don't sing of time,
He's hackney'd, stale and worn, and should
Be cast amid the moles and bats
Of long ago."

Not sing of Time, because he's old?
[illegible]
Been my friend, and led me by the
Hand, unharmed, along the slippery
Paths of life, through fifteen score of
Moons, the last of which to-night is
Tottering, Moses-like, high up
The star-gem'd steep of yon
Ethereal Pisgah in the sky,
Anon to view o'er Jorden's wave
The funeral of the year

Yes, yes —
Of him — Old Father time — I first
Will sing, and then communion hold
With Mars — the bloody god.

Old!
There's something holy in that word,
It twines itself around the soul
And melts the heart in tenderness,
The hills — the green old hills — who does
Not love them? Old as love itself,

With all its devotees they stand.

And then, the old homestead, the old
Woods, and the old folks — the poor old
Folks, God bless them — they'll not be with
Us long. Each year adds silver hairs,
Makes coffins, and digs graves.
But father Time, though old and gray
Still jogs along, through wet [illegible]
Through sunshine and through shade.
Come weal or woe, 'tis all the same
With him. He holds the scythe and spade,
And wields the magic wand.
He smites the rock and opes
His icy gates [illegible]
And stern, when limpid waters come
Forth creeping from beneath
The melting snows, and fill the ruts,
And swells the creeks, and bears along
The rafts of ice dissolving
In the flood, till all is gone, and
Gentle Spring, with babbling music,
Flowering vales and grazing herds
On verdant hills appear. Then
Summer, Autumn, and again the
Winter winds, its cold, white moons and snows.

Indeed, it seems as though
This old man Time has full control
Of all things here below, (except
The Devil and old Death, who play

Conspicuous parts upon life's
Checkered stage.) The first ensnares the
Soul and lures it from the narrow way,
And haunts us to the tomb, where Death,
Assumes control. Ah me, and
After all, Old Time, unpitying,
Still by some strange project enters
Through th' unseen door and revels
O'er the sleeping dust.

Strange power. Eccentric monitor,
The future, present, and the past,
Hope reality, and sailor
On oblivion's sea remorseless,
Even in the grave.

Sixty One!
The Battle Year; baptized in blood,
And pregnant with events, is dead!
The poor old year, alas, is gone,
Gone forever. In after times
Methinks when these, my locks now in
Thick Summer bloom, will be
With frosty hand made white
From snowy Eld adown
My dusky cheeks will roll a tear,
In memory for the dear ones
Fallen on the tented field,
The bloody plain, the road-side, and
The mountain pass, and tottering
Down the hill of life dependent

On my cane, I through my glasses
Oft upon their mossy tombs will
Read their names, their deaths, the Battle
Year, and where they fell.
And oft, I ween, in fancy search
For those who died "unwept,
Unhonored and unsung."
Who mouldered down to dust in graves
Unknown e'en as the one
The angels dug in Moab's
Ancient vale.

Aha, the king of terrors —
That wolf-like guest, who comes
Unwelcomed to each fold,
And steals away the lambs, fears not
The pomp and pride of glorious
War, but lurks about the camp, and
Courts the sword, and prowls amid the
Battle's rage, regardless whom he
Grapples with. A Lyon yields; an
Ellsworth, young and brave; a Winthrop,
And a Baker fall, and millions
Mourn, but cannot lure them back.
They're all, all gone; gone with hopes and
Joys and tears. Gone, gone home with
The Battle Year.

And Sixty Two is born!
Fresh from the hand of God it comes;
A nation's prayer ascends for it,

And sanctifies its every day
And hour. Rebellion must be quelled,
The fires of liberty must burn.
Six hundred thousand men in
Rank and file, firm, and true and brave,
And armed with muskets, swords, truth,
And prayer, with God to lead the van
And strike the blow, will conquer, through
The heavens fall. Speed on, speed on,
The holy war; let every bellows
Blow, and every anvil clang, till
All the pruning hooks and plow shares
In the land be beaten into
Swords and spears to strike and hew the
Traitors down. Let selfish England
Come with fleets and navies strong, our
Good good old ship of State will not go
Down, her stripes and stars are too near
Heav'n for [illegible] hands to touch.

Monmouth, Ill.

THE POWERS THAT BE
MA Sept. 26, 1862

Hail, Banner, hail! We'll guard thee well,
No traitor's hand shall mar
The luster of a single stripe,
The glory of a star.

Columbia rising in her might
Is like the swelling sea,
As louder blow the warring winds
High leap the billows free,
Then Union, gird thine armor on,
Cheer up, we're all with thee,
To bravely fight to win the right
And guard the Powers that Be.

Cheer, Union, cheer! A mighty host
To day is marching forth,
To swell the ranks of glory
In the army of the North —
A mighty host of loyal men,
Six hundred thousand strong,
To conquer and return again
With Jubilee and song.
Then Union, cheer, and never fear
They're all, they're all with thee,
To bravely fight to win the right
And guard the Powers that Be.

Cheer, Union, cheer! Thy songs of War
Enchant the Bondman's ears,
As Angels were when first arose
The music of the spheres.
There's language in the whizzing balls —
The "hundred pounder's" roar,
That tyranny and treason soon
Shall be with us no more.
Then Union strong, oh sing the song

We're all, we're all with thee,
To bravely fight to win the right
And guard the Powers that Be.

Hail, Union, hail! That powerful One
Who forth the lightning hurls,
Who rides upon the thunder car
And guides the rolling worlds,
Is ever in the battle's van,
The center and the rear,
To aid us through the fiery charge
And shelter us from fear.
Then Union strong, trust thou in God,
Thy surest hope is He,
To bravely fight to win the right
And guard the Powers that Be.

Monmouth

THREE CITIES
MA Oct. 24, 1862

How stirring the city, to-day!
More noisy than usual, it seems,
From the rattling of wagons,
And driving of teams —
From the click of the mills,
And the hum of machines;
The clang of the anvils,

The roar of the fires,
The banterings and dickerings
Of sellers and buyers —
The shoutings and clamors
Of hucksters and boys
[illegible]
Nuts, candies and toys.
The changing of money,
The weighing of grain,
The dunning of debtors,
The building of fame;
And houses and blocks
From the mortar of gain
And the granite of strife.
Thus thriving the city,
The growing young city,
The city of trade —
The city of life.

A sorrowful sound
Breaks from the church bell:
Solemnly, mournfully,
Speaking a knell,
As the funeral train
Moves slowly along,
Nearing and passing
Through life's giddy throng,
As the wheels of the [illegible]
Turn round and round,
Tracking their way through
The dust of the streets;

Threading their course
To the burial ground;
To the city of shade,
In the valley of dreams
Where all is lonely and still —
Where nothing is heard
Through the long, long years,
Save the grate of the spade
And the dripping of tears —
Where summer comes not,
Nor the music of spring;
Where the flowers never bloom,
Nor the birds never sing —
Where the coffined ones sleep,
Undisturbed in the halls,
Where the sun never shines,
Nor the dew never falls —
Where the trampling of feet
Never crosses the floors,
And the dwellers within
Never open the doors —
For moveless they lie
There, taking their rest,
With their bony hands crossed
On the cold, hollow breast,
In the silence supreme,
For alone can it be
Down in the deep grave
[illegible]
And the graves are the houses —
The mansions I ween —

And above them the streets,
And hillocks of green,
All mute with the spirit of Death.
Thus stands the old city —
The growing old city
The city of shade —
The city of Death.

On a marble step, cold,
Stained, mossy and old,
At the door of a grass-hidden tomb,
I sat in my dreams —
And on the long beams
My fancy climbed up to the moon
For I thought her a trundle
Of silver on high,
Or hitherward wheel
Of a ponderous Car,
Where mortals might ride
Up the walls of the sky,
To the home of the weary ones,
Thitherward far.
But nothing I found there,
Save a lone world,
And "the man of the moon,"
In his great rocky chair,
Who gave me a seat
By his side on a crag
Far up on the mountain-side
Barren and bare.
"From whence cam'st thou?

What dost thou here?
And whither dost go?"
Quoth the man of the moon.
I told him I came
From a far-distant sphere —
From the haunts of the grave;
From the door of the tomb,
That the moon was a wheel
Of a chariot, I dreamed,
Whereon I could ride
Th' ethereal hills o'er,
To the city of God;
Where death, as I deemed,
Was fettered and barred
From window and door.
"Very true — very true," quoth
The man of the moon.
"That Monarch of Terrors
Can never go there —
But alas! man, alas!
You must leave in the tomb
The mortal, through time,
Unsealed in his care —
Then the spotless undying
Shall swiftly arise,
On pinions celestial,
And soar to the skies —
And not on a chariot —
No chariot, save one,
Will be there, and its gleamings
Shall vie with the sun —

Wherein the Lord Jesus,
In royal attire,
Will in majesty drive
Th' fleet coursers of fire,
But come, and I'll show thee
That city of light,
Where time has no end,
And the day has no night.
That city without either
Graveyard or tomb,
A place without sorrow,
Tears, sadness and gloom,"
Quoth he. "Then your vision
Obliquely advance
Upward, away,
Through yon ether expanse."
Lo! myriads of miles
Of gold-dotted blue,
And orbits of planets
My vision passed through,
Till it came to the city of God,
And thus it appears.

Four mighty walls of Jasper,
In stately grandeur rise
Around the shining city —
The golden Paradise.
Three pearly gates of glory
Outward swing on either wall,
And ceaseless floods of splendor
On gates and city fall.

They're not the brightest shining
Of the clearest mid-day sun,
They're from the beaming countenance
Of God — The Holy One.
The radiant love of Jesus,
His pure and spotless Lamb,
His Counsel in Eternity,
Long ere the worlds began.

Through golden streets untarnished
Troops of Angels to and fro
In perfect time to music
Step as liquid numbers flow;
And oftentimes the legions
Of the city meet in song
And swell celestial anthems,
In grandeur, loud and long.

No trades, nor petty strivings,
No net-work to ensnare,
No tired limbs or weariness,
Nor restless longing there.
No death, no tears, no sorrow,
No storms do ever come —
The City of the Angels;
The bright, eternal Home.

Monmouth, Ill.

THE OLD YEAR AND THE NEW
MA JAN. 9, 1863; <RR JAN. 28, 1865>

[Irvine titled the much shorter 1865 version "The Old And The New Year." It ended with the words "dawning year" and did not include the parts about the morning and evening. — Ed.]

DECEMBER 31ST, 11 O'CLOCK P.M.

The night in silence glides along,
My watch ticks quick and clear,
As even-paced, the second-hand
Is spanning off the year.
One solemn <*lonely*> hour, and all with him
Will be forever gone;
The thunders of his battle-days —
His merriment and song.

We then will lift his coffin lid,
Unfold his winding sheet,
As round his bier we congregate
And quiet vigils keep.
We'll talk of all t'was said and done,
In low suppressive tones <*solemn under-tones*>,
By those who shared his pilgrimage,
Now in their "narrow homes."

How the old grew weak and weary,
And burdened down with pains; <*From tott'ring down the hill,*>

And how they walked with *<leaned on>* Providence
And leaned upon their canes. *<Obedient to His will.>*
And how, when called to cross the tide *<And how, when called [illegible] Jordan's flood,>*
Of Jordan, tossed with storms, *<Beyond the stygian realm,>*
They threw them down, and cast themselves *<They hurried o'er with dauntless Faith,>*
Into His mighty arms. *<As Pilot at the helm.>*

And then there's been a thrifty trade
In coffins large and small;
Stern Man, sweet Youth and Innocence,
Alike have filled them all.
New grave stones and new monuments,
Each passing day we see
Uprising from the burial grounds
Of Earth's mortality.

But marching down the track of war,
The mold be lightly pressed;
Beneath, in clay-walled sepulchres,
Poor fallen soldiers rest.
No weeping willows shade the spot,
No mounds above them swell,
No marble slabs or polished shafts
Their mournful story tell.

But on a Nation's mighty heart
A fadeless record stands,
For them a deep memorial

Inscribed by grateful hands.
More sanctified their noble deeds
Will grow in after years —
More glorified their sacred names,
And cherished o'er with tears.

O, Earth, make strong their thin roofed graves,
Heal up their battle scars; <*The wounded, heal their scars;*>
Wave proudly, O, ye stripes for them;
Wax brilliant, O, ye stars,
Their brothers fill the vacant files;
To be revenged they stand;
For God requires their sacred blood
From every traitor's hand.

Unheard the night still glides along;
My watch ticks quick and clear;
'Tis midnight, and I stand beside
The coffin of the year.
Farewell, a long farewell to him;
Once gone, he comes no more —
The selfish past gives nothing back
Of all his precious store.

Unheard the night still glides along;
My watch ticks quick and clear —
But hark! the tolling bells announce
The funeral of the year.
Aha! <*Hark! hark!*> they ring in joyous peal
For dawning Sixty-Three; <*For Sixty-five is here,*>
Each one a sounding anthem swells

For God and Liberty! <*For th' young and dawning year.*>

New Year's Morning

The welcome day — the New-Year's van —
By seers and statesmen oft
Has come with blessed news for all
God's loyal host. Oh let us sing
Our Hail Columbia doubly grand,
As forth in might and majesty
Our armies march, with swords unsheathed,
To cut the shackles off and let
Oppressed humanity — the poor,
The panting fugitive, go free.
The holy issue consecrates
And sanctifies each coming day,
While anxious millions waiting stand
Its consummation to maintain,
Though every rebel, North and South,
Be butchered or be hanged. Then fate,
Mcthinks, will metamorphose them,
And, allied with the Peace Democracy,
And intervention from the French,
The English, and the infernal gods,
They, undisturbed, can have "their rights" —
A warm confed'racy below.

[illegible]
Old years, long gone, and numbered with
The ancient times, still backward cast
The brightness of their beacon lights,

High blazing from the hills and plains
Of liberty. Wilt thou, New-Year,
The bondman's chains unloose, and speed —
Speed on the righteous work began?
Light up the world with Freedom's fires,
And let them burn unquenched till time
Shall cease to be.

New Year's Evening

Ah! the loom of time has woven
A checkered web to-day —
Some threads have sable proven,
Some silken, bright and gay.
And another web to-morrow,
Will be surely woven, too —
Shuttles filled with mirth and sorrow
Will be driven through and through.

Sun, and calm, and stormy weather,
Will alternate come and go,
As the future travels hither
Freighted down with weal and woe.
For whom has weal been treasured?
Would to God we knew it well:
And to whom shall woe be measured?
No human tongue can tell.

Oh! for a Prophet's vision,
Their destiny to see;
We then would make provision

To meet futurity;
For its issues all be ready,
And always waiting stand,
Resigned, and calm, and steady,
Always strong of heart and hand.

Thou God of Hosts uphold us
By thine almighty power;
Beneath thy wings enfold us,
From danger's threat'ning hour.
Our Nation, in her anguish,
Wilt Thou remember Lord?
For Thee we long and languish
To sheathe the bloody sword.

Thou King of Light and Angels
Oh! take us to thine arms!
Thou alone canst work our changes
And calm the battle storms —
Still the awful strife so gory,
Restoring peace to men.
Thine is the power and glory
Forever, Lord, Amen.

Monmouth, Ill.

LETTER FROM NIAGARA FALLS
MA Mar. 6, 1863

Niagara Falls, Goat Island, Feb. 14, '63

Friend Clark: There are four places under the sun, from which Editors always receive letters, to wit: The Camp, the Gold Diggings, the Holy Land, and Niagara Falls. The subscriber writes from the latter place.

To begin at the beginning, we left Buffalo on the morning train, and after a run of an hour and a half, we alighted from the cars at Niagara City. Here, as usual, we were assailed by a brigade of impudent professional "Bus" drivers of all sizes and complexions. Like Tennyson's Charge of the Six Hundred, we were surrounded.

Bus drivers in the front of us,
Bus drivers in the rear of us,
Bus drivers to the right of us,
Bus drivers to the left of us,
Shouted and bellowed,
Plucked us and pulled us,
Sought and besieged us,
In the brogue of "Fardowners,"
And bloody "Corkonians,"
Dutch badly broken,
And half butchered English;
Then once in a while,
By way of variety,
A contraband's voice

Would ring in some changes,
Or perchance a live Yankee,
Would switch in his tongue —
All versed in the phrases
Of omnibus lingo.

We elbowed our way through the modern Babel, this bevy of rag, tag, and bobtails, without paying the the least attention to them, until we gained the [illegible] of the crowd when one polite chap, an English ignoramus, with a face deeply frescoed from small-pox, and a crooked nose, came forward and gently informed us that he would drive us to the Falls, a distance of half a mile, "in a [illegible] two-'oss' sleigh, for three cents a 'ead!" I told him he was my man — to drive up his two-"oss" sleigh — and in a moment, off we dashed for the Falls; and the next minute our man Friday drew a tight rein, halloed "Ho!" at the "osses" — the "osses" came to a halt — the Hinglishman twisted his ugly face over his shoulder and said, "These ere is the Hamerican rapids, on the Hamerican side. In horder to see the Falls as they hare, you must go the Canada side." Here the three cent per "ead" contract was [illegible] Friday. He was evidently skilled in omnibus craft, [illegible] was his tune to improve it. Said he, "Shall I drive you over, Sir?" There we sat in his easy cushioned sleigh, intoxicated with delight at the roaring, plunging river, plumed in his white-capped surges, and leaping forward like an unchained giant to battle in the awful cataract. Neither the American or the Canadian Falls can be seen to any advantage, save from Goat Island or the Canada side.

The best view, however, is from the letter. "Shall I drive you over, sir?" shouted the Englishman. Said I, "Where do you cross the river?" He answered, "On the Suspension Bridge." This was another feast for the eyes. I forgot to make a contract with him, and told him to drive over. A gleam of ineffable satisfaction rolled over his frescoed physiognomy, thinking he had caught a "green one," and "I'll stick him" to the tune of "one dollar per hour." He jogged along at a slow trot, and in the course of three-fourths of an hour, halted at the great Suspension Bridge, a distance of two miles from the American rapids. I climbed out of the sleigh and asked the tollman for two tickets — one for myself and one for the person in company. He said "The toll is one dollar. One dollar, sir, for yourself, your lady and your team." I turned about and asked the man Friday if he expected me to pay toll for his team. He said he did. I told him I would see him and his sleigh going over the Falls before I would do it; at the same time offering him fifty cents, telling him I could dispense with his services. He said his charge was one dollar. I told him he could take fifty cents or nothing. He said the law allowed him a dollar; if I did not pay it, he would have me arrested. I told him to arrest me. He said he would. I told him to do it, at the same time purchasing a couple of toll tickets, and starting through the bridge. He followed, saying, "I'll take the fifty cents!" I paid it over, and the English swindler started back, swearing like a trooper.

As we walked through the great Suspension Bridge, when looking upward, it seemed as though Art were a victor over Nature; but looking downward hundreds of feet, until the eye caught the boiling, foaming, and swiftly dashing current, the grand old walls, rough, iron-ribbed, fearfully high, and ancient as the sun, on either side, the dark green hemlocks low moaning in the breeze, and yielding back the spray in dewy tears — Ah, how small the bridge grew in the eye of comparison. Are they who reared this magnificent bridge, mightier than He who built the mountain and scooped out the hollow for the sea? Art is great, but Nature wonderful, mysterious, past finding out.

After crossing ever into Her Majesty's dominions, we had another "set to" with a second pack of unprincipled scoundrels, claiming to be licensed guides, but who in reality were a set of impostors and swindlers. Some had one kind of conveyance and some another — all misrepresenting the difficulties, the dangers and the distance connected with the Falls. Suffice it to say, the two miles intervening between the Canadian end of the bridge and the Falls were soon passed over, and we stood for the first time in life before Nature's great water works — the mighty cataract of Niagara. All I had ever read or heard about them, instantly flashed across my mind. Yet neither pen or pencil has ever portrayed or painted them. I had not gleaned the least idea of their appearance. Niagara Falls are too mighty, too grand for paper or canvas.

While standing on the bank at the head of the long icy stairway running underneath Table Rock, on a parallel with the river, in a descending grade of about 45 degrees for a distance of five or six hundred feet, and stopping abruptly at the foot of the great cataract, another guide — a hireling or rather circulating medium for an old Canadian curmudgeon, who keeps a large museum, a green house, and a wardrobe well stored with water or rather spray-proof over-alls, for the accommodation of those who wish to go under the cataract [illegible] guide came up, and very affectionately bid "good morning" — and his oily tongue slipped off the following — "Sire, the Falls look beautiful this morning." (I suppose he had heard some sentimental boarding-school Miss say *beautiful*, which they indiscriminately apply to every thing, from a wax doll up to Mt. Blanc. But let them pass.) The guide continued: "You can't see their beauty here, Sir. You must go to the foot of the stairway there, under the sheet of water, sir. Shall I furnish you and your lady with suits of spray-proof clothing for fifty cents [illegible] an experienced guide, sir? You will see the most beautiful sight of your life, sir," &c. I replied, perhaps I would go over the Falls — would he go over with me as a guide? He smiled, and said he believed not. The stairway being too icy and dangerous for a lady to descend, I told him I would go down with him myself, after retiring to his wardrobe and dressing myself in a suit of oil-cloth, from head to foot, he called up a big negro, and told him to take me to the Falls, &c.

Down, down, we went, cautiously, holding to the railing, until we arrived under the sheet below. The sounding of the water was like the voice of severe thunders. We stood swaddled in spray upon the ice-clad floor, and looked up, upward till the sense grew dizzy and the brain reeled. I was awe-stricken. I backed up again [illegible] wonderment. Strange thoughts flittered through my imagination. I thought of old Neptune, the God of the ocean — of water nymphs, water spouts, sea devils, and shower baths — then of the deluge, of little man, and the great God of the Universe pouring the floods from the hollow of his hand. Sounds like the rushing of many winds, the gathering of the tempests, the roar of the hurricane, continually and unceasingly rolling upward. How strange it seems. That deep voice sang bass in the anthem of the morning stars. Six thousand years lie buried in the vale of Forgetfulness; yet wild Niagara, untamed by age, still rolls on in might and grandeur. Behind the cataract stood the stout old wall, cold and sullen, over which the flood poured. At its base great piles of ice, slippery and ragged, stood like winter sentinels or white guardsmen of the passway.

I found the "contraband" guide quite intelligent. One would not think that an institution without a soul would have been so well posted. I know some of our democratic brethren who might have been taught by him. But I don't wish to bring up the "nigger question" here, so let him pass.

Turning from a darker to a whiter subject, the waters underneath the cataract have the appearance of a great pot of boiling milk, foaming and splashing, bubbling, surging and waltzing round and round, gradually settling into a deep, dark, sluggish tide, dragging its slow length along until it reaches the rapids below the Suspension Bridge.

The guide informed me that Table Rock was yearly shelving off — that it was considered dangerous, and consequently nothing could be seen from it.

After doffing my yellow oil-cloth suit, and resting a little, guide No. 1 — the circulating medium — intimated that the next room contained a museum of the first order — "would we walk in, sir?" We consented and were well paid for our trouble. There we saw a little of everything, from the bones of a whale to the bird that scratched up the seeds of original sin — stuffed birds of all kinds, snakes, lizards, alligators, fishes, monkeys, lions, tigers, rats and mice; mummies, said to have been embalmed 1500 years B.C. The guide did not say he was present at the embalming exercises, but I am convinced he would have done so for half a dollar. You can find men all round the Falls, who will lie to any amount for a few cents.

But returning to the house of bones, or in other words the museum. We would say before leaving, always pay it a visit when you go to Niagara Falls. It certainly contains an immense stock of natural curiosities of all kinds. And never fail to purchase the "Niagara Album," a little book in pamphlet form, containing the remarks of visitors, in prose and verse, in relation to the Falls. For example, one visitor writes: "What would have been the result, had Demosthenes stood under the cataract with the pebbles in his mouth, and lifted up his mighty voice with the flood?" Some wag writes immediately below it: "He would have got wet, and tore his breeches." You will find it contains some beautiful and some ridiculous things.

After re-crossing to the American side, and receiving some refreshments, we visited Goat Island, where I now write. I need not describe it, as time and space is growing short.

A little advice, and I close. When you visit Niagara Falls, look out for [illegible] and impostors. You [illegible] at your elbow every time you turn round, demanding fifty cents. Either pay no attention to them, keeping a tight hand on your pockets, or else cut a good stout club and crack a few of their [illegible]. Niagara City, I am told, has no law against visitors pounding and pummeling them. If you take my advice, for I claim to have purchased some experience, you will never regret a visit to Niagara Falls.

Yours truly,
J.P. Irvine

THE 36TH ILL. VOLUNTEERS
MA Nov. 20, 1863

Full ranked "the 36th," and strong
Its iron heroes stood,
With dauntless wills to smite the wrong,
On fields of strife and blood.
As hope in thickening clusters hung,
And faith in mystic tendrils clung
Upon each arm the while,
Our full hearts forth a blessing gave
For every soldier stout and brave —
Thousand, rank and file.

Methinks there were no Trojan band,
Though mailed from head to heel,
Could battle with them, hand to hand,
Or measure steel with steel.
Nor fabled knights of olden times,
Nor legions known in classic rhymes,
With poniards, shields and spears,
Could ward their minnie balls away,
So schooled in battle craft were they —
Our Union Volunteers

With zeal, I've watched, through calm and storm,
How, 'neath the knapsack's load,
In long blue lines of uniform,
They trudge the rugged road,
Sore-footed, through each gap that opes
Its craggy pass through mountain slopes,
For many a weary day —
E'en when the night hung black and dire,
Without a star or cloud of fire
To light the fearful way.

Their ranks are thin to-day — suffice
To tell, the absent names
Have offered up, as sacrifice,
Their lives in battle flames
Yet still a handful firm and strong —
The living foes of hell and wrong —
Remains a fearless band,
All ready by the altar side,
Like patriot martyrs, brave and tried —

God, hold them in Thy hand.

Chicago

INK DROPPINGS
MA JAN. 8, 1864

ON THE LAST DAY OF THE OLD YEAR

Loud wails the winter blast to-day;
Like chaff, the drifting snow,
In fearful gusts is whirled about
And winnowed to and fro,
As shivering brutes unsheltered stand
And hungry cattle low.

I in my cozy chamber sit,
And wish His hand divine
Would teach His "handi-work" to build,
In Autumn threshing time,
Thatched booths to shelter from the storm
The patient meek-eyed kine.

Yes, wild and fearful is the day,
Loud wails the piercing blast,
Compassion for the Old and Poor
My heard binds like a clasp.
Would to God the storm was o'er —
Would to God the winter past.

Let not the Old Year in his wrath
In death depart to night;
Let War his [illegible] dagger sheath,
And stern revenge her might;
And calmly as a Christian dies,
So let him take his flight.

But soon the "storm king" of the North
Will drop his icy spear,
And soon the "Queen of Spring" will come
And plant her violets here,
Then Summer bearing bearded sheaves,
And so the changing year.

ONE HUNDRED THOUSAND SLAIN
MA FEB. 19, 1864; <RR FEB. 20, 1864>

Throughout the bloody Union,
Beneath the crimsoned waves,
One hundred thousand soldiers
Are mouldering in their graves:
In chill and sunny forests,
Where tower the palm and pine;
'Neath fallow-grounds and wilderness,
The cluster and the vine;
In swamp and moor <*moor and marsh*> and fern-land,
Where plagues and fevers are;
On every slope and mountain
That flank the trail of war;

Within the church-yard's sacred mould <*ground*>,
As brothers, side by side,
Cut down, as lofty cedars,
In their glory and their pride.

We miss them at the altar,
When the family meet in prayer,
We look around the circle
And we see the vacant chair;
And then the heart grows sorrowful
Beyond the will's control,
And swells with grief until it chokes
The flood-gates of the soul.
About the streets the mourners
Go, in sable raiment <*garments*> clad;
I know <*Methinks*> they mourn a brother —
A noble <*fallen*> soldier lad.
We meet the long procession
It slowly moves along,
In the ears a spirit whispers
"Another soldier gone."
Ah! but few posts and lintels
Have been sprinkled, as of old,
Were the doors of chosen Hebrews
When Egypt's doom was told;
But the mourners' name is legion,
And they mourn the brave and fair,
For the angel's crossed each threshold,
And slain a victim there.
Oh, bloody deluged Union
How sacred hast thou grown!

As new wine at the marriage,
Our lavish gore has flown
No Union, precious Union,
We will not give thee up,
Though priceless be the sacrifice
And bitter be the cup;
God knows how oft we've drained it <*To the dregs, God knows we've drained it*>
And it filled and filled again,
We will drink, yea thrice repeat it,
And loudly shout, Amen!

Ho! courage, Union, courage,
Our foes we'll o'erwhelm,
Our loving good All-Father
Is standing at the helm.
His armies are a million,
And his ruling power they feel;
Their bosoms are united,
And their arms are true as steel;
And then, in ceaseless numbers, <*And then in countless millions*>
The upward march of prayers,
Is subduing more than armies —
Than he the sword who bears.

Take courage, Union, courage!
The victory is won,
The rebel host is vanishing
Like mist before the sun;
The shackles of the bondman

Are cut from off his bones,
While Kings and haughty monarchs
Are trembling on their thrones.
Yet still a weighty sadness
Is lurking in our souls,
For the broken cords of silver,
For the shattered golden bowl,
For the noble hundred thousand
'Neath the sod and crimsoned waves —
The hundred thousand soldiers
Now mouldering in their graves.

Rockford, Ill.

OUR PILOT
RR APR. 2, 1864; MA APR. 8, 1864

Three long and weary years the storm
Has tossed its billows mountain high,
Still, black as death, portentous clouds
Low brooding over-pall the sky,
As veins of lightning nimbly dart
Around the rumbling thunder-car
Through frowning gorges draped in gloom
And pregnant with the fire of war.

High rides the good ship "Union" yet,
Sea-worthy as when newly launched,
Though battle-scarred her trusty hulk,

Her rigging torn and weather-blanched.
What though the white cap't waves run mad,
The storm-king rend away the shrouds,
There is a Pilot at the wheel —
A master helmsman in the clouds.

Have faith, a little longer wait,
For tried our Pilot is and true.
Have faith, the helmsman in the clouds
Will guide him and the good ship's crew,
He in His own good time and way
Ere long will still the surging sea,
O'er board more Jonahs must be cast
Ere blissful calm and sun there be.

Then let us sing as Miriam sang,
And, Moses, when the Hebrews crossed
And saw the Red Sea walls fall down
On Pharaoh and the Egyptian host.
"What though the white cap't waves run mad,
The storm-king rend away the shrouds,
There is a Pilot at the wheel —
A master helmsman in the clouds."

Rockford, Ill.

THE BEAUTIFUL LAND OF BEULAH
RR May 7, 1864; MA May 20, 1864

Beulah is an ideal land located immediately this side of the Death Jordan, where aged Christians dwell near the close of their lives, anxiously waiting to be called through the golden gales. Bunyan's Pilgrims journeyed through it on their way to the Celestial City. It is also spoken of in Isaiah LXII, 4-12. It probably signifies married to Christ.

Far, far away, is a beautiful land,
And a river hard by, where the Pilgrim awaits,
As a weary sojourner, still watching the hand
That shall beckon him soon through the golden gates.
From that evergreen clime where the myrtle-tree blooms,
And the grass-mantled crowns are undotted with tombs,
And the name of the land is Beulah.

Where the landscape and mountain are strangers to storm,
And the balmy air sweet with the fragrance of May;
Where the children of Jesus are drawing near home,
And soft are the notes of the turtle dove's bay;
Where the roses are blooming all the year long,
And the voices of heaven are echoed in song,
In the beautiful land of Beulah.

They tell me in yonder bright kingdom on high,

Is a sanctified host who shine as the sun;
As stars with each other in brilliancy vie,
So they in the home of the glorified One.
And these are the martyrs and prophets of eld,
Who within a stone's throw of the river-side dwelled,
In the beautiful land of Beulah.

Come, then, let us go to that beautiful land,
But a few weary years the journey will seem;
Then a few years of waiting and watching the hand
To ferry us thitherward over the stream
To the gates of fine gold, ajar standing long,
Where we heard the sweet voice of the angels in song,
From the beautiful land of Beulah.

Rockford

PLANTING CORN
RR MAY 28, 1864

Scarce half an hour the rising sun
Had climbed his crystal way,
As golden tip't the hills around
Stood green in merry May;
Now merry May had roundly filled
Her silver moon that morn —
A time when farmers mostly choose
To plant the Indian Corn.

I chanced in riding by a field,
Which near the road-side lay,
In viewing round [illegible] my eyes
On charming Olive Gray,
Who'd set aside her spinning wheel
By well assuring "Ma,"
That she could save at least a man,
By dropping corn for "Pa."

Her father, (old man Gray,) was skilled
In farming rocky land,
And kept (as farmers often do)
A rather seedy hand;
A song of "old man Brown's" was he,
And ranked as seventh brother,
Because he was the seventh son
Of Mrs. Brown, his mother.

He was tall, and lank, and limber,
Cross-eyed and freckled-faced,
And in shanghai locomotion
His limbs were somewhat graced;
His arms were loosely hung, and long,
And rough his burly hands,
His feet were small, yet none would fit,
Save "No. 10 brogans."

His hat had felt the kicks of time,
His vest was shabby, too;
His coat threadbare, the buttons off,
And both his elbows through;

Then his linsey woolsey trousers
Made the fellow look forlorn
As he strided through the furrows
And "kivered up the corn."

But 'neath that rough exterior beat
A warm and loving heart,
And on the stage of action,
It played a noble part;
For a young industrious farmer
'Ere reaps no pride or scorn
From plowing up the mellow ground
And planting Indian Corn.

But Olive Gray was rustic
A "Country Girl," and poor,
Yet sweeter than the rose that grew
Beside her father's door;
Her hair in auburn tresses hung,
Her eyes were liquid blue,
Her weight an hundred twenty,
And she wore a "No. 2."

'Tis true her pleasant face was tanned,
Yet half so sweet had none,
'Ere won the wooings of the wind —
The kisses of the sun,
So artless, pure and innocent
Did she appear that morn,
Whilst tripping thro' her father's field
And dropping Indian Corn.

Old Gray, her father, "furrowed out"
With Dobbin, poor and blind,
And Olive, with her little [illegible],
Came dropping close behind.
Three grains she drop't in every hill,
'Mid smiles approaching laughter,
While awkward Brown, with hoe in hand,
Came slowly striding after.

And as she drop't the golden grains,
Some grains of love fell down,
Which seemed to rise in magic spells
Into the heart of Brown.
And strange to say, they proved as free,
From that advent'rous morn,
To germinate, and bud and bloom,
As grains of Indian Corn.

I passed the field, almost a score
Of long eventful years
Had flown, and brought their [illegible]
Their pleasures and their tears,
When once again I passed the farm,
Where on that pleasant morn
I first saw charming Olive Gray,
When dropping Indian Corn.

But now her name was Olive Brown,
And where she first began
By leaving Ma and Spinning Wheel,
"To save at least a man,"

She was happy 'mid the light of home,
And [illegible] a pleasant morn,
And seven bright eyed Little Browns,
To drop the Indian Corn.

Rockford

My Soul and I
RR July 16, 1864; MA July 22, 1864

All day upon the mountain,
My soul and I, alone,
Together held communion
By a rugged mossy stone;
As the far off booming thunders
Spake as with a solemn tongue,
And the pillar'd smoke of combat
O'er the field of battle hung.

Out quoth my soul — thus saying:
"O'er yonder cloud on high,
Are dying soldiers' spirits
Fleetly trooping up the sky,
To that great celestial country
Where no hostile armies tread
With iron heel the verdure,
Nor heap on heaps the dead.

"While below, the mangled corses

Of the mortal strew the hills,
And from many a wounded hero
The limpid gore distills;
Amid the rushing squadrons,
The bugle blast, the shout,
As perchance his sacred living
Drop by drop is trickling out.

"O, thou hast not learned the sorrow,
Nor canst thou ever know
The host of mourning Rachaels
Who have drained the cup of woe;
Nor count the narrow houses,
That so thickly flank the way,
Nor teach your children's children
Each unnumbered battle day.

"As thitherward and hitherward
I watch the passersby,
From country walk or city,
There greet my ear and eye,
The haltings of the cripple,
Moving slowly up and down,
And wooden legs and crutches
Hobbling o'er the beaten ground.

"I hear the sobs of mourners
By the coffin side and biers,
The jostlings of the ambulance,
The waterfall of tears;
All to sanctify the Union

And re-unite her bands,
Plucked ruthlessly asunder
By strong rebellion's hands."

Rockford

OUR DEAD CAESARS
MA SEPT. 9, 1864

"BEAR WITH ME, MY HEART IS IN THE COFFIN WITH CAESAR."

A stone's throw back from the market road,
An old church stands in the wood hard by,
With a kirk-yard ample and broad,
Where the dead of the neighborhood lie.
And the mason who builded those walls —
Grew old, toiling early and late —
Now sleeps where the long shadow falls
From the gable not far from the gate.
And the pious folk say he sleeps well;
That he said, 'ere his spirit had flown,
That the temple wherein he should dwell,
Had Christ for the chief corner-stone.

As th' years rolled by with unceasing tread,
The flock and their shepherd met there,
Oft times, alas, to bury the dead,
Or commune with the Father in prayer.

Year after year, on each Holy Day,
The pastor propounded the Word,
Till the gospel seed fell by the way,
And the harvesters gleaned for the Lord.
Reaping thus where the sower had sown,
And gathering the sheaves that were bound,
Till to-day, under yonder white stone,
The good pastor sleeps in the ground.

Blithely and sweetly the wild-thrush sings
In the boughs of the elm tree near;
On the gray church walls the green ivy clings,
As memory encircles the bier.
The wild-thrush sings — Whom cans't it be for?
Ah, my poor heart is heavy to-day,
I can heed but the thunders of war,
As they heavily roll up the way.
I can see but the yellow clay mounds,
When my soul burrows into the grave,
And there bathes the blood-clotted wounds
Of our dead Caesars sacred and brave.

Their church pews are empty and still,
Their ranks have grown thin — but full grown th' tomb;
There's a poor widow's cot o'er the hill
Hangs a ball-riddled coat in the room.
In a house at the foot of the lane,
Is a hat that will never be worn,
A Bible deep crimsoned with stain,
And a lock from the smitten head shorn.
There's a sword in yon house to the left,

With [illegible] and cracked hilt
But its well-tried steel two rebel skulls cleft,
And the blood of disloyalty spilt.

But the true hand that drew it lies cold,
Yet the fire it gleamed forth blazes high,
A million tried boys still troop o'er the mould
With the watch-word — "We conquer or die."
In the old church yard, dear soldiers, sleep well;
May our gratitude grow with the years,
Our hearts like the summer clouds swell,
And we rain out the burden in tears,
May you dwell where the old mason said
He would rest, ere his spirit had flown,
In that temple where Christ at the head
Stands for aye as the chief corner-stone.

DAVID
RR FEB. 25, 1865; MA MAR. 3, 1865

[This poem forms the end of "In Memoriam," where Irvine uses My Soldier Boy in Heaven instead of David's name. — Ed.]

* BEFORE NASHVILLE, DEC. 16TH, 1864

For thee my tears have filled the cup
Of sorrow, from the world apart.
Yet heavy thoughts come struggling up,

And sore oppress my wounded heart,
As thither strolling down the way
To where thine infancy was rocked,
The mile-stones call to mind each day
Whereon we laughed and sang and talked,
David!

Alas, my boy, that tongue is still,
Thy voice is mute, those lips are sealed.
Not thine alone but His good will
That thou thine own sweet life shouldst yield.
Though hard it seemed, while meek-eyed Peace
Stood braiding 'round the clouds of war
Her rainbows arch with promises
Full clearer than the morning star,
David!

But be it so — His will be done;
Such blood atones the Nation's ills,
Nor oil, nor wine in rivers run.
Nor cattle on a thousand hills.
Nor corn, nor gold, nor sheaves suffice,
But fervent prayers in sack-cloth bound,
And human lives in sacrifice,
Will heal the grieved Jehovah's wound,
David!

Then all is well, from far away
A hand beside the great white throne
Through every hour along the day,
Keeps hither beck'ning me to come.

A voice within the night-time seems
To whisper "Come: Christ is the vine,"
These visions be no empty dreams,
That spirit voice and hand are thine,
David!

I'm clay within the potter's hand,
And Christ the Lord will me remold,
As grain by grain ekes out my sand
He fits me for the streets of gold.
Each day in silver numbers run
Ye sands, a ceaseless stream out glide,
Oh, blessed time, oh quickly come
When for them I am sanctified.

Rockford

* David S. Irvine, killed in battle before Nashville, Dec. 16th, 1864.

How Are The Mighty Fallen
RR Apr. 22, 1865

Be skilled my hand, touch thou no note of mirth,
For Lo! to-night I sing of death,
In sorrow's minor keys.
All day long the solemn bells have tolled, and
O'er each door the festooned drapery hung,
And half-mast flags from staff and steeple drooped

In dark habiliments of woe;
I did not heed, I only heard the griev'd
Heart of the nation sob, my thoughts dwell with
The murdered Captain of the host, for like
The bulrush bowed, my fellow men and I
Were sick and faint from weeping.

No narrow homes of thine, O Death, has e'er
Been tenanted by one so honorable,
So noble, and so true a friend of man as he.
Thither shall the soldier — the war-scarr'd vet'ran
Of a hundred battles, go, and here the
Dusky freeman, whose shackles he ungirt,
Shall turn aside with reverent step and drop
A dear of homage on the grass.

The people whom he loved, and who loved him,
From heart-spun threads a shroud hath woven,
And rolled him in a winding sheet
Of non-forgetfulness.
And is there no revenge? No balm
In Gilead for this dreadful wound?
[illegible] and doubly damned
The fiendish brute. Amen! so let it be.

Rockford

THE ATLANTIC MONTHLY PUTTING ON FRENCH AIRS
MA Oct. 20, 1865

A young man wishing to express a thought in a certain article in course of preparation for the New York *Evening Post*, asked Mr. Bryant the propriety of using a foreign phrase, to which that learned and venerable man replied: "Use good, sound, plain English in all you write. I have never found a sentence or thought that my native tongue did not convey better than all others." So say I. A thought dressed in the reader's mother tongue is more beautiful and winning to him than in a foreign garb. Keep out your italicised foreign proverbs and sayings; your jaw splitters and tongue stammerers. They mar the fair proportions of smooth, dignified English page; they are not there because the writer [illegible] for good king's English. Our vocabulary is wonderfully wordy, and if properly arranged, conveys wonderful thoughts and unfolds wonderful mysteries. Nevertheless we have seen persons afflicted with a kind of chronic wordy diarrhea, who were constantly shooting off their mouths and firing blank cartridges, never hitting their mark with an idea. We have also seen men who looked as wise as owls but never were known to say anything. But we have never met the individual with a thought fully matured in his brain, who could not plainly express it, however awkwardly, with more distinctness and force in his mother tongue than in any other. A thought in the noggin knocking to get out had better knock itself to death than to be introduced into Yankee Society so Dutchy, or Frenchy, or Spanishy that it will never be fully known or recognized. Neither does the writer use them because they are superior to the English. No, that's not the reason; but a trumpet blown, a classical toot announcing the blower to be a college bred gentleman, that he is the possessor of a "sheep skin" with a Latin inscription thereon, translated thus: "Know ye that I have graduated, run the curriculum from end to end, had the triangular corners and uncouth bumps ground off against the bricks of the college. Ugh, me big Ingun."

Well, the blower may have rubbed against the walls of a college or he may have never seen one. When we remember that these phrases are all selected from a dictionary of foreign proverbs and sentences, with an English translation in the opposite column, so that the most illiterate may copy if he chooses, the fellow who wrote a long epistle using but one capital letter, (D in the word God,) might have correctly copied a Latin or French proverb in the next line. We presume every army correspondent carries one of these dictionaries in his pocket, and if allowed to judge from his letters, he uses it more than he reads his Mother's Bible. How often when reading his splendid description of a battle, with a rhetorical flourish, perchance in company, may be in your own parlor, with your framed diploma hanging in bold relief on the wall, you have suddenly run against one of those classical snags. First you are brought to a dead stand still, then visions of the sheep-skin flit across your mind, and you make a dash at the snag, blunder and flounder over it, lucky indeed if you are not asked by some of your listeners to translate it.

Some days since the *Evening Journal* announced the reception of the October *Atlantic* proof sheets, also its table of contents and the respective authors — among them, "Noel" a poem by Prof. Longfellow. We read Longfellow closely and as zealously admired him. By and by the magazine arrives, we cut the leaves, and "Noel" appears, covering two pages in solid French. We felt "snubbed." It has the air of Boston about it. It has been published to please the "hub of the Universe." Mr. Longfellow is a fine linguist, and it is doubtless a fine poem, but those who are not French scholars must content themselves with knowing that some of the *Bon tons** of Boston can read it. *The Atlantic Monthly*, forsooth, must be a tool for Boston. Perhaps the people of the west are illiterate, and if it suits Boston, the west will think it all right. True, the western people are a plain, plodding people, somewhat matter of fact, not given so much to [illegible] and shoddy as your eastern people. They can readily choose between dross and gold, cockle and barley, notwithstanding, they are not devoid of culture. They read the *Atlantic*, *Harper's*, and all the leading periodicals of the day. Can appreciate their merits, and readily detect their errors; and although its scholars are not so ripe and aristocratic as those of the "hub of the Universe," [illegible] it makes Presidents, molds Generals, equips armies who march undismayed "right into the very mouth of Hell" and rescue a tottering and shattered Union.

If Prof. Longfellow has a passion French verse, and Mr. Agassiz loves the French muse (the gentleman to whom the poem is dedicated,) let them and the Boston mutual admiration Societies have a little French periodical printed and circulated among themselves. With the same propriety let them advocate church rites and ceremonies to be read in Latin, so that every illiterate commoner will not be able to comprehend it, and every poor devil frequent the sanctuary.

J. P. I.
Rockford

* A capital article, the above, and we only regret that the writer should have been under the necessity of introducing that horrid "French" phrase. If short fellows, like us, friend I., may do such things, what may we not expect of Longfellows! — [Eds. *Atlas*]

THE NEW YEAR
MA JAN. 5, 1866; <RR JAN. 6, 1866>

<Title: *Carrier's Address to the Patrons of the Rockford Register*>

PRELUDE

To Him whose mercies fell around
My pathway day by day,
As thither to the ferry bound,
I plod my erring way,
I gladly lift my soul and sing

A hymn to Pilgrim time,
Though old its euphony, I'll ring
On silver bells of rhyme,
Full sounding flow the major tones
In tranquil harmony,
And like the ocean's troubled moans
Be sorrow's minor key;
For right and left our fates have run
Between our hopes and fears,
As shadows alternate with sun,
So pass the dappled years.

GONE

He has gone beyond the River,
Through the valley chill and dark,
With his twelve erratic children,
A snow-haired Patriarch

II
Yet ere his crossing over,
Peace from out her horn had poured
Her lavish balm of Gilead
Through the gashes of the sword.

III
Cut deep in fearful struggle
On the carnage field, alas!
Where the blood of martyred heroes
Turned to gore upon the grass.

IV
Well, these were times of trouble <*sorrow*>;
And we never shall forget
Our agony and tossings,
Through nights of bloody sweat.

V
But a telegram at morning
Our pent up tears unsealed;
"In their army blankets shrouded
"They were buried on the field!"

VI
Then came the tender <*gentle*> spring time,
With clover nooks and birds,
To woo away our grieving,
Like a Nun's consoling words.

VII
And doves came to our windows
With their plucks of olive spray;
And the roll of battle thunders
Grew fainter day by day.

VIII
Then, as a flash of lightning,
From the azure heavens sent,
Came the news that smote us speechless —
Our murdered President!

IX
We did not weep; the flood gates
Of our souls were choked with grief;
We could only grieve <*groan*> in spirit,
We so loved our murdered <*martyred*> chief.

X
At length the flood gates bursted,
And our sorrow deluged forth;
Then we rose and swore revenge,
And we well fulfilled the <*our*> oath.

XI
Then Spring to Summer glided
Flooding fields with amber grain,
Healing o'er the scars of battle,
With the sunshine and the rain.

XII
And the soldier, turned to farmer,
And to market drove his beeves,
And the hands that bound the Union,
Now bound the golden sheaves

XIII
And the swords of haughty Rebels,
By the sweat of manly brows,
Were beaten into pruning hooks,
And shares for Yankee plows

XIV
To break the wilds where bondmen
From blood-hounds lay concealed,
The war trail worn and trodden
To a thrifty cotton field.

XV
Ho! Southward! men of action,
With your Bibles and your looms;
Go, chase away the darkness
From the land of Rebel tombs.

XVI
Ho! Southward! singing anthems
To Him whose mercies gave
The year foretold by prophets,
A land without a slave!

Forward and backward, stand I on the juts
Of time and look; somewhat I've wandered
Through the Past, foot-sore, scrambling up its steeps,
And sauntering here and there, sometimes in woods
And wilderness, perchance by hamlets, on
The farm through town and thorough-fares where trade
And traffic roar and babble all day long.
In passing thus <them> I've read the signs,
And numbers on the doors, and dates engraved
In marble in the Kirk-yards far and wide,
The mile-stones every one I've numbered
In my strolls, and kept a note of all the landmarks,
You see I'm full familiar with the little

Corner of my life, and like the Hebrew King
Have found that all is vanity,
Hence I'm weary of the Past, and wish
To know no more.

The far Beyond —
I seem to see its castles built of air;
I seem to hear a sweet voice singing,
"Come this way," Beware! the rainbow and
Bag of gold no mortal e'er hath gained.
I go. Of course my destiny lies there,
But how uncertain to this timid mind,
To Him alone who doeth all things well,
Let's give our hand, and uncomplaining go
As He shall thither lead.

Rockford, Ill.

Two Taverns
MA Aug. 3, 1866; RR July 21, 1867; <CA July 18, 1875>

On the river slopes I tarry,
Where the flakes of clover grow,
As moon beams o'er the waters <*The moon is in the waters,*>
Their silver pontoons throw <*The silver stars aglow,*>
When all my thoughts a-rambling, <*And musing martial numbers*>
Troop over to and fro. <*Are trooping to and fro.*>

To southward thrice a furlong
On airy-sandaled feet;
Through the care-encumbered city,
Through the toil-beleaguered street,
Now, like the sea from tempest,
In the holy calm of sleep.

Then northward, light as fairies
In their dance of sylvan rounds,
To the clumps of thrifty maple
On yonder burial grounds,
Where supple feet grow heavy <*lagging*>
Amid the crowded mounds.

Come hither, from the maples, <*So come, my musing members,*>
So weary <*heavy*> grown ye seem;
Come, sit down amid the clover,
My Paradise, I ween;
Come, nestle in my bosom,
My beloved, while we dream.

And so they came and nestled,
And we dreamed, in visions sweet,
That Sleep and Death kept taverns
On either side the street;
That one kept transient lodgers
And gave them wine and meat.

And the other, entertainment <*halls of slumber*>
For comers <*the weary,*> night and day,

Whether straggling in at evening,
Or morning's twilight gray,
Through the doorway wreathed with cypress,
But they never went away.

Rockford <*Kirkwood*>

Going Westward, Going!
WC Oct. 17, 1867; MA Oct. 25, 1867

Rocky Mountain Excursion, Oct. 11, 1867

We are on the wing, one hundred and fifty editors, "staging it," through to the Rocky Mountains! It's a big thing on wheels. Nothing like it in point of magnitude and novelty ever before rumbled and thundered over iron. Eight shining and flashing chariots like fleet coursers chase the steed of steam and fire to the rocky haunts of the grizzly, and wild slopes where the antelope gambol.

The irrepressible Yankee "is a joy forever." His jack-knife, in peace, is even more active than his two-edged sword is terrible in war. How it has whittled for progress! It is never in his pocket. It should be made the symbol of American ingenuity.

This train is a marvel of its skill — very beautiful and elegant. Carved and polished walnut panels and silver trimmings; ceilings of colors and tints, rich and delicate, fantastically blending and intermingling.

Lamps girdled with globes flowered as with a gauze of frost. Crimson curtains shut out the sharp light of day and filters it into a mellow flood over all within. Every time you move, you are reflected in a mirror. You lounge on puffed seats which temporize each rough jog into a delightful teeter! You step on soft Brussels. If your fingers are skilled to the touch of ivory, you can let them stroll among the keys of an organ to tickle your ears with sweet sounds.

We left Chicago at three o'clock in the afternoon after dining on frogs and everything palatable at the Sherman House. The bill of fare was long and "Frenchy." After grub we formed a procession headed by the Wilmington Brass Band, which can melt the heart with "Daisy Dean," or make one step staccato to "Get out of the Wilderness" — marched to the Depot — all aboard and away for the Mountains. Fleet as the sea-bird.

"We cross the Prairies, as of old
The Pilgrims crossed the Sea."

We do not stop for water tanks or towns, but Westward, ho! we rumble and thunder. We have all the humanity, eatables, and drinkables afreight we desire. We have brilliancy, stupidity, self-esteem, humility, experience, learning, wisdom and wit in all these Knights of the "gray goose quill." Yonder stands a group. The centre figure is the most irrepressible Yankee on the globe. He wears a "shad-belly" coat, a round-crowned stiff-brimmed hat; his breeches set so tightly that his legs resemble huge sausages; his feet are large and bumpy from corns; his hand is plump and white. A ring with a twinkling diamond is on his finger; his eyes are large, dull and gray, but he can light them at will; his hair is raven, intermingled with gray, and curling. Thus I have described the person of Geo. Francis Train. He is a perpetual motion machine. As a talkist, he is beyond doubt a success; he can talk to anybody, in any language; his tongue can roll off a brogue, double-round the Dutch, accent the French and switch off the Yankee, with every syllable sharply cut, like the inscriptions on a new coin; he can make a speech against time, on the shortest notice, on any subject named, and treat it in the most novel style of any man living. Yesterday, while on the ferry boat, before crossing to Omaha, I heard him extemporize rhyme, which was sung by all hands to the "Camptown Races," for a round half hour. Geo. Francis Train is a phenomenon. To my left is a little knot of four. They are writing a song; two are scribbling and fishing for a jingling rhyme, while Ossian E. Dodge composes music which Frank Lumbard will assist in singing at complimentary dinners. To my right and left are reporters and letter writers busily driving their pencils, and sending reports to the rear; others are playing at cards and chess, drinking Champagne, and one thing and another. Some are sleeping, some are lounging, telling stories, reading and giving themselves, as it seems, wholly up to "lotus eating." Care — that load, the weightiest of all — which so bends the back and oppresses the heart, cuts wrinkles on the cheek, and threads our locks with premature gray, seems to have been rolled off at Chicago. I say it looks so; but I know of one who brought a little along with him; for who knows his heart, better than himself. We sleep as the train moves westward two hundred miles through the darkness of the night. We awake in the light of the morning, wash in a marble bowl, and arrange our toilet before a mirror. Then we breakfast in the spacious dining car, on the most sumptuous fare.

The country we have passed through thus far to Omaha, I think is the richest and finest on God's green earth. Hundreds of thousands of acres of rolling prairie only await the Yankee plow-share to make it yield its fruits for man. There is land enough to supply all demands, so long as the Star of Empire Westward takes its way. And now since this great Railroad has been finished, lumber can be obtained for building and fencing purposes, at tolerably cheap rates. For a long distance between Boone and twenty miles east of Council Bluffs, the prairies are entirely uninhabited, save where we find streams and timber.

As we move swiftly along, someone says: "What hill is that?" It is one of the Council Bluffs. These bluffs multiply in size and steepness as we progress Westward. They appear to be composed principally of sand, and where the Railway cuts into the base a kind of clayey rock crops out. The first tier on the East presents a stunted grass, no other vegetation growing thereon. As we still dash Westward, they become more and more numerous, more and more precipitous, but crowned with a heavy growth of trees, shrubbery and grasses. The monotony is broken, however, by wild glens and gorges threading and cutting into them. Now and then the inevitable Irish hut is seen squatting in filthy humility with a hog pen by the door, while Bridget and the dirty-faced children stare at the flashing and rushing train. On one side is the scenery I have described; on the other we have a long, long stretch of corn-fields, flats, here and there a lake, now a slough, vocal with quacking ducks and hoarse-voiced cranes. I thrust my head out of the window, and behold the steeples of a town! We are turning on the brakes for a brief halt at the city of Council Bluffs. In the days of the ox teams and mules, when the gold fever put the cruel lash and goad into eager hands to lash and stab the weary, sore-footed cattle, toiling away to the far off land of Ophir, this city was famous in newspaper history, and was considered the jumping off place. We have met the mail bound eastward, and I must close until next week, when I will take you through Omaha, and farther Westward, ho!

Going Westward, Going!
WC Oct. 24, 1867; <MA Nov. 1, 1867>

Rocky Mountain Excursion, Oct. 13, 1867
No. 2

Omaha

Is not an old city, or a large one; but a city notwithstanding. She has great expectations and her citizens are full of drive and push. In the year 1853 an adventurous pioneer by the name of Jones settled on the present site and laid out a city. Jones was a prophet, inasmuch as he surveyed and staked its streets a hundred feet in width. To-day the wheels of traffic and the coming and going of busy feet quite fill them. Wide streets for a thriving city. Jones is sensible. I wish Jones had laid out Rockford <Monmouth>.

The city does not appear to much advantage from the Iowa side opposite — nothing more than a large village of straggling wooden buildings, with here and there a dingy brick overtopping its more humble neighbors. But as you cross the river and pass through to the eminence in the rear, upon which the State House stands, you will be fully convinced that Omaha is a city. Many fine brick blocks with magnificent stores — a large number being wholesale — loom up on every street. W. R. King & Co., wholesale grocers and liquor dealers, transact a business of one million dollars per year. A new brick is being built 180 feet front and running 100 feet to the rear. The Herndon House is five stories high. The State House is a long, brick structure, which can be seen at a great distance as you approach Omaha by rail from the East. It is painted white and is in a rather dilapidated condition. It has never been fully completed, the stair railings are not up, many of the interior Halls unplastered. Seated on the steps of the front door you have a full view of the whole city below, also of the valley up and down and beyond the muddy Missouri. The name of the city is derived from a tribe of Indians, who formerly inhabited this region. As intimated before, the site of the present town was an uninhabited wild in 1853. In 1860 the population was but 1,884. In 1865 it had increased to 4,500, and it is now estimated at 12,000.

The good people of Omaha extended to the excursionists the right hand of fellowship. The party was ferried across the river aboard the steamer Elkhorn, and drawn from the landing to the Cozzens House in conveyances gratuitously furnished by the city. The Cozzens House is a splendid new building, erected and finished from cellar to garret in just sixty days! Hospitality and a generous welcome were extended to us at every hand. A magnificent supper was given us by the proprietor of the Cozzens House, at which the Mayer, Senator Thayer, the ex-Governor of Nebraska and many other distinguished guests were present. In the evening the festivities closed with a Ball where "bright lamps shone on fair women and brave men." The next day (Thursday at 12 1/2 o'clock p.m.) we waved good-by to the "New Chicago," and again the train thundered Westward.

A MEAL ON THE CARS

Since starting towards the land of sunset, let us stagger forward through several coaches and across their quivering platforms into the dining cars. On our way thither we pass a corner where the hob-nobbing and clinking of glasses, the dense cloud of cigar smoke, boozy groups, boisterous laughter and hilarious talk are indicative of a saloon on wheels. As we carefully cross the next platform the olfactories divine the smell of potatoes and beef steak. We open the door and potatoes and beef steak "it are," with the addition of coffee in the morning, alkali water at dinner, and tea for supper; sometimes a little variation in the way of poorly cooked ham and sausage. Six short tables in a dress parade flank either side the aisle. Each is covered with a white oil cloth, and steams with hot grub. As we are a little late, we shall have to take our turn, and accordingly a motion chucks us behind the car door until some hungry brother is filled, when he reels out and we hobble and zigzag into his place. The aisle is filled with the children of Ham, who walk not exactly after the flesh, but step like blind dogs through high rye. They are gentlemen — every one of them — they come willingly forward, freighted with the inevitable rations; but the way is narrow, the rocking of the cars heavy and sudden, the filled are lumbering out with uncertain step, and the hungry, staggering and elbowing for a vacancy, so that the legs of the Press not unfrequently become tangled with those of the culinary department, when corns are pinched and profane language is heard above the confusion of tongues, the rattle of cups and the clink of tumblers. The bumps of the Union Pacific Railroad have completely jammed and thumped out the grace and suavity of the Kinsley Opera House waiters. Four men occupy each table and face each other as at euchre. A waiter, after some eccentric motions, sets you a dish of a decoction called coffee. The cream goes into your cup with a splash — the cup to your lips with an awkward flourish, and the coffee into your mouth with an impetuous gulp. Your knife and fork attacks consist in a series of pokes, prods, parries, thrusts, cuts and jerks. With all this skirmishing you lift the teetering and jiggling fork full in the direction of the mouth which meets it half way, when the morsel disappears singing, as I imagine, "Farewell, vain world, I'm going home." Appeasing hunger thus, is novel, to say the least of it. The fast whirling car wheels grind a man's appetite to a keen edge, and he eats by the league. We dart by three telegraph poles while buttering one biscuit and thunder over a score of miles at every meal. Fast living, yet good for digestion.

WESTWARD HO!

A sparsely settled country, resembling that of western Iowa, with rolling prairie, traversed by small creeks flanked with timber of an ordinary quality, extends about one hundred miles west of Omaha. The advantage of a ready market coupled with the Railway will make it very desirable for stock dealers and farmers, so that it will doubtless soon be thickly settled.

The North Platte River stretches its sand bar and island dappled length a long distance parallel with our line of travel. It is a very singular stream; the snows fall to a great depth, gorges the darksome cuts, and plumes the far off peaks of the Rocky Mountains; the Sun puts forth his warm hand, melts them into rills and brooks which laugh and leap into the valley. Thousands of these are tributary to this river. Byron said truth was in a well. Woodward said the "Old Oaken Bucket, filled with the emblem of truth overflowing and dripping with coolness arose from the well." But I say the symbol of truth wimples over the silver sands of the North Platte.

The Union Pacific R.R. from Omaha to Cheyenne threads a distance of 513 miles. The country after leaving the river, seems intended only as a floor for the railway and nothing else valuable; a long, long monotonous sea of arid waste covered only with a stunted bunch-grass, wild sage, cactus, ant hills, and prairie dog towns is all the eye detects, save occasionally sterile sand bluffs at some distance to the right or left. Dew is unknown in these regions, and rain never falls save in June and November. Sometimes, as we speed along, we see a jack-rabbit, as Josh Billings would say "with ears as large as snow shoes;" now an antelope is seen scudding towards the bluffs, with its white erected as a flag of truce, or a coyote skulking away, with backward look at our approach.

J.P.I.

Going Westward, Going!
WC Oct. 31, 1867; MA Nov. 8, 1867

Rocky Mountain Excursion, Oct. 14, 1867
No. 3

Twenty or twenty-five stations have already been established on the road, generally bearing Indian and geographical names. The average distance between them is about fifteen miles. A brief schedule of these stations will afford perhaps, a better idea of the primitive features of the great pathway than any other I could produce.

After leaving the "New Chicago" (Omaha) we scud westward 3 1/2 miles right onward through "Summit Siding" — a switch, no houses. Papillion, 12 1/2 miles — a "one mule" town if it may be dubbed, a wood and wagon station, a filthy Irish hut tenanted by a section hand and family; country rolling and fertile. Papillion some day will be a thriving village, only this and nothing more.

Elkhorn, 28 miles. At this point the eastern gate of the great Platte Valley swings open, and we enter in. A long curve in the road, like a graceful bow sweeps a mile to the right. I put my head out of the window, and lo! a picture — a landscape painted by the hand of the Creator! You drink in the breeze, and revel in its delight. A mile forward the pilot engine darts onward like a swallow. Now the great locomotive throws the fleecy steam from his hot nostrils, his great heart beats, and the pulses of his fleshless arms leap with floods of living fire, as the long train chases after, obedient to his will. The Platte Valley stretches 500 miles, from the Missouri River to the Rocky Mountains. Two or three scattered houses in sight; country rich.

Diamond, 33 miles. A wood and water station; choice prairie region. Here we met a passenger train in which were Gen. Rawlins, of Gen. Grant's staff, returning from an inspection tour among the western forts, and Gen. Dodge, chief engineer of the Union Pacific R.R., to whom we were introduced, and who made brief speeches.

Fremont, 46 miles. Called so in honor of John C. the original surveyor of the Platte Valley to the Rocky Mountains, where he caught the "woolly hoss," and dined on mule meat. Fremont is a town of eighty or a hundred small houses; good farming region, well settled for several miles around.

North Bend, 61 miles. Say twenty frame structures; two rival eating houses — price of grub, $1 per meal. No wine, oranges or nuts. Can't say I'd like to board here. This burg derives its name from the bend in the river to the north, where the railroad runs to within a few yards of it, but the track usually threads along several miles north of the stream.

Shell Creek, 75 miles. Only a wood and water station; extensively laid out, but thinly settled. Several houses can be seen on the old coach road, two miles distant.

Columbus, 91 miles. Is a "right smart" place, containing probably a population of 500 souls, and several millions of mosquitoes. Is located near the old town on the old coach road. The two have joined hands in marriage and so make a respectable village. Here George Francis Train claims is the geographical centre of America, and accordingly George has driven stakes for the future capital of the United States. He has wheedled many into that belief, and hence the secret of its thrift. Columbus is also the Capital of Platte county. In this vicinity is located the remnant of the once powerful Pawnee tribe, who have a fine reservation of land, and are supported by the Government. There are some four thousand of the tribe — men, women and children. Several hundred of the braves are now out hunting the Cheyenne and Sioux. We are to witness a war dance on our return.

Silver Creek, 109 miles. A house or two; fertile country.

Lone Tree, 131 miles. A lone house, but no lone tree in sight; wood and water station.

Grand Island, 153 miles. Half a dozen houses; good eating station; meals one dollar.

Wood River, 181 miles. A wood and water station only.

Kearney, 190 miles. The railroad feeder of Fort Kearney, a few miles distant on the opposite side of the river; eight or nine houses, one or two stores. Will hunt buffalo here on our return.

Friday morning we pass Elm Creek, 211 miles, one or two houses, miserable country. Towards daylight the cry of buffalo is raised, and an enthusiastic sportsman rushes to the window and lets fly at a small herd of peaceable cows.

Plum Creek, 230 miles. Four or five houses and near the scene of the massacre last summer. The ties with which the Indians threw the train off the track, and the debris of the cars are still visible. Just beyond is a new adobe fort. Presently a dozen antelope are seen north of the track, and the Nimrods, all excited, spring for their guns. Soon a squad of three or four more, and now a large wolf which is fired at but escapes unharmed.

Antelope Running the Gauntlet

Did you ever see an Antelope? Horace Greeley was right when he said they were the poetry of motion. To see one of these beautiful and timid little creatures is to look upon the very perfection of grace and elegance; the soft liquid eye is as clear as the limpid water of the Platte, the ear is transparent as a shell, and the nose sharply cut and very delicately formed. I think the Creator first apprenticed his hand on the fallow deer, and then molded the beautiful antelope. After breakfast as we rattle along between the last station named and North Platte, three of these little animals spring from the grass and lithely bound forward. All pity and compassion is lost in the fever and lust for sport, and men forget their humanity as they eagerly grasp their firearms and nervously level them from the car windows. The river runs parallel a mile to the right; the bluffs a half a mile to the left; the little fellows are not philosophers and trusting their speed try to head off the iron horse and thus gain a safe retreat among the hills on the other side. The eye of the engineer is on the game, and his hand upon the throttle; the antelope are running a gauntlet for their lives, the engineer urges and reins the fiery steed for the aim of his riders — bang, bang, bang from a hundred guns and carbines, now a whole volley rings sharply on the air, and the whizzing bullets cut the dirt about and beyond them, now they sheer off a little from danger, again leap forward, fleet as the wind and quickly oblique towards us, when a storm of mingled fire and hail opens with a terrific crash, but onward they bound and spring, and terrible as the rush of the whirlwind the train thunders on their flank. Hurrah, light footed antelope my heart is with you in your danger; ten miles and your speed has not abated, not a hair has been cut; twelve miles and you have baffled half a thousand bullets, and unscathed have won a safe retreat in the distance; three cheers for the antelope.

Next week I will describe a war dance and Julesburg.

GOING WESTWARD, GOING!
WC Nov. 7, 1867; <MA Nov. 22, 1867>

ROCKY MOUNTAIN EXCURSION, OCTOBER 1867
NO. 4

The town of North Platte is located 290 miles west of Omaha, at the confluence of the north and south branches of the river. This station was the busy terminus of the road until Julesburg sprang up and stole away her enterprise, everything moveable shifting in the direction of that modern Sodom. An eating house of considerable size, where meals are served at $1.25 each, twenty or thirty nondescript wooden buildings and shabbily constructed, a railroad round-house, and a number of repair shops make up the external appearance of North Platte. Two companies of cavalry and one of infantry are stationed here.

A War Dance!

This was the first place we saw Indians. A short distance back from the town was a small encampment of the Sioux tribe under Big Mouth, a chief. The appellation is just, for a mouth extending almost from ear to ear he has. He is a very large, muscular man, about 40 years old, and dressed in the attire of the pale face. Big Mouth and his small band were in readiness to regale us with a war dance. Our party formed a large circle, all eager "to see what they could see" of the red men. About thirty of the dusky devils walked in, and humbly squatted in a semicircle, many of them with their blankets half drawn over their faces as though they were ashamed to be seen. Not much I fancy as they appear at a real war dance after deliberately murdering white men, women and children, elevating their gory scalps on poles and howling like demons. I doubt not that these same humble, peaceful appearing "young men" of the forest would have cut the top knot from the head of any editor in the party, could they have caught him alone five miles from the railway. A bass drum was procured and a steady monotonous beat kept up by the squaw of Big Mouth, the only woman who participated in the powwow. Quite a number of squaws stood short distance off and looked admiringly on. Many of them were miserable old hags, wrinkled with age and covered with filth. One of them, a young squaw, was pointed out to me as the wife of "Spotted Tail." Mrs. "Spotted Tail" was evidently much charmed with the drumming and was one of the first to be moved by the spirit of the war dance — she jumped "straight" up and down, and made many demonstrations of delight. Mrs. "Spotted Tail" is the mother of a very bright-eyed, fair-haired little pappoose. One of two things is clear. "Spotted Tail, Jr." is either a half-breed, or "Spotted Tail, Sr." is a very light complected chief. Two others, sisters of the one first alluded to, were also designated as being wives of this blood-stained savage. All who participated in the war dance were daubed with paint, not spread on so evenly or quite so well blended as that on the cheeks of Rockford <Monmouth> belles, and much brighter in color. By this time the drumming has moved the spirit of one or two of the braves and they throw off their blankets, spring to their feet and go through a series of spasmodic jerks, whirls and jumps, accompanied with hideous grunts and whoops. In a moment, they suddenly stop, again squat to the ground, and sneakingly hide in their blankets. Probably two or three more will go through the same maneuvers. Then a single "big injun" will arise like a sinner under conviction, and recount his experience in hunting and scalping Pawnees. During the ceremonies while a brave, whose only costume was a very brief shirt and spare breech clout, is jerking, kicking and stamping among the wild sage and cactus, some wag asks if Mr. "Lo!" the poor Indian is present, when Geo. Francis Train, ever ready with his tongue and wit, replied:

"He is here —

Lo the poor Indian whose untutored mind
Clothes him before, but leaves him bare behind."

Big Mouth during the performance sat still as a stone, with his elbows resting on his knees and looking very despondent and sad. I could but recall the verses which passed before Hiawatha when told by Iagoo that he had seen "the

Coming of a bearded people
From the regions of the morning
From the shining land of Wabun."

After hearing this Hiawatha says:

"Then a darker drearier vision
Passed before me, vague and cloud-like,
I behold our nations scattered,
All forgetful of my counsels,
Weakened, warring with each other;
Saw the remnants of our people
Sweeping westward, wild and woeful,
Like the cloud-rack of a tempest
Like the withered leaves of autumn!"

The interpreter said Big Mouth was offended at some remarks that had been made. Train said that some white gentleman present also felt very much hurt at the conduct of the Indians, but that if Big Mouth was sorry for it, and would make a suitable apology, it would be acceptable, and that while the subject was under consideration he would introduce the celebrated Chinese war dance. Throwing off his coat he went at it, going through the most laughable gyration around the ring. Getting in front of the old chief — who evidently couldn't see the point — Train flapped his arms and legs about in the most extravagant manner, amidst the roars of the whole party.

After this, Ossian E. Dodge and Frank Lumbard sang a song, improvised by the former for the occasion, a box of presents was distributed among the Sioux. Our artist took a photograph of the Indians on the spot, and we returned to the train.

J.P.I.

Going Westward, Going!
WC Nov. 14, 1867; MA Nov. 29, 1867

Rocky Mountain Excursion, Oct. 1867
No. 5

Julesburg

If I were asked if hell has a geographic location, I think I should render a decision in favor of Julesburg. Sodom was a moral and religious city in comparison, yet it was cleaned out with fire and brimstone for its iniquity. We presume no such a burg as this same Julesburg exists on the face of the footstool. I have heard of "Natchez under the hill" as being most desperately dissolute and full of devilment. Paris is said to be a "tough place." Chicago has an unenviable reputation, little towns on the Mississippi river are low-lifed, filthy and full of abominations, but Julesburg trumps 'em all. Julesburg "knocks the persimmon," she is the most damnable of the damned. One may walk through the streets of any little village and see nothing but industry and morality; at least they will be the predominating features, but this collection of shanties on the plains exhibits the opposite side of the picture, idleness and the most wanton dissipation, the *ne plus ultra* of all cussedness. Last June this thing of evil sprang up like a mushroom — by the dog days it contained a rough-and-tumble population of 3,000, as the railway passed mountainward Julesburg, like an old shoe, began to run down at the heel, so that by the time the Editorial Excursion decamped there, for the night only, it looked not like a deserted village but an improvised one-horse Babylon decaying and falling away by piece-meal. A dreary country stretches itself over a dead flat as desolate and monotonous as the dead sea, bare sand bluffs rise here and there in the distance, and these are all the eye rests upon, no green trees or shrub, or flowers but the lone sandy plain.

The Excursion arrived early in the afternoon, the Mayor made a speech, and invited us to strap on our revolvers and take a stroll through the streets to see the sights. The streets are wide, no sidewalks, the threshold of each particular shanty is on level with the ground, sometimes the floors are below the common level; the buildings are all board shanties, mostly occupied as saloons and dance houses, a description of one of these houses will be a picture of all the others; eighty feet in length, forty in width, built of rough boards, a good solid floor. As you enter you hear fiddling and dancing — fiddling the most bewitching hornpipes, and the tipping and tapping of feet as perfect as a tattoo on a tenor drum; on the right hand is a bar where cheap cigars and forty-rod tangle leg are vended through all the hilarious hours of the night, on the left a faro bank, and all the tools for gambling.

The centre of the room is where the dancing is done, four brazen faced, blear eyed prostitutes sustain the female half of the cotillion, four "bullwhackers" (ox drivers) the other half thereof; these women, if so they may be called, are the most mournful spectacle of human depravity I have ever seen. A drunken prostitute smoking a cigar and cutting the most vile antics is a common sight in a Julesburg dance house. Each man participating in the dance is obliged to treat his partner.

The correspondent of the Sterling *Gazette* describes them as follows:

"Take pardners fur a dance," sings out the leader of the band, and the she devils go for the motley group of cut throats congregated around the bar. The set full away they go through the form of a cotillion, ending with "all promenade," which means you must take your girl to the bar and treat. The ladies respond without urging. One says:

"I'll take a whisky straight."

"Lemonade with a fly in it," says another.

"Here Jim, I want a gin-cocktail," is the gentle repartee of the third; and the fourth says:

"I'll take a cigar in mine."

And so it goes for hours, every night, Sabbath and week days, without intermission. Inflamed with liquor, these male and female specimens of depravity, keep alive these seething cauldrons of perdition and sink themselves so far down in the scale of degradation as to cause Babylonish harlotism to sink into utter insignificance in comparison. In our country, where the God of day casts his bright rays on civilization and Christianity, one such cesspool would be looked upon as sufficient to sink the whole community far into the regions of everlasting torment; but what will our readers think of Julesburg, where just such places are counted by the dozen — the rule and not the exception? But enough of the shameless devils who inhabit this God forsaken country. We have tendered them our compliments, and may God have mercy on the worms of the earth when the polluted carcasses of these beings shall be laid in a nameless grave on the adjacent sand hills.

"Verily I say unto you it shall be more tolerable for Sodom and Gomorrah in the day of judgement, than for" — Julesburg.

J.P.I.

Going Westward, Going!
WC Nov. 21, 1867

Rocky Mountain Excursion, Oct. 1867
No. 7

[This letter follows number five without a chronological gap in the newspaper issues, so it is almost certainly number six, incorrectly labeled as seven. — Ed.]

From Julesburg the train proceeded westward until we arrived a short distance from the end of the track. After coming to a halt we proceeded on foot about half a mile, when we overtook a regiment of workmen, armed with spades, pick axes, spike drivers, and all tools peculiar to the business of railroad building. The grading is done very rapidly, at some distance in advance, then the ties are thrown across and placed at equal distances apart almost as rapidly as the thread of a weaver is whipped through and through a web with a shuttle. The continuous line of rail grows longer and longer almost as fast as you can walk, and thus westward threads the great Union Pacific Railroad, the mightiest enterprise of the nineteenth century. The day of our arrival 4 1/2 miles of track was laid and completed. At this point, we endeavored to obtain conveyances to Denver via Cheyenne, it being 36 miles distant to the latter and about 140 to the former place, but we did not succeed as an excursion; only a small number being accommodated.

From this point the excursion started homeward,

running as far as Julesburg and there remaining over the Sabbath. I attended divine service in "Matcalf's Variety Theatre." The exercises were conducted by Rev. L. P. Tschiffely of Green Bay. The building is on [illegible] an 'alf principle, the front half being [illegible] part of canvas like a circus pavilion. What would be a vestibule in a church is in this one a drinking saloon and gambling hell. Now and then during service a citizen would step in, listen a few moments, and steal out in to the saloon to commune with a more congenial spirit than the one of whom the clergyman was speaking. I never spent so desolate an hour in my life. The wind moaned dismally and rattled the loose boards driving the dust and sand through the spreading cracks between them. The stage, upon which the minister stood, was in ridiculous contrast with a pulpit. On the front of the first screen was a [illegible] warning to the congregation to "BEWARE OF PICKPOCKETS!" On the opposite one another notice with the following bit of information: "25 CENTS FOR A STRAIGHT WHISKEY." In the rear of the pulpit one could discern empty bottles, short stumps of tallow candles sticking in square blocks of wood, which served for a "stick," oyster cans, and all kinds of "leavings" peculiar to a Julesburg Variety Theatre. The sermon was on "Progress."

Early in the evening the locomotive steamed up, and we soon left this modern Sodom in all her glory. We stopped over at Fort Kearney during Monday and until 4 P.M. on Tuesday, engaging in a buffalo hunt. About eighteen of these animals were killed. Our stop at Council Bluffs was very pleasant. We arrived home on the Saturday following, thankful for a safe journey, &c.

J.P.I.

IN MEMORIAM — A POEM
MA JAN. 24, 1868

[Irvine incorporated "David" at the end, but at the conclusion of each stanza, he swapped David's with My Soldier Boy in Heaven. Several early stanzas here also appear in "Arlington."— Ed.]

DELIVERED AT JACKSONVILLE, ILLINOIS, JAN. 8TH, 1868, BY J.P. IRVINE, ESQ., OF THE WINNEBAGO COUNTY CHIEF, ROCKFORD, ILL.

I
For th' soldiers a monody,
(Who breathe not a breath,)
All tenting in th' valley —
The shadow-land of Death.

II
A kingdom of no laughter,
Where th' lute is never strung;
No campfire merriment,
No battle ballads sung.

III
Where reveille and tattoo,
The drummers never beat;
Nor ever sounds the bugle
To advance or to retreat.

IV
No skirmishers on dusty,
No foeman lurk about,
The pickets have come in
And all the lights are out.

V
From the dusty rank and file,
To the wearer of a star,
Chief and private altogether,
Sleep the deep sleep of war.

VI
Friend and foeman altogether,
The rebel hordes in gray
And the blue hosts of Union
Are mouldering away.

VII
I saw them trooping thither,
To this dark vale of shade,
Full thrice an hundred thousand,
Till my heard became dismayed.

VIII
Ghost-like I saw them stalking,
Through weary night and day,
Hungry, haggard skeletons,
From Bastilles far away.

IX
From dank and noisome dungeons,
Where famine calls the roll;
From cells of plague and fever
Their ghastly spectres stole,

X
From the whirlwind of battle,
As flaming anger runs;
Hot as lurid lightnings
Out flashing from the guns.

XI
As deeper grows the carnage,
And redder grows the fight,
Alas, all slain and bleeding,
They vanish from my sight.

XII
From Antietam and Shiloh,
In combat hand to hand;
From Fair Oaks and from Frederick,
In green-hilled Maryland.

XIII
On Lookout, bald and rugged,
Were spread a thousand palls,
As up through flame and thunder,
They scale the craggy walls.

XIV
Three days from Murfreesboro,
They went, they went, alas;
And blood at Chickamauga,
Turned to gore upon the grass.

XV
O'er Malvern Hill the buzzards
Look downward soaring by;
And in the lonely [illegible]
The hungry ravens cry.

XVI
For th' fallen have been gathered
To the dust of kindly years,
The winds have chanted dirges,
And dews have drop't their tears.

XVII
The clouds have wept their fullness,
The heavens smiled serene,
The sun has poured his shining
O'er the mounds of mantled green.

XVIII
Sweet nature, ever mindful
Of darkness sorrow brings,
Is sure to send the morning,
With healing on her wings.

XIX
Yet still a weighty sadness
Is lingering in our souls,
For the loosened cords of silver,
The broken golden bowls —

XX
Sad tokens of their memory,
Cause ebbing griefs to swell
The full heart over-brimming,
As their mournful stories tell.

XXI
In hamlets and in palaces,
In cottages and halls,
Their canteens and their knapsacks
Hang empty on the walls.

XXII
Many coats are in the garrets,
Deeply crimsoned with stain;
And many are the blankets
Once a cover to the slain.

XXIII
There are hats pierced with bullets,
That never will be worn,
And locks and bonnie ringlets
From smitten heads are shorn —

XXIV
In all their mute eloquence,
Like talismen they are
Calling up the memory,
Of them who died in war —

XXV
Of the brave heroic soldiers,
(Who never breathe a breath,)
All tenting in the valley —
The shadow-land of Death.

In olden times, the morning stars high up
In yon ethereal world together
Trooped and sang an anthem to th' new born earth.
Fresh from the hand of God, she like a bride
All glorious and beautiful stood still.
The green-sward of her meads and swelling hills
Was by a plow-share yet unscarred; a scythe
Had never mown the clover from the nooks,
And kidlings ne'er had cropped the daises yet;
No axe had bled the young tree's tender trunk,
Nor pruning hook the thick'ning vintage trim'd;
Nor ship's prow vexed the crystal seas, or shook
The stilly waters of the lake.

'Twas long ere toil and traffic had grown busy
In the [illegible], and care had lain his heavy
Weight upon the human heart; ere age turned
Raven locks to gray, and cut his wrinkles
On the brow; ere death skulked like a leopard
In, with noiseless step, and stole away his prey.
Blood had not stained the grass, nor sounds of war
The mountain solitudes awoke.
The anthem o'er, the fleet-paced years take up
The march of Time. To-day we stand and look
Far backwards down the winding way
Full thickly flanked on either side with graves.
Consumption, wan and hectic, claims a part;
While fever, flushed and fitful, claims its share,
And suicide and murder, blood-be-dabbled
Stain the willows.

But most of all
In armor clad, with flashing sword unsheathed
The cruel War-God tears and groans hath made,
And filled the earth with horrid cruelty.
This goodly land of ours so sorely scourged
Has learned to know him well, and bear,
Her wounds yet scarcely healed to scars.
But yesterday we heard the drums
A-beating far and wide for volunteers,
And soon the march of armies knew no halt,
Save only when they grappled in the fight.
The tingling wires told many a sorry
Tale; and all the columns of the Press
O'er teemed with stories making hearts already

Sick with dread suspense, to throb and ache, with
Woe more keen than was the anguish of the
Hebrew King, when mourning for Absalom
"His son, his son;" and mothers, Rachel-like
Refusing for their smitten offspring to
Be comforted. O, those mothers weeping
A slain son, and binding the sash upon another
To fill his vacancy. O, heroic
Fortitude and Christian submission.
In the solemn stillness of the night, I
Hear, methinks, a mother singing to her
Soldier Boy in Heaven:

For thee my tears have filled the cup
Of sorrow, from the world apart.
Yet heavy thoughts come struggling up,
And sore oppress my wounded heart,
As thither strolling down the way
To where thine infancy was rocked,
The mile-stones call to mind each day
Whereon we laughed and sang and talked,
My Soldier Boy in Heaven.

Alas, my boy, that tongue is still,
Thy voice is mute, those lips are sealed.
Not thine alone but His good will
That thou thine own sweet life shouldst yield.
Though hard it seemed, while meek-eyed Peace
Stood spanning 'round the cloud of war
Her rainbow arch with promises
Full clearer than the morning star!

My Soldier Boy in Heaven.

But be it so — His will be done;
Such blood atones the Nation's ills,
Nor oil, nor wine in rivers run.
Nor cattle on a thousand hills.
Nor corn, nor gold, nor sheaves suffice,
But fervent prayers in sack-cloth bound.
And human lives in sacrifice,
Will heal the grieved Jehovah's wound,
My Soldier Boy in Heaven.

Then all is well, from far away,
A hand beside the great white throne,
Through every hour along the day,
Keeps hither beck'ning me to come.
A voice within the night-time seems
To whisper "Come, Christ is the Vine,"
These visions be no empty dreams,
That spirit voice and hand are thine,
My Soldier Boy in Heaven.

I'm clay within the potter's hand,
And Christ the Lord will me remold,
As grain by grain ekes out my sand
He fits me for the streets of gold.
Each day in silver numbers run
Ye sands, a ceaseless stream outglide,
Oh, blessed time, Oh quickly come
When for them I am sanctified.
My Soldier Boy in Heaven.

As cunning Time moves slyly by, his hand
Will smooth each battle-furrowed field,
Full rounding every sapling's trunk
Erst shattered by a cannon ball.
We children of a day, from humoring
Desires, and chasing phantoms, will, amid
The snares concealed along the way become
Entangled and perplexed, forgetful of
The sheaves once reaped and gathered there.

Now Ye who wield the sceptre quill, with whom
The power to bless or bane doth rest;
Ye guardians of the Union gates,
Still singing, "Printer's Ink is King;"
Throw ope each column of the Press and urge
Each County where your power is felt, to build
Its soldiers dead a monument — a shaft
Of snow white marble towering up, in mute
Perpetual Eloquence:
Ever telling of th' soldiers
(Who breathe not a breath,)
All tenting in th' valley —
The shadow-land of Death.

TO THE BOYS IN BLUE
MA OCT. 23, 1868

"Come rally round our Flag once more," and for our country go

[illegible] people know,
Who led us safely through the war, was always seen before,
We've seen enough of war, my boys, and don't want Seymour.

With "Ulysses" for our Captain, and at the helm "Colfax,"
Our good old ship will ride the storm, and soon reduce our tax,
Our country then will prosper, the wars will all be o'er,
We've seen enough of war, my boys, and don't want Seymour.

We still have brothers in the South, who hopeful look to you
To do your duty at the polls, and they will still prove true,
They love the North, they love the South, their country they adore,
They've seen enough of war, my boys, and don't want Seymour.

There is a ship a building, whose timbers are all green,
With "Horatio" for her Captain, "Frank Blair" for a swain,
She's bound for the "Salt River," in November leaves the shore,
We've seen enough of war, my boys, and don't want Seymour.

Our ship is large, our crew well tried, we're bound to make good time.
Then step on board all ye who wish to fight upon that line.
"Salt River" is no place for you, who fought so brave before,
You've seen enough of war, brave boys, and don't want Seymour.

To Johanus Leonidus Murpheus, Esq.
MA Mar. 26, 1869

We do not think much of the following as [illegible] genius of one of our citizens, we let it slide. — Eds. *Atlas*

I've been thinking, dear friend, you might relist a line
From the city of Springfield, if done up in rhyme,
And have just dipped a pen in this inkstand of mine,
And there's a beginning;
But where it will run to, why, He only knows
"Who knoweth all things," both beginning and close
Of a yarn, e're yon start a spinning.

I left your famed city, perhaps you may know,
At seven a.m., thirsty-first ultimo,
To-wit, on the last of December.
And I'll tell you the most I have seen since that time,
Or, all I can possibly force into rhyme;
Or, all I distinctly remember.

We came by Mendota, Decatur, and "sich,"
Through a country wide, level and fertile, and rich,
And as "nice as a woman."
No, that I'll take back, that is rather too strong;
Though the country is nice I am certainly wrong,
Because it's not human!

You may talk of nice houses, nice pictures, nice books —
[illegible]
But you still can't deceive;
You may say they are nice, and they are without doubt,
But to my mind the nicest thing ever "let out"
Was a "daughter of Eve."

There are some things down here that to my mind ain't level,
But don't let it out or they'll give me the devil —
As sure as a gun!
If I only dare tell you the "tricks of the trade,"
Of the "grabs" on the green ones by sharp fellows made
You would think it rare fun,

But money still makes the "mare go,"
And money makes names in the papers show,
And money makes reputation.
There is another thing, but [illegible]
I have been told — but it can't be so —
That money makes legislation.

There's a fellow round here who is ready to "do us"
In the papers of Springfield, Chicago, St. Louis,

Or any great town.
A few plain facts he wants to know,
As a starting point from which to "blow,"
And then — "Come down."

[illegible]
And a goat for a sheep in his hands would pass,
For a small consideration.
A saint of the veriest sinner he'll make,
A model man of the wildest rake,
If he pays for the transformation.

But after all don't you think with me,
That a man's own self he had better be,
And fill a more humble station,
Than to be puffed up above one's peers,
A target for all the fleers and jeers
Of this very irreverent nation.

Now hoping this letter will find you O.K.,
As "fine as a fiddle," and festive and gay,
And happy and pleasant,
I will "cut it off" e'er it gets too long,
And "wind it up" with that "same old song"
Of — "nothing more at present."

Springfield

The Jewel in the Casket
WC Aug. 26, 1869

In Memoriam

When a fond father sits down to write the obituary of his only child, whom he loved as he loves his own life, his heart must needs be heavy and his soul sorrowful. If to-day I could throw open the doors of the secret chambers of my inner life, where darkness broods and desolation sits in solitude, I would refuse to do so, lest a sunbeam should glint in and make me forget the cause of this darkness and desolation. Only a faint shadow of what bereaved parents feel, when the light of their house is struck out by a blow, can fall upon paper. Every father's and mother's sorrow for a lost offspring is peculiarly and sacredly their own. No one but he or she who is crushed with affliction realizes what strange and mysterious yearnings there are in the human heart. Mysterious, yes, to-day my heart yearns with pain, yet revels in a sweet remembrance; pain for everlasting absence of Lizzie, the dear one; a sweet remembrance of her silver laugh and genial face; a wave of grief for the half-worn little shoes which shod her delicate feet and a joy to know that she walks the streets of gold and that she can never go astray; a sigh to realize that she will never run to meet me and a pleasure to know that she beckons me to heaven; a sad thought that her voice is hushed on earth, and a sweet one to know that she sings with the angels; a tear for a future without her kisses, and a smile for the fond ones she left. Oh how much more happy to-day than her father and mother, and how we rejoice that she is safe from temptation and pollution. The [illegible] and this is a hard world, and the little ones who set out to try its realities will grow footsore and weary on the journey, for the hills are rugged and the way is long; dangers lurk in the hedges, and seductive hope fills not her promises. There are no rough places in the land where Lizzie has gone. There is no night or darkness there. There she will never grow weary or know that pain is. The footprints of the years will never mar [illegible] the affection that prompted her to throw her arms around my neck and say: "Papa, I love you," will be lavished upon a better Father than he who pours his soul out for her to-day. Alas my child — thou dear one of my heart — it is hard to give thee up, hard to miss thee at the table and the gate, to know that thou will never light this darkened house again. That shower of brown curls that fell about thy snow white shoulders, and clustered closer when it rained, is now a pillow for thee — my jewel in the casket. Thine eyes, so full of light and joy are closed, closed forever, and their lashes lie like silken fringe upon their lids of alabaster. That rounded brow and silver skin so laced with faint traces of azure veins will fade and yield to death's imperial reign. But what of that? Some time — not long — we will meet — when all shall meet — a regal company, I think. Kings and Queens and little children robed in white and crowned with love and "beautiful with all the soul's expansion." Lizzie has only gone before, only gone to heaven to be educated. In the language of another: God makes no mistakes, so all is well with us, and the jewel we have locked in the casket.

Resignation

There is no flock, however watched and tended,
But one dead lamb is there!
There is no fireside, howsoe'er defended,
But has one vacant chair!

The air is full of farewells to the dying,
And mournings for the dead;
The heart of Rachel, for her children crying,
Will not be comforted!

Let us be patient! These severe afflictions
Not from the ground arise
But oftentimes celestial benedictions
Assume the dark disguise.

We see her dimly through the mists and vapors;
Amid these earthy damps
What seem to us but funeral tapers
May be heaven's distant lamps.

There is no Death; What seems so is transition;
This life of mortal breath
Is but a suburb of the life elysian,
Whose portal we call Death.

She is not dead — the child of our affection,
But gone onto that school

Where she no longer needs our poor protection,
And Christ himself doth rule.

Is that great cloister's stillness and seclusion
By guardian angels led,
Safe from temptation, safe from sin's pollution,
She lives, whom we call dead.

Day after day we think what she is doing
In those bright realms of air;
Year after year her tender steps pursuing,
Behold her grown more fair.

Thus do we walk with her, and keep unbroken
The bond which nature gives,
Thinking that our remembrance, tho' unspoken,
May reach her where she lives.

And though at times impetuous with emotion
And anguish long suppressed,
The swelling heart heaves moaning like the ocean,
That cannot be at rest —

We will be patient, and assuage the feeing
We may not wholly stay;
By silence sanctifying, not concealing,
The grief that must have way.

To Our Readers

We know our readers will, one and all, sympathize with us in our bereavement and excuse our columns from the dearth of local news this week. Nothing but the death of our child, and the sad circumstances which surround it, occupy our mind. We trust, however, that many who read what we have written (with a very sore heart) will be benefitted thereby. By degrees the waves of sorrow will in a measure ebb away, and we will then give you all the news.

Those who are not familiar with this sad calamity will learn that she died on Sabbath morning last, from injuries received by being thrown from a runaway carriage on the evening of the 16th Inst.

A Card of Thanks

To all those kind friends and neighbors who assisted at the bed-side of our unfortunate little girl while she suffered, and for every deed they performed after she passed away, and for the warm and Christian sympathy extended, we return our most grateful thanks.

J.P. & Hattie Irvine

At the Golden Gate She'll Meet Us
WC Sept. 16, 1869

A Father's Tribute

At the golden gate she'll meet us,

When the weary years are gone,
And she'll loudly kiss and greet us
With her angle plumage on
As the song of sacred story
In its numbers sweetly falls
She will lead us home to glory
All within the Jasper Walls.

CHORUS
Weary years, then cease to tarry
Yet we sigh and long to go;
Tow us, boatman, o'er the ferry,
Though white-plumed the breakers flow;
For we know, she'll run to meet us,
And she's watching while we wait
And the whitest soul to greet us,
Will be Lizzie at the gate.

All within, where every tomorrow
Brings its joys without its woes
And no bitter cup of sorrow
Ever brims, or overflows,
Where from grieving and [illegible]
[illegible] no longing souls in vain
But, as precious jewels, shining
In the sunbeams after rain.

CHORUS: WEARY YEARS, THEN CEASE TO TARRY, &C.

[illegible]
And the way so rough and long,

And the night so dark and dreary,
And the days devoid of song;
Yet, there's joy to know she'll meet us,
And, in patience, we must wait,
For the whitest soul to greet us
Will be Lizzie at the gate.

CHORUS: WEARY YEARS, THEN CEASE TO TARRY, &C.

MY LITTLE GIRL UNDER THE SNOW
WC NOV. 18, 1869; MR NOV. 26, 1869; <GL MAY 1891>

[The version Irvine used in his book, with many changes, appears in full below. — Ed.]

My heart, in the ripeness of sorrow,
Grows mellow as winter draws near,
All alone I stand by the window,
Looking out on the fall of the year;
For ceased have the sleeting and raining,
And now in the stillness, I know,
By the vagrant flakes that are falling,
That all the night long it will snow.

And I think of my beautiful darling,
In her little grave under the leaves,
Only dressed in a shroud of Swiss muslin,
Cut low in the neck and the sleeves;
For she died when the manifold lilies,

And woodbines and asphodels blow;
But the meek little face in the coffin,
Was as pure and as white as the snow.

And now I remember, while thinking,
How a year ago she and I stood
Talking here by the window together,
Of the robins and babes in the wood,
And kissing me, ask'd if the birdies
And God loved all little childr'n so?
But little thought I that my birdie
To-night would sleep under the snow.

But she needs not the care of the birdies,
Though the robins may gather and sing,
Where grasses come up, and the roses
Blow full in the beautiful Spring;
For I know she is Queen among angels,
In the land of no longing or woe,
Where all the year long it is Summer,
And nothing lies under the snow.

<1891 version, same title>

I am standing alone by the window
A looking out on the infinite gray,
As it deepens and darkens to silence
At the close of a desolate day:
There's a lull in the sleeting and raining,
And now in the stillness I know —
As the flakes feather aimlessly downward —

That all the night long it will snow.

And lo, as it falls in the valley,
In the deep, still woods and the sea,
There's a fall, as of flakes, in the darkness
Of the life that God gave unto me;
For the clouds have been heavy and rainy,
But now there's a lull, and I know
That my sorrow is soft'ning to longing
For my little girl under the snow. —

This night, for my poor little darling,
In her little grave under the leaves,
Only dressed in a shroud of Swiss-muslin,
Cut low at the neck and the sleeves;
For she died when the manifold lilies
Were a-bloom in the garden below,
But the meek little face in the coffin
Was as mute and as pure as the snow.

And now, I remember, while thinking,
How a year ago — this very night,
That she and I, here by the window,
Stood watching the snow-birds alight;
And coaxingly calling she fed them
With little white pellets of dough,
But alas, did I think that my birdie
Would sleep to-night under the snow.

But why should I weary with longing,
When to cease, if for e'en but a day

Or a night, would be proof of forgetting;
Ah, sorrow, stay with me, I pray;
Stay with me, that I may be humble
And patient in bearing the loss
Of the dear little idol that keeps me,
So near to the foot of the cross.

1870-1879

Farewell
WC Oct. 22, 1870

With this issue of the CHIEF, as its editor and proprietor, I bid my patrons farewell, having sold all my right, title and interest in the same to Mr. Hiram R. Enoch, who will hereafter continue its publication and assume editorial control.

In retiring from its cares and duties I feel as if released from a burden, that during the past year has been very heavy, yet, at the same time, my heart aches for I had become warmly attached to the CHIEF, since it was the object of my own enterprise, and that someday it should out-rank all secular weeklies in the great State of Illinois was the goal of my ambition. But I had not the money to sustain it, and a lack of money and hard times and domestic trials and afflictions, crushed my ambition until I became aware that I was neither doing my patrons justice nor carrying out the intent of my motto, and hence my object and my only object in parting with my cherished enterprise. During its existence of two hundred and five weeks, or four years, almost, I have been absent from the city but nine or ten days, and only [illegible] publication, except during a severe illness.

What the CHIEF has been in point of independence, the public well know, whatever may have been my faults and failures, I have mostly published my opinion, and for the simple reason that the naked truth was often exposed and vice handled without gloves, I have received only a little credit with a large balance of censure charged on the debit side of my account. Yet, if I edited a paper for a thousand years to come, I should pursue the same course, only with a keener lance and a more vigorous pen.

In the hands of Mr. H. R. Enoch, I have no doubt the CHIEF will prosper. That gentleman was for some time associated with me in conducting it, since which time he has been engaged in the management of his job printing office in the same building. Mr. Enoch has had considerable newspaper experience, is an industrious, prudent man, and well known throughout the county, and we trust the business public will extend to him a liberal patronage.

Towards our contemporaries, we cherish nothing but the most kindly feelings. True, Mr. Griggs of the *Register*, and I have had many a tilt, I have shot a good many arrows at him and he has thrust lances back at me, but if they wounded at all, it was only for the time being for it was never thought of when we met. Mr. J. E. Fox, associate editor of the register, also has our thanks and well wishes for his uniform courtesy.

The *Gazette*, for some time past has been our nearest neighbor, and we have found Mr. Smith, its editor, to be a very civil and obliging man, one who to all appearances attends strictly to his own business. In times past we "pitched into him" occasionally, but since he made no "fuss" about it, we concluded to quit. We cannot but wish the *Gazette* success.

In speaking of my contemporaries, I regret to say, that there is, and always has been, a deplorable lack of harmony between them, while they have agreed in politics — that is of the same party — they have made it a rule, without an exception, to disagree upon every other question, hence, they lose their moral influence and the public learn to mistrust them. As local newspapers, neither of the three has come up to a proper standard. The reason of this is that their editors have either confined themselves too closely to their offices, or given too much time and attention to the business matters of the paper. For this the public, too, are much at fault, inasmuch as it is a notorious fact that people do not pay the printer with that promptness they do others.

And now, in retiring as editor of the CHIEF, permit me to thank all my patrons and friends who have been both generous and forbearing during our business intercourse, and I do so from a full, warm grateful heart, ever wishing for the prosperity of the CHIEF, and trusting that the blessing of heaven may rest upon all.

J.P. Irvine

AT NEW YEAR'S DAWN
CA JAN. 7, 1872; <GL MAY 1891>

A poet wove at Near Year's dawn <*At New Year's dawn a poet wove*>
A tinkling rhyme in divers keys:
Behind, he saw <*him lay*> the darkened hills,
Beyond, the light of <*him rolled the*> purple seas.

And Time is young and Time is old
He made the glad and sad refrain,
Sweet mingling each with each as fall
The amber <*glinting*> sunbeams and the rain.

And Time is young and Time is old,
And nimble feet aweary grow,
As round and round the seasons roll
And cypress buds and roses blow.
<*The woodbine and the cypress blow.*>

And <*Aye,*> Time is young and Time is old,
Said He, who sends <*With Him who marks*> our joys and tears,
A thousand years is but a day,
A fleeting day a thousand years.

ORGANIC REMAINS
CA Jan. 21, 1872; MR Oct. 18, 1872; <CA *June 28, 1874; DG Apr. 7, 1875*>

<*The following choice bit of rhymed humor, worthy the pen of Tom Hood, first appeared in* The Capital *some two years ago. Since then the lines have been going the rounds of the press, latterly without credit to us, and generally abused by careless printers. To correct these wrongs, we republish them to-day:*>

Six tunes <*times*> in all, I think he ground,
Six rasping, whee-whaw, wheezy tunes;
All summer long he came around
And ground away the afternoons.

One darned eternal <*'Twas one demnition*> horrid grind
Of "Captain Jinks," and "Not for Joe,"
A German waltz, and "Auld Lang Syne,"
An Irish jig, and "Jump Jim Crow."

This organ-grinder had, I ween,
A look all humble and forlorn,
And, furthermore, of red and green,
A monkey dressed in uniform.

His monkeyship <*This monkey he*> was keen and cute,
So clever, too, that I began
To side with Darwin, and to boot,
I thought the monkey most a man.

<*He'd walk upon two legs and chaw*>

<Tobacco — so I've heard it said —>
<And pick up every cent he saw,>
<And doff his hat and scratch his head.>
One afternoon the two came 'round,
As usual and a-grinding stood,
When lo! an earthquake shook the ground,
And buildings of the neighborhood.

There was a sudden stampede then
From basements through to attic nooks
Of children, women, dogs, and men,
And bottle-washers, and chief cooks.

Pell-mell, the cultured and ill-bred,
Without regard to courtesies,
They found the organ grinder dead
To all intents and purposes.

And since <*At least*> the fragments, lean and lank,
Looked somewhat like him, when adjusted;
Also, a surplus tail and crank
Proved clearly org. and monk. had busted.

SEQUEL

Some wag the organ lock had sprung
The night before, as could be seen,
And hidden in its wheezy lung
An ounce of nitroglycerine.

And when he ground, of course you know,

The earthquake came, when suddenly, <*monk. and he,*>
He, and the monkey, and Jim Crow <*And Jinks and Syne, and Joe and Crow*>
All jumped into eternity.

MORAL

And now, beware, since he "went up,"
Oh! organ grinders it is seen, <*Ye grinders, for 'tis plainly seen*>
That deep damnation is pent up
In wags and nitroglycerine.

THE NEXT DAY AFTER THE DISASTER.
Washington, D.C.

DEFUNCTUS NIGER
CA MAR. 3, 1872

[*The Capital* titled its recurring humor column "Graduatcd Grins" and "Capital Grins." — Ed.]

Not a very fitting ballad
For a "Graduated Grin,"
But I rather guess I'll tell it,
And accordingly begin:

He was a ranting rouser,
Of the pedigree of Ham;

His name was Samuel Johnston,
For short they called him Sam.
His head was round and woolly,
And his visage black as jet,
And his lips curl'd like the bottom
Of a German clarinet.

His heels were like the jaybird's,
And a question grave arose
Amongst the monkey-naturalists
Regarding Johnston's toes.

But in time they did develop,
Thus convincing Johnston's friends
That all was right concerning
HIs pedal odds and ends.

And as he peddled oysters,
(In a horn) his life sublime
He made, by leaving footprints
Upon the sands of Time.

This "d—d infernal trumpet" —
Or words to that effect —
Had rasped my nervous system,
And my social being check'd.

I could prophecy his coming
Upon his daily walks
by his cussed snorts, and shoutings,
And lacerating squawks.

I think it was a fortnight
Or a month ago, or sich,
When a-shouting, and a-squawking,
That he fell into a ditch.

And there he flopped and floundered,
By fits, and starts, and jerks,
And he swore he wished the devil
Had the Board of Public Works.

An infuriated madman
He resembled in his rant;
And then he prayed to Gatchell,
And called on Captain Grant.

And grabbing up his trumpet,
He blew with such a vim
That *terra firma* trembled
And the sandy ditch cav'd in;

Which rather put a veto
(Because he greatly sinned)
On Johnston's calculations
By shutting off his wind.

And as the sewerage piping
Had been lain, as could be shown,
They left him in his glory,
Uncoffined and alone,

Till Life in ample fullness

Shall overflow its cup,
And the resurrection angel
Shall come and trump him up.

Notice

There's a deep and yawning sewer
Near my dwelling, and I know
The Fates have left it open
For oystermen who blow,
And should any tumble in it —
As Johnston on his route —
I'll leave the job to Gabriel
To blow the fellow out.

Something Rotten in Denmark
CA Mar. 12, 1872

A certain scissor-grinder,
The style of Jeremy Diddler,
A bilious-looking harpist,
And a melancholy fiddler,
The other night were groggy,
Which accounts, as clear as noon,
For th' blood and thunder rumpus
In a Murder Bay saloon.

It appears th' scissor grinder,
Who was cock'd on apple jack,

Had hit the fuddled fiddler
On the head, a thund'ring whack
With an empty ketchup bottle
Which upset him from his legs,
Into his proper level,
Down amongst the empty kegs.

At this the harpist's dander
Riz, and ran so fiercely high,
That ere he knew he put a
Mansard roof on grinder's eye;
Then grinder grab'd a roller —
For rolling rumpled towels —
But, with a pair of scissors,
Harpist jabbed him in th' bowels.

Then grinder shied the roller
As if nothing had mishap'd,
With such exact precision
That, instanter, something drap'd!
Whereon he fell, for want of
Breath as stiff as any post,
And, like unto the others,
Then and there gave up the ghost.

Of course the brave policemen
Somewhere else had urgent calls,
(They always have a chronic
Taking leave from midnight brawls,)
So sudden fell the terror
On the devil of the hell,

That he lock'd th' door and scampered —
Which accounteth for the smell!
MORAL

What! vulgar in my language?
Nay, good reader, understand
That slang can only picture
Well the rum-holes of the land.
Profane? Ah! truth is sacred:
Go ye down to Death, as soon,
As th' damned infernal precincts
Of a Murder Bay saloon.

ARLINGTON
CA MAY 26, 1872; MA SEPT. 27, 1872; <PG JAN. 1874>

<Title: *Death's Encampment*>

[Several stanzas here also appear in "In Memoriam." The following introduction prefaced only the Monmouth version. — Ed.]

Arlington was the name of the homestead of the late General R. E. Lee, commander-in-chief of the Confederate army during the rebellion. It is located on a wooded height, on the Virginia side of the Potomac river, opposite the City of Washington, D.C. It will be remembered that it was confiscated by the Government and dedicated as one of our National Cemeteries. About

22,000 soldiers lie buried here, 2,000 of whom are colored, and 4,000 rebel.

How very mute the soldiers,
In these solemn tents of death;
I often pause and listen,
But I never catch a breath.

I never hear a foot-fall —
Nor a murmur, nor a sigh,
Nor peal of jocund laughter,
And I muse and wonder why.

For years are brief between us
Since the muster roll was long,
And <*Where*> camping grounds were noisy
With the roll of mirth and song.

Though these bivouacs be narrow,
Still content and hushed are they:
The Blue who loved the Union,
And the valiant Rebel Grey.

[Monmouth and Pension versions, stanza 5 — Ed.]
And they, who once <*late*> were bondmen,
Lie in level state between,
Their mold <*dust*> is just as sacred,
And their mounds are just as green.

[D.C. version, stanza 5 — Ed.]
Sweet Charity is kindly

And responds to Nature's call
With daffodils and roses
And violets for all.
<And nature in her roses,
For each, conceals regrets,
Yet in spite, her tears are welling
In the eyes of violets.>

The North has grasped and shaken
The warm hand of the South;
And her web the spider's woven
Across the cannon's mouth.

The sword is in its scabbard,
And in cottages <*attics*> and <*in*> halls,
Their canteens and their knapsacks
Hang empty on the walls.

No reveille nor tattoo,
The Drummers ever beat;
Nor ever sounds the bugle,
To charge or to retreat.

No skirmishers on duty,
Nor foemen lurk about;
And the pickets have come in,
And all the lights are out.

Washington, D.C.

My Angel Visitant
CA June 8, 1872

Stay, oh stay, my sainted sister,
Yet a little, let me be
At thy feet an humble learner
While I frankly question thee;
For I know thou hast the knowledge —
By the glory of thine eyes,
And the whiteness of thy raiment,
Of the Golden Paradise.

Hast thou seen a dainty angel
With a wealth of sunny hair;
Has she grown in radiant beauty,
Are her foot-falls light as air?
Did she smiling run to meet thee,
Were her kisses sweet and bland,
Through the open gates of jasper
Did she lead thee by the hand?

Has the flash of Time between us
Quickened darkness? does she know
Of the cruel grief that smote us
When our hope was changed to woe?
But I'm told that the Immortal
Is unshadowed by the Past,
And the burden of remembrance
At the door of Death is cast.

There was one of ample promise,
By the cannon's thunder jar
From the family cluster shaken
As a windfall — of the War.
He was truthful, he was tuneful,
And he wore the blush of Spring;
In his sanctified perfection
Does he ever smile and sing?

Have you seen the meek and guileless
King of Kings — who died for men —
Are his garments like the morning,
As the sun his diadem?
And do Truth and Love and Mercy
Ever woo him to be kissed;
Or his head upon his bosom
Leans the dear Evangelist?

Come, draw near me, now, make answer,
Let me touch thee, feel thy breath;
Reach thy hand, and I will clasp it
Half across the dark of Death.
Yet I would not lure thee hither,
Back to earth, nay if I could,
Though we grieved so when you left us
And put on your angelhood.

This world is still a paradox,
Still so hard to understand:
There's sunlight on the ocean
And there's shadow on the land;

Our freighted ships go sailing
And we never see them more;
The sea is wild and wrathful
But there's calm upon the shore.

Come then, oh! beautiful sweet spirit,
Lend me wings and let me fly
Far with thee across the vastness
To the ever peaceful sky —
Through the open gates of jasper,
To the Eden of the bless'd,
Where the wicked cease from troubling,
And the weary are at rest.

And I 'woke and she had vanished
Like a vision from my sight;
And I lay and heard Time flowing
Far adown the vale of Night.

Washington D.C.

A Hymn
CA JULY 7, 1872

Come, oh! blessed Savior, woo me
From this bondage of regret,
Call across the darkness to me,
Once again — a little yet.

What is pleasure but a fancy
Lost to wisdom while we wait —
Cunning game of necromancy,
In the nimble hands of fate?

Well I know the world, and love it —
From its wounds my heart is sore —
Still, its sweet allurements covet,
Reaching out and crying more.

Oh! the nameless pain of longing —
Tossing night its fever brings —
Blessed Savior, send the morning,
And the healing of its wings.

Make my faith and patience stronger,
Let me live, and let me try,
In its light, a little longer,
How to live and how to die.

Washington, D.C.

THE WOODEN LEG
CA JULY 21, 1872; <MR APR. 14, 1876>

Have you heard of the fate of poor Gregory McGregg,
Who was leal to the Union and gave it a leg,
That was shattered away by a fragment of <*piece of a*> shell,

For <*When*> the battle was red like a fierce, panting hell?
But a life is a life, so he crept to a wood,
Where he lay in a thicket, hard by, in his blood,
Till the enemy yielded, and faltered, and fled,
When they gathered the harvest — the wounded and dead. <*Where the harvest was gathered of the wounded and dead.*>

So McGregg was borne off to the hospital then,
On a stretcher between two utility men,
And there doctored and soothed by the kindest of hands,
Through the Christian Commish and the singing of psalms,

Till at last he got well from his anguish and such,
Was discharged, and went home, 'twixt a staff and a crutch;
But his old Uncle Sam taking kindly to him,
In his goodness of heart went and bought him a limb.

'Twas a patent concern, as the stamps on it shows,
Though how to describe it the Lord only knows,
But it bends at the knee and it works at the toes,
It is shapely and smooth as a woman's, but still

It is bloodless, and cold, and it has not the will
Of the one which he lost in the fight on the hill;
For the muscles, and tendons, and nerves, and such things,
Are inanimate tackle of staples and rings,

And of garters elastic, and fine tempered <*fierce-tempered*> springs,
And of Yankee clock wheels and bass fiddle strings.

When he walked it came up with a jerk and a twitch,
And then down with a sort of a chuck and a hitch,
But he shambled <*stumbled*> along, and was happy and kind,
Till he met with a woman of muscular <*masculine*> mind!

She seized <*besieged*> his affections and gave him a banter,
He right-about-faced, and they married <*wedded*> instanter,
But from loving too quickly they should have refrained,
For the honeymoon filled, but the honeymoon waned.

Soon a captious, cavorting virago she proved,
And she made him walk Spanish whenever he moved.
On his works, which she frequently did, as Mc. said,
With a spittoon or skillet bombarding his head.

And she ogled him much, and a queer notion took
That McGregg was too thick with the Hibernian cook,
But she flirted herself, hence she dare not him chide
On his browsing around, just a little outside.

Her feller <*fellow*> was spawned in the Arkansas bogs,
Talked "hoss" and delighted in rat-and-tan dogs,
Played poker and sneered at the virtue of women,

In short, he was more of a brute than a human.
Well, so things ran along, and continued to run,
Till one morning Mc. rose with the lark and the sun,
When he found — by the gods! — that he had but one leg,
And the wooden one missing with Mrs. McGregg!

For shouldered had she both his leg and her Cross,
And eloped in the night with the chap <*man*> that talked "hoss,"
So pursuit by McGregg would have all been in vain,
And he sighed and <*And hence he*> hopped off on his crutch and his cane —

Hopped off to his breakfast and a hearty meal took,
Then he told the whole tale to the Hibernian cook,
When she hove a deep sigh, said, "the divel! do tell,"
And they winked at each other, and said "It is well."

MORAL

Revenge to a single-legged husband is sweet,
When his tormenting spouse and her paramour meet,
And then and there leave him in life's giddy rounds,
With a gushing young cook pouring balm on his wounds.

DOORSTEP SOCIETY
CA AUG. 11, 1872

Along the airy line of streets
And avenues, and alley mouths
The lighted lamps are glinting out,
Like jewels from the maple boughs.

On marble and on granite steps
Are seated family knots and cliques,
The negro boy, with hose attached,
I mention here, has wet the bricks.

These family knots are "cooling off,"
And scarlet bows, and gauzes white,
And blinking of Alaska pins
Blend mildly in the tempered light.

Quite pleasant, too, the gossip is
Of trifles, which may bless or mar.
Of chips from Farmer Greeley's axe.
Or fleecy whiffs from Grant's cigar.

The blade of Wit is fine and keen,
The javelin of Satire stings,
For Poverty is jealous of
Those water guzzlers at the Springs.

But memory runs to ale and beer
The beaded cup I quaff and prize
In lieu of draughts which smack of sal-

Eratus — then I sympathize

I pity those imprisoned snobs —
Those bilious Thompsons with a P —
Who roost in attics — charming nooks
For damaged aristocracy!

Deserted steps and windows closed
Proclaim the family "not about,"
But from an alley I this morn
Saw Amy hang her parrot out!

Now when the Season 'gins to close,
And every swallow homeward flies,
These sallow folks will reappear
With rainbow crescents 'neath their eyes.

Along the airy line of streets,
An avenues, and alley mouths,
The lighted lamps are glinting out,
Like jewels from the maple boughs.

So take it all in all, I think
I'd sooner be of common blood
That sweetens underneath the stars,
And draws me nearer unto God.

Washington

A Pair of Dainty Gaiters
CA Oct. 27, 1872

A Father's Tribute

When the airy gold of morning
Like a benediction falls,
And woos away my slumbers,
And lights my chamber walls,
Then I grow so heavy hearted,
And I ponder and I muse —
They hang beside the window —
Just a pair of little shoes.

A pair of dainty gaiters
That shod the dainty feet
Of a very dainty darling
Who used to trip the street,
As light as any fairy
In innocence and glee,
The sweetest Balm in Gilead
In all the world for me.

But alas, there came an angel,
At early dawn of day,
And the two went out together
And went and went their way;
And she never comes to see me,
Still better, after all,
For she's free from all pollution
And the gaiters on the wall.

If her nimble feet were in them
They might be led astray,
And her fragile limbs grow weary
On life's uncertain way;
Then I know the streets are golden,
And the dear Redeemer takes
Her hand in his and leads her,
And He never makes mistakes.

Washington, D.C.

To The Author of "Life in Death"
CA Nov. 2, 1872

An Open Letter

My Dear Madam: Anna thinks no trouble like her own, so you think of yours and I of mine. Ah! my good woman, when I read your story of "Life in Death" the tears unbidden came. I couldn't help it, indeed I couldn't; the flood-gates of my heart would leak in spite of my will. It was more sorrowful than the old, old one of common death. I never read a drama that so moved me, nor a poem of such pathos. You are only one of a great multitude who bear, and have borne, a full knapsack of troubles and disappointments, and, worse than all, regrets. It is the most natural thing in the world that each should think their own the most burdensome. Shall I unstrap one I carry and make known its contents? At times it is heavy now, but not so grievous as it used to be, for each intervening year kindly lightens it, just as time has yours.

In the year 1866, then a young man with a wife and one child — a little girl bright with the sunshine of four summers — I resigned a position I held, at a very fair salary, and embarked in that most hazardous of all enterprises, the "newspaper business." I was totally without experience, either as an editor or publisher, and, to make the prospect more dismal, I was in a city of twelve thousand population (Rockford, Illinois) that supported two excellent papers. My bank account footed up just $550, and my face was good for $500 I borrowed. With that thousand and fifty I bought an office, minus a press, and "job office." The press work I had done at another office.

My first issue was five hundred copies, and fully half that number of subscribers — to quote their own vernacular — "took the thing conditionally," the condition being "If you hold out six months I will renew my subscription;" the remaining two hundred and fifty patronized me out of a sort of duty or charity. I was painfully aware of this, but it served to set the teeth of action on edge and stimulated me to the most vigorous efforts. Steadily from the beginning did my list of patrons increase, and with them, of course, came friends — they are always plenty in prosperity — so that at the close of the third year I printed an edition of three thousand five hundred, and my advertising patronage was correspondingly large. Thus you see I was successful. I was out of debt, respected, industrious, ambitious, happy. I had a home, a blessed little girl who met and kissed me at the gate every noon and night. That child was the idol of me and mine. I loved her with all the ardor of my nature, and the depth of that ardor none can ever sound. She was as bright as a sunbeam, nimble-footed, and lithe as a fairy. Her eyes were like the dawn and fringed with the blackest of silken lashes. Her features were delicately cut and well defined, and a wonderful wealth of brown hair flowed backward in clusters. To me — in the language of Massey — she "was the wee white rose of all the world." Day by day I read a new meaning in her face, and her eyes were always preaching the most eloquent of sermons. But, alas, my cup of happiness was too full for one of the children of men, and fate, devilish with envy, reached out her cruel hand and dashed it over. Now listen:

It was 5 o'clock p.m. August 16, 1869. While seated at my desk in the office I heard a peal of silver laughter, and looking around I found her at my elbow — she was always capturing me by surprise. She said: "Papa, I am going with my class to the Sunday-school picnic tomorrow, and I want a pair of yellow gaiters like Annie Dinsmore's," at the same time showing me the half-worn slipper on her dainty foot in proof of her need. She well knew she would get them, and hand-in-hand I accompanied her to the nearest store. I wanted her to wear them home, but she thought "they might get dusty and not look so new the next day." So, after kissing me, off she started with the new shoes she never wore in life, under her arm. I returned to the office, and after a lapse of twenty minutes a thunderbolt fell from the clear sky and struck me dumb.

I had casually stepped to the door, when I saw everybody running up State street in the direction of my house, which was located fully six squares distant. Supposing it was a fire, I naturally looked for the smoke and the engines, carelessly asking, "Where is it?" I had not received an answer when I saw my next-door neighbor coming in a buggy at a furious speed. In a flash he halted his horse close by the door, turned suddenly around, and nervously said: "Get in quick and ask me no questions, I will take you home in a minute, there is trouble at your house." I sprang to the seat by his side without the power of speech, for I saw that something terrible had occurred.

His driving was terrific, and everything gave way before us.

On Elm street, within a square of my house, we passed the wreck of a buggy and the body of a dead horse. "My God," I stammered out, "what does all this mean?" But he made no answer.

By this time he had reined his fleet steed in front of my door. The street was filled with people, and everybody about the house seemed to be in confusion, but I neither caught a glimpse of Lizzie nor her mother.

I sprang out and dashed in. A good old woman whom I always called "Auntie," met me in the hall and seizing me by both arms hurriedly said, "Go into the parlor and try and save Hattie, (my wife,) for Lizzie is dead!"

I don't know how, but I found myself in the parlor, and I vaguely remember to have seen a number of women working over her, as she lay prostrate and apparently dead, on a sofa.

From the parlor I rushed frantically into the bed chamber, only to find the idol of my heart broken, bruised, speechless. Two physicians were in attendance, one of whom seemed to be feeling for her pulse, and the other wiping the tears from his cheeks, for she had been his favorite and had ridden many and many a mile with him on the rounds of his practice.

But of what avail was human skill? What could medical aid do for an arm broken near the shoulder, the bone thrust through the flesh, the ball of the shoulder thrown from its socket, the hinder part of the head cut, and the skull indented on the forehead until it lay on the brain?

In the mad delirium of agony I demanded, "will she live?"

"She is badly hurt, my poor man," replied the physician, who held her wrist. I knew just what that meant.

Again, I demanded, "Will my wife recover?"

"Oh, yes; she was on the street, and seeing Lizzie thrown from the doctor's buggy, fainted, and was carried home insensible. Yes, she is all right," said he.

Here a third physician, with a case of surgical instruments, walked into the room.

"What are you going to do with those?" I frantically inquired.

"Trephine her," said one of them. I had seen this operation performed in the army, and I knew that it consisted in sawing a hole through the skull, and in this instance they said it was necessary in order that the compressed portion be lifted up from contact with the brain.

"Doctor," said I, "can't you get along without performing that cruel business?"

"No," he replied, "I must do it in order to save her life."

At that word "life" my dead hope quickened into fortitude, and I think it must have put on the absolute power of death, for I held her on my lap while the fearful operation was performed. Then I saw them force the dislocated shoulder into place, set the broken bones, and bind the poor crushed arm to her body with strips of adhesive plaster. They then bade me good night and left for their respective homes, saying they would call early next morning, to keep Lizzie quiet, and not be uneasy regarding the illness of my wife.

In a half hour afterward she came staggering into the room where Lizzie lay, and dropping into my arms we stood and sobbed and moaned in one common anguish. I whispered heavily in her ear, "Hattie, while there is life there is hope." She answered, "Yes," and turning to the bed knelt down and put her troubled and anxious face close to that of the little sufferer, and I, only I, could measure the length and breadth and depth of her grief by my own. For a moment I mutely stood and watched her, but feeling that the pent-up fountains of soul were about to break loose I left the room and walked away into the night. I wanted to be hidden in the darkness, to be lost in the vale of forgetfulness. I don't know where I walked, but I remember to have seen some one with a lantern, and approaching I saw a man taking the harness from the dead horse. I asked him if he saw the runaway and he answered, "Yes, sir, and I never want to see another one like it. Oh! It was terrific."

It appears that Lizzie, after leaving me at the shoe store, had fallen into company with another little girl, and on their way home, noticing a spirited team of horses, which were attached to a carriage, and hitched to a post, and recognizing them as Dr. Ritching's, they climbed in to await the coming of the doctor so that he might drive them home. For some reason unknown the horses broke away from the hitching post and ran with the rush of a tornado up State street, turning onto West and again onto Elm, when in turning the corner one of them fell down, dashing its brains out on the foot of a lamp post, the buggy in the meantime being hurled over and smashed to flinders. The companion child was fortunately thrown away from the wreck uninjured, but Lizzie was picked up, as one dead, bruised and mutilated. Her mother happened to be on the street at the time, and seeing the awful occurrence, swooned away, and she and Lizzie were carried home together.

"What became of the other horse?" I asked.

"One of his legs was broken and we shot him."

I had learned enough, and turning on my heel, I walked homeward.

Arriving there I found my wife at Lizzie's side, and through six dreadful days and nights we nursed and waited. Like two sentinels we stood watch and ward at the outer gates of a dear life, for we knew that Death lay somewhere near in ambush. I wish I could have met him hand-to-hand in mortal struggle, for the blade of my desperation was fine-tempered and keen, and had he vanquished me it would have been better than it was.

I had seen deeds of heroism on many a sanguinary field of conflict, patience stretched upon a hospital bed, and sick in the trenches, human endurance worn out in a Southern prison, and fortitude putting on an angel's power, but until now I had never seen them mustered and handled at the will of a frail, smitten woman. In her and me Death had two powerful enemies in that room.

The weather was warm, and the days and nights long and tedious. I think, however, that she suffered but little, for the life-tide was very low. She only spoke one sentence, and that was, "I want papa to give me the medicine, it don't taste so bad."

I mutely slipped out of the room, went upstairs to another chamber, and the pent-up fountains of my heart broke loose. I wept myself sick. But presently I felt relieved, and again went to her bedside.

Death came, just as the morning blushed in the east, so gently and so quietly. I pushed the blind ajar and looked into her face. I saw him imprint his great white seal there. She opened her eyes and there was a strange glory in them, and then the lids closed down forever. Her mother and I unbandaged, stripped her of her clothing, shrouded her in Swiss muslin, laid her on her side, and then I combed her beautiful hair. Her skin was transparent and of unearthly whiteness, and her temples laced with faint traces of azure veins, and the sweet smile that beautified her mouth was proof of her angelhood.

It was the Sabbath day, one of sorrow and unforgetfulness, still and solemn. Everybody spoke in an undertone, and walked so softly. Little children slipped by, went to the casket, looked in, kissed her, and silently stole away. The neighbors would come in, take us by the hands, look full into our faces, but say nothing. A friend of mine, a man who knew me, met me in the hall, threw his arms around me, and wept, for I had been one of the pall-bearers to three of his little people.

There was no empty pomp about her funeral, none of the cursed mockery which characterizes some of those of the present day. On Monday afternoon we carried the casket to the graveyard a mile distant, and hid it away under the daises. I don't know whether there was one or ten thousand followed us, neither did I care. I had but one great heavy thought, too sacred to share with the curious outside world.

When we arrived home we found the house almost deserted. It was lonely and desolate. Lizzie was nowhere to be seen or heard, not even at the gate. The gathered waters of grief had dried up, and our hearts were sick with the dull ache of a deep-stabbed woe.

The first night following is a blank to me, but not the day after. I had not been to the office for a week — in fact, I didn't know I had an office. Consequently, no paper had been published. The publication day was Thursday, and the next issue demanded immediate action. I pulled the brim of my hat down over my eyes, sat down to my desk, and penned "The Jewel in the Casket." Then came the generalities of the paper.

Heretofore it had savored of wit and humor, for I always felt generous and funny. But not so now. As the weeks and months rolled by it did not improve, but as steadily lost ground as it had gradually grown into life. To borrow the sweet and sad language of the "Author of a Woman's Poems":

> "The very sunshine seemed to wear
> Some thought of death caught in its gold."

I couldn't for the life of me be bright or funny, though I tried hard to be so. I became involved in debt, and in order to extricate myself I sold my possessions and came to this city in the capacity of a Government clerk.

Now be assured, my dear madam, that what I have written is true to the letter.

Private griefs, I am aware, are too sacred to be paraded before the public, but as you have told yours, I add mine in proof of how much the human heart will endure and not break.

J.P.I.
Washington, D.C.

JEMIMA JACKSON
CA Nov. 10, 1872; WO Dec. 5, 1872 [NO INTRODUCTION]

The following ballad is from the pen of the gentleman

who gave us last summer "Organic Remains," a touch of humor not excelled by anything done by Hood or Holmes. We have caveated everything from this source at a heavy outlay for the benefit of our readers:

A gust of wind blew sharp and stout,
She was alone without a fellah,
I saw her tack and veer about
And struggle with an umbrella.

It eddied 'round those knobby charms,
(I saw her feet, I'm only human,)
I rushed and caught her in my arms —
Delicious waif! that breezy woman.

"Oh! thank you, sir, for this relief,
I thought I was about to blow up."
Said I, "That umbrella reef,
Or Miss, or Madam, all will go up."

She did it, as I saw the name,
"Jemima Jackson," on the lining,
Date, eighteen thirty, which the same
Would make her forty and declining.

I read her age as in a book,
The faded blue spoke of the bygone,
The handle with its curious crook,
Also the dog's head with an eye gone.

Jemima's face was in a veil,

Although her ways were frank and open;
As home I saw her through the gale
She chattered and was loosely spoken.

Said I, "What are you snuffing for?"
Said she, "There's something burning, stranger."
And then I thought of my cigar
I dropped when snatching her from danger.

Then, peering round in anxious thought,
I quickly saw the art of man were
Mockery, since the flames had caught
The news department of her pannier.

I worked and shouted out of breath,
And jerked away her loose adjustables;
But wind and fire are strong as death
When on the rampage in combustibles.

So up Jemima Jackson went,
A prey to fashion and to folly;
No insurance — no, not a cent —
Which makes it rather melancholy.

Hymn of Thanksgiving
CA Nov. 24, 1872

[This poem shares several lines with "Song of Thanksgiving." — Ed.]

NOVEMBER 28

Oh! grand is our wonderful Union of States,
Our temples are granite and golden our gates,
And high on the walls is our banner unfurled,
Oh! glorified land of the beautiful world.
Full skirted and jeweled our lowlands and leas
With crystalline lakes and amethyst seas;
And woodlands are dappled with amber and green
As the mellow sun sifts through the leaf-woven screen;
And the rivers flow oil and murmur the rills,
And cattle are pastured on thousands of hills;
And vintage, and hives, and the new milk of kine
Are sweet with the fragrance of honey and wine,
Till the heart overflows with gladness and sings
A thanksgiving hymn to the Good King of Kings —
A jubilee, swelling through valley and glen,
For His manifold gifts to the children of men.

Washington, D.C.

THE "FREE-LUNCH" CLERK
CA DEC. 8, 1872

Some days since an ignorant little fellow, who signs himself "Clerk," assassinated the King's English through a dead flat of nearly a column of the daily *Chronicle*, in order to prove that a Government clerk ought to live comfortably and "lay up" a few hundred on a salary of $1,200. The little fellow "reflects" after this manner. Listen:

"When I reflect on the position I fill, the desk put in my charge, and the very light duties imposed, with the slight demand made on my time to properly discharge those duties, together with the very handsome remuneration for the time given, I cannot, with honor to myself, extend my open palm to an already overburdened country and beg for more wages."

Beautiful, isn't it? How resigned, and how charitable not to extend that open palm of his!

Now I have not the least doubt that this individual, whoever he is, and it makes but little difference, is amply paid for the "light" duties imposed upon him, from the simple fact that he is a very light clerk. He runs on a narrow gauge, and is what we clerks term a "free-lunch man," that is, a chap who goes to one of those cheap restaurants precisely at 12 o'clock each day, calls for a glass of lager, lays down his nickel five cents, and then "free lunches" over fifty cents worth of a concoction known as bean soup. He knows just where each and all of these establishments are located, and accordingly makes way with their bean soup in regular order. If he have a wife and children, and that household calamity, a mother-in-law, he can't live in a store box, and consequently, must pay a fair rent, which can't be done on bean soup, for landlords don't bait gudgeons in that way. If he have his "washing done" (or perhaps his wife does it) he is out of pocket five dollars the month, cash, for a washerwoman's bill can never be "sponged out." Then his little ones kick holes in the toes of their shoes, his wife is a modern woman, and his blooded mother-in-law won't knead dough nor darn stockings. Then there is eating to be done at home, and since he is not allowed to carry away and unswallowed supply from the free-lunch hell-holes, he is obliged to repair to the market and again pay out cash. And so it is for the light and fuel, and every necessary of life, to say nothing of comfort.

I do not wish to be understood as condemning a proper economy, nor in burlesquing that spirit which provides for the future, but stingy persons are to be despised. I have never exactly seen them biting a shingle nail in two lest the scales might overbalance, but I fancy I have seen them keeping an eye on a loose button in fear that it might drop off and roll away. I have seen them slipping around armed with a claw-hammer pulling rusty nails from hitching-posts and empty store boxes, tucking away bits of strings, collecting cast-off boots, and fugitive horse shoes until their premises resembled a vast junk-shop, and when a five-cent nickel drops into their pockets it can be heard singing the well-known line of a familiar hymn:

"Farewell vain world, I'm going home."

All of which is mournfully true.

But I ask, in the name of the commonest kind of common sense, can one be extravagant, and at the same time honest, in a city on a salary of $1,200? Now you see I know how it is myself. I am a $1,200 clerk, I am honest, I don't contract debts, I don't dissipate, nor play at games. I am a husband and support no wives by brevet. I am free from tobacco and club houses. I don't loaf nor fool pennies away on organ grinders. I keep my accounts thus: I, at the close of the "fiscal year," write $1,200 on the debit and $1,200 on the credit sides of the ledger of memory, sit down and look at the result with a sort of melancholy pleasure, saying to myself: "How is that for financiering, my boy?" I then become thankful to my Government for so faithfully keeping its contract and not kicking me overboard.

It will be seen, then, that by close economy I have lived, but where have been the comforts and amusements of the year? "Don't need 'em," says some old fossil. "They would unfit you for heaven," cries another bigoted mummy, and the ignorant little fellow referred to above says, "study clerk life."

We may here remark that the study of "clerk life" is demoralizing even to the patience of Christians, inasmuch as the ways of clerks are so dark and their tricks are so vain.

I wish to announce to the world that although poor, I am a social being. I believe in the orthodox faith, but I love to dance and to joke and laugh and sing, for my nature is full of music and fun. Were it not so, what would we do with the sorrows of the heart? Now, in order to do and see and hear all these joyful things one must have full-dress suits and some loose change in his pockets.

The common comforts of life are so manifold that we cannot enumerate them. And then what is comfort for one would be a burden for another. But in the case of clerks it narrows itself down to this: the necessaries of a common livelihood, which consist of plain victuals, plain bedding, plain clothing, and an humble home, furnished in a plain way. And in this roaring, rolling, fast age you must look out, keep a clear conscience, keep down the breaks of a fast nature, pay everything as you go, and square the books, as I do, at the end of the year.

Now a word to the gentleman who hides behind the nom de plume of "clerk." You, sir, are the first honest (?) man I ever heard of who did not possess a human nature, but it is sweet to know that you are a creature of "modest ambition." If you were possessed of human nature you would "extend that open palm" and ask more wages, and if you were innocent of "modest ambition" you would have written your name to that article. Oh! You are a jewel, you are. Call and see me, it shan't cost you a cent. Seriously, though, I'll tell you the kind of a man you are thought to be.

To begin with, you are very ignorant, if not so, you would never have undertaken to have proven an absurdity. You lack respect for your mother tongue or you would not have kicked about so loosely amongst its parts of speech and violated its rules of syntax in the manner you did. Are you not ashamed of yourself? You are evidently a sycophant, and are doing the bidding or courting the notice of a superior, with an end of higher position in view. That, probably, is the truth of the whole matter.

That, by close economy and humble living, a man and his wife and child, without a nurse, denying themselves of much which is not actually necessary, but things of simple comfort and enjoyment, can live on a salary of $1,200, has been proven over and over again. If nothing is saved, and sickness and calamity come, then the pangs of poverty are felt, and often their victims become the objects and recipients of charity at the hands of their fellow clerks.

I think the reform needed is this: Pay large salaries to competent, industrious men and women such as you find in the banks and business houses of New York and other cities. Discover their merits and habits by practical test, and not by what they knew of school books, when in youth.

Washington, D.C.

Ye Umbrella Mann
CA Dec. 22, 1872

[Irvine reused much of this poem, minus the flowery spellings, in "The Old Umbrella Man." — Ed.]

When e'er the morning drizzle-eth,
Then see and hear you cann,
This sorriest of vagabonds —
Ye umbrella mann.

But never in the afternoon
In either miste or fogge,
For then ye umbrella mann

Is overcome with grogge.

Ye gentle folk he devileth,
Yea, muchly so, indeede,
For he altogether kicketh,
At any moral creede.

His broken ribbs he shouldereth,
And walketh without paine,
And a second-handed handle
He useth for a cane.

But he shamble-eth, and limpeth,
And ogle-eth for a friende;
Righte lustielie he holloweth:
"Umber-ell-er-ers to mende."

And whenever one he findeth
He squatteth on the grounde,
And boreth with a pegging awle,
And bindeth rounde and rounde,

With wire, the dislocations
Of whalebone and rattann —
This eccentrickest of mortals —
Ye umbrella mann.

And so much the fellow chargeth
It aggravateth you,
For the cobbling bill exceedeth
The price when it was new.

So in damp and churlish weather
He earneth and he errs,
But he's one of Adam's children —
The Imp's philosophers.

Thus through his life and character
I see his sinful ways,
As an open umbrella
Its holes in rainy dais.

Washington, D.C.

THE MOTHER-IN-LAW
CA FEB. 2, 1873; <MR MAR. 24, 1876>

I'm only thirty-five today,
Yet anything but hale and thrifty;
Why, darn it, Joe, I'm bald and gray
As any patriarch at fifty.

Ah, no! it isn't cards nor wine,
But woman — that's the shoe that pinches —
That stately mother-in-law of mine
Has almost finished me by inches.

Why did I marry? Well, you see,
I blindly loved sweet Nellie Pruitt;
And then <*Besides,*> the family crowded me,
Till I was just obliged to do it.

We wed at morn — no cards — at noon
We moved into our little cottage;
But shadowed was my honeymoon,
And bitter was my mess of pottage.

I felt a disappointment gnaw,
As though my social life were cankered,
When there I saw my mother-in-law
With both her gout and baggage anchored.

I would have brooked her swollen joints
But for her cussed <*constant*> domineering;
Also <*Likewise*> her exclamation points
Concerning me, which weren't cheering.

Before the advent of the twins —
Both boys — her crankiness and flurry,
Solicitude, and dubious whims,
Inflamed me to a chronic worry.

Yet time was kind in passing on,
Still, she was short and overbearing;
The twins had passed the Rubicon
Of birth — and boots and pants were wearing.

Said she, "Them boys <*twins*> are badly sp'iled,"
That she "could raise and train 'em better,"
But that "it gits their mother riled,"
And that "their father, he won't let her."
The truth is, Joe, from time to time,
She loomed <*bounced*> right up and made things tingle;

And as for those twin boys of mine,
She daily spanked them with a shingle.

Oh, no, she didn't die of gout,
Some thought it might have been bronchitis,
And others, that her sands run out
Because of spinal meningitis.

It wasn't that, an error huge
She did commit by drinking poison,
'Twas thought to be a vermifuge
The doctor left to dose the boys on.

Joe, that old woman was a fraud,
I know she's dead, but then, confound her,
She's better underneath the sod
Than dev'ling everybody 'round her.

A Kiss
CA FEB. 8, 1873

I had met her at the ball, and our feet
Had twinkled together in the busy maze
Of the waltz; I had whirligigged around
Her airily in the "Boston" and
Capered nimbly in front of her in the jig
Of square dances until I was in love,
And loving, longed to taste the ambrosial
Sweets of her lips — yea, as a humming bird —

To there manipulate honey without
The shadow of foul suspicion.

One eve —
In the dewy stillness I spied her fair
Form leaning languidly on her father's
Gate. I approached and timidly slipp'd
My arm lovingly about her waist. She sighed
Not — sweet girl — but spasmodically drop'd her
Head — face upwards — on my shoulder.

I went
For those lips, and touching with mine she hove
A sigh which blasted my love and knocked the
Kiss into nonforgetfulness. She had
Been eating onions!

Washington, D.C.

The Washington Monument
CA MAR. 2, 1873

[Irvine revised and expanded this poem for an illustrated chapbook published in 1875: *Concerning Washington and His Monument.* — Ed.]

SACRED TO THE MEMORY OF GEORGE

I've just been gazing on it, George —

(George Washington, I mean,)
And wond'ring if your spirit eyes
The thing had ever seen;
Mount Vernon isn't far away,
And then I know, you see,
That ghosts are very often moved
With curiosity.

I truly hope you haven't, George,
For if you ar'nt tough
Those women dubbed a "Regency,"
Have bored you quite enough;
They've dug away the very stump,
That hatchet made of thine,
And all your heir-looms modernized
With paint and turpentine.

The monument's unfinished, George —
I grieve to tell you so,
According to the plans devised
Some forty years ago;
It was to rise six hundred feet,
And then and there to stop,
And you in copper uniform,
To stand upon the top.

I furthermore regret to say,
George Washington — by George —
Of money in the treasury
There wasn't such a gorge,
That so when we had built it up —

The Lord knows only how —
The glory sort o' petered out,
And there it standeth now!

It looks so like a light-house, George,
Half wrecked upon the main,
Or wind-mill Don Quixote
Thought, a giant on the plain;
The mortar's crumbled from the joints —
A hint of time's reproof —
And a thing they call a derrick is
A-rotting from the roof.

I know it's awful shabby, George,
And I regret it sore
Because we love thee just as well
As in the days of yore;
The heroes of the war of wars,
So lately known to fame,
Dim not the golden luster of
The halo of thy name.

The public's patriotic, George,
But Uncle Samuel grieves
Because of reckless habits so
Peculiar unto thieves.
Now there's been a million dollars if
There's ever been a cent
Of "penny contributions" paid
To build the Monument.

At all the noted places, George,
Throughout the lavish land,
Were contribution boxes stuck
To reach the willing hand,
And drop by drop, for years and years,
In showers the money fell,
But where it went is something which
No honest man can tell.

Of course there's a committee, George,
Who carryeth the keys —
All very worthy gentlemen (?)
Of leisure and of ease
Whose bowels are filled with yearnings
And patriotic cramps
For the tardiness of people
In coming down with stamps.

Now really to be honest, George,
I'll tell you what I think,
The monumental money has
Been mostly spent in drink,
Or, the said committee lost it,
Without regard to law,
By playing necromancy, or,
At poker known as "draw."

And I furthermore remark, George,
As I have said to Jones,
Since they stole away the money,
They should have hooked the stones,

With the wooden roof and derrick,
So that Uncle Sam's disgrace
Might be blotted out forever,
Leaving not the faintest trace.

Washington, D.C.

TWELVE HUNDRED A YEAR
CA Mar. 23, 1873

Since the class of a clerk
Very often depends
On the standing and work
Of political friends,
He may frequently shirk
At the odds and the ends.

But the same is not true —
I would hint to recruits —
That because of a few
Which the metaphor suits,
That the shirking is due
To a congressman's boots.

If a man be a thing
He is careless of gains;
If you solve him you bring
Away naught for your pains:
Take nothing from nothing

And nothing remains.

Civil Service, you see,
Is of fruitless avail,
When it tests a monk-ee
With a view to entail
An improvement per se
By curtailing his tail.

Can a learned baboon
With his monkeyshines part?
No, he'll climb to the moon
In the face of all art,
And profoundly assume
To be owly and smart.

"Like the crew of the Ark,
They're an animal show,"
I am free to remark
Was the lie of a foe,
Though clerks' ways are dark
And eccentric, we know.

But it seems unto me
That the thing would be meet
If the "Board" should agree
To a Fool Killer keep,
Whose commission should be
To kill every dead beat.

Let him squelch every leech,

Every loafer and sham,
It will heal up a breach
That afflicts Uncle Same,
And for whom say their speech:
"We don't give a damn!"

In addition, I say —
And I think it is clear —
Give the worthy ones pay
As their worth may appear,
But more we do pray
Than twelve hundred a year.

Now I don't play at games —
And I'm honest, I think —
For I pay all my claims
Of food, washing, (and drink,)
But in spite of my aims
My salary I sink.

We are keeping at house,
And by hook and by crook
We flank the remorse
And expense of a cook;
But my nature ain't coarse
And the thing's hard to brook.

Yes, my nature's at strife,
And the thing is a bore,
For there's so much of life
That a clerk must ignore;

Keeping house and a wife
In a manner so poor.

But we'll anxiously pray,
And await with good cheer,
For a little more pay
Than twelve hundred a year;
And come when it may,
You can bet it will be
An acceptable day
To a fellow like me.

Washington, D.C.

Unknown
ES May 30, 1873; <MA June 13, 1873>

[This is the poem Irvine read to President Ulysses S. Grant, Frederick Douglass, and 10,000 spectators. Many similar lines and imagery appear in his other war poems. — Ed.]

<At Arlington Cemetery, near the National Capitol, is a conspicuous granite monument, erected over the remains of 2,131 unknown soldiers, gathered from the various battlefields. It was as a part of the memorial ceremonies there, that the following poem was read:>

A sigh is as old as the primitive years

And a minor refrain as the song of the stars;
And the children of men were weary with tears,
Ere sorrow was crowned in the kingdom of wars;
Yet, when the grim Harvester calls for his own,
And afar to the angels he carries a sheaf,
Our sickles we drop and away all alone
We hide in the shade of a sanctified grief;
Alone, with the poor stricken heart that is bowed,
Till at length it is quickened and breaks with its pain,
And weeps out its woe as a low brooding cloud
When riven with lightning its burden of rain.
But the sadness that lingers is softened, I ween,
And the vagueness of longing is tinged with delight,
Till the love that's remembered becomes as a dream,
Or a voice that is lost in the hush of the night,
But to-day we come forth, and in fancy review
The silent encampment here tenting about,
For it seems but a night since it beat the tattoo
When the pickets came in, and the lights were put out.
And the valiant are here; and the weak, and the strong;
The known, and unknown, and the army is Fame's —
And the roll is a wonderful roll, and so long
That we weary of reading its dearest of names.

Unknown, did I say? Ah! none are unknown
Though strangers to us, and it may be to art;
Though engraven the baffled endeavor on stone,
The name is recorded in somebody's heart;
There's a brother somewhere who's bereft of a joy,
Or a sister, mayhap, of a brother's fond trust;
Or a father who grieves for his beautiful boy,

Here only a handful of fugitive dust;
Or a Rachel, lamenting the fruit of her womb,
With an anguish too sharp for the healings of time,
For I have a brother asleep in the tomb
And the love of our mother I think is divine;
Or a child in its orphanage, knowing not yet,
Of a father enthralled to an absolute fate;
Or a widow, perchance, in her tearful regret,
Long watching and waiting alone at the gate.

And there's somebody, still, who is singing the lay:
"When Johnnie comes marching" to ne'er again roam,
For hope is the same with the Blue and the Grey
But Johnnie — poor Johnnie — will never march home.
Yes, the nameless are legion who come nevermore,
And these are but skirmishes bivouacked here,
Alas! they are scattered abroad the land o'er
As the leaves of the wood in the fall of the year,
Ah! the Union is wide and they sleep as of eld
The prophet of God, in a Moabite plain,
In a sepulchre never by human beheld,
And angels alone in the funeral train:
They're hidden, I know, in the wilderness shades;
In coves, and lagoons, and fen-lands and leas;
In the plains of the palm, and the evergreen glades,
In forests of pine and the depth of the seas,
Away in the mountains, and lonely ravines,
In thickets, and wilds, where the wounded have crept;
In the shadow of cliffs, on the margin of streams,
Where they perished alone, unnursed and unwept.

In the corners of fields, and old camping grounds:
By springs, and the windings of hoof-beaten roads;
By the hedges, and lanes, and by-ways and mounds,
On the skirting of creeks, and the flanking of fords;
In prisons and hospitals noisome and damp,
On the march, in all weather, in the day-time and night,
Of wounds and exposure, and the fevers of camp,
And the bullet, and sword, in the obstinate fight,
Oh! the story were sad, if the story were told,
And the roll would be long were it mustered and called;
But neither, the wisdom of years can unfold,
And dear-hearted love will remain unappalled.
'Tis wisdom sufficient to know that they died —
A wonderful army — at home and afar, —
That loyalty triumphed, and valor was tried
When the Union was racked in the thunders of war

To know that they died is a truth that reveals
The kinship of men to be more than a breath,
And a knowledge, baptized in affliction, that seals
The proof of a love that is stronger than death.
Then cease ye to mourn, and list unto reason,
For the way is not far to the white-tented land,
They will ne'er come to us, but ere a brief season
We'd deploy unto them at the word of command;
Away to the camp where the weary retreat,
Where toil is a stranger and war is unknown;
Where the roll is uncalled and the drums never beat,
And the charge is unmade and the bugles unblown,
But the world they have left is a beautiful world,
And Freedom has gone from its manger of birth,

And the angel of Peace with her pinions unfurled,
Is bearing the news through the glorified earth;
And the sword in its sheath, and the bayonet rust,
And the haversacks hang in the attics and halls;
And the rations remaining have mildewed to dust,
And the canteens are empty and hang on the walls;
And the North is extending a hand to the South,
And the tides of their blood will again never ebb,
And the cannon is silent and over its mouth
The spider unfrightened is weaving her web.
Then their low-lying graves let us garland with flowers
Full blown, and profound, and of manifold hue,
They are delicate gifts, these symbols of ours
And born of the heart, and the sun, and the dew;
And join, oh! ye minstrels — ye blithe-hearted throng,
Dear blue-bird and robin your roundelays sing,
And thrushes, and bob-o-links tipsy with song,
For the dull ear of death may be quick when ye sing.
And ye, wooing winds blowing wildly and free,
And ye, of the crystalline army of stars
Unite in the hymn of the great jubilee,
At the crowning of peace and the ceasing of wars.

Change Baggage
CA Aug. 3, 1873

My Dear Mr. Reed:

I want to kill a railroad man! Is there any objection? I understand that you are a lawyer as well as an editor; therefore I wish to inquire if the killing of one of these emissaries of the iron horse is, in the eye of the law, a crime? Suppose that in traveling a distance of about a thousand miles on the line of a main trunk, right through the heart of the United States, you were obliged to suffer all the torments of an orthodox fire-and-brimstone sort of agony, extending through the slow length of four days and almost three nights, what then? Honestly, would you not be tempted, at least, to thrash somebody? Now my good sir, you once related an experience of yours, which occurred on board the cars from Chicago to New York, in language quite as elegant as the English you employ in writing your editorials, hence I was somewhat in doubt lest you had clothed your very amusing account in the purple and fine linen of fancy rather than the plainer garb of truth. I had always known that traveling people have no rights which railway officials respect. I once rode from Cleveland to Toledo roosting on the wood-box, the result of common politeness, having surrendered my seat to an old fat woman who didn't even thank me, and who snored terrifically through the whole distance, for it was in the night-time, and the old creature was too stupid to realize where she was. The car was crowded, and I hinted to the conductor that I would like to exchange my perch for a seat. He snubbed me. I remember to have measured him from head to foot, and had it not been that he was about double my own weight I should have gotten down and flogged him, as he deserved.

Recently, while on the trip mentioned above, I was

in a devilish mood of temper during the entire journey. And right here, dear reader, let me assure you that I am giving the exact truth, and if I succeed in finishing this article without growing profane, I shall feel that I am amply fitted for membership in the Y.M.C.A. I was victimized on the start. Mrs. Tompkins — the better half of Timothy, a neighbor of my father's — with a brace of boys — Paul and Silas — aged respectively five and six, (and a sweet pair of juvenile apostles they proved to be,) was about to visit a married sister residing at Moundsville, West Virginia. Mrs. T. proposed to travel under my wing, inasmuch as I was about to start for Washington, District of Columbia. My direct route was via Chicago, Pittsburg, Harrisburg and Baltimore, but in order to accommodate Mrs. Tompkins I was obliged to take other lines. Tompkins had been consulting a "railway guide," and of course the common result followed — insanity. Those "guides" have turned the brains of more people than either love or whisky. I have known passengers to become raving maniacs, at one sitting, while endeavoring to trace a connection of lines through their maps.

But to resume.

The following is an exact copy of my diary kept during the trip:

Young America, Illinois, Tuesday morning — 1873; met Mrs. T. accompanied by Paul, Silas, and baggage, at the depot; one big trunk strapped with a bed-cord, a large partnership lunch stored in a paste-board box and secured by the diverse crossings of a cotton string — looks as if the bottom would drop out; a hand basket with a tin cup tied to the handle; an extra shawl and pillow; a satchel; my own overcoat, my trunk, and in my hand a violin case; train an hour behind time; train arrives; kissing, hand shaking and tears; on the wing; Mrs. Tompkins leans out of the window and blows her nose; not a good-looking woman, rather stout, stubby hands, thumb-nail purple from the bruise of a hammer; hair light, thin, leading back from the forehead in two limp strands and twisted into a knot about the size and shape of a pear, and tucked by the aid of pins under waterfall, kept in proper limbo by net; eyes a dull gray, lids a little red; ears punched for drops, (but no drops;) face wears an anxious expression, expects disaster; whistle blows, jumps; says "getting sea-sick;" head out of window (just in time;) Paul and Silas on the move; Paul wants a drink, Silas a drink; Silas asks for a lunch, Paul do.; Mrs. Tompkins pulls down the box, bottom falls out, milk bottle breaks and apples and hard-boiled eggs roll over the floor; I say "d—n it" and passengers giggle; I am afraid they think the family belongs to me; noon; Mrs. T. worse, boys getting tired, both asleep; Silas falls off seat, cries; Paul awakes and bellows; passengers very unsocial; Mrs. T. begins to look like the last rose of summer; Chicago, "change baggage;" I lift and pull and tug; cross city in a bus; man drunk and leans against the sea-sick sufferer; she protests and I affect not to notice it; "change baggage;" again I work like a sailor, and in my supreme disgust talk like a Dutch uncle to a brakeman, who threatens to "lick" me; off we go again; I put my three tormentors to bed; gave the "nigger" a dollar; tells him "if that woman dies before morning come into my car and let me know it;" "Eh?" said he; I repeated: "If that woman dies during the night come forward into my car and tell me of it;" whites of nigger's eyes roll up, colored troupe is alarmed and says, "Oh, de Lord, she ain't gwine to dun gon and die is she, eh?" "Yes I think she will." Ethiopian looks at dollar and says, "Yes Sah."

The night was black as the face of the negro, and the great train was roaring and plunging onward far into the dark, and quickening a dream in the vastness behind. You've groped your way from a platform of a car forward, have you not? It is risky business at best, but more so in thick night. How nervously one clutches for the iron guards, and how ardently he grasps the knob of the door. After crossing four or five of the connections I drop into my seat and am soon oblivious to care and turmoil.

Here again referring to my diary I find the following:

Colored individual calls me at 1 a.m. "Think, sah, she's agwine to pass in de checks; she's ben aheavin an dem air youngsters of hern's ben a bawlin' all night, so dat de passengers mity mad." Stumbled and felt my way back; found her about dead; brandy, six flasks, simultaneously presented from as many different berths; a voice. "Give them boys a horn big enough to put them asleep." Brandy was given, and soon everything was quiet on the Potomac. Next morning, Alliance, Ohio; "change baggage;" raining; Mrs. Tompkins lying in the depot so sick as not to be able to raise her head, waiting for train to Wellsville, Ohio;

train five hours behind time; infant apostles clinging to me and growing more and more familiar; 12 1/2 p.m. train arrives; "change baggage;" all aboard; Wellsville, Ohio, 4 p.m.; the place where John Morgan, the rebel raider, was captured; indolent, smoky little town on the Ohio river; train to Bellair behind; "change baggage;" raining; we all get out, lifting Mrs. T.; says she wants to die, (a consummation devoutly to be wished for;) carry her into the depot, so nearly exhausted that I think of shuffling the mortal coil myself. Evening; baggage and all aboard; run thirty miles back over the line we came in upon during the afternoon; why? (an unanswered conundrum;) was told at Wellsville that we must again change baggage at Bridgeport, opposite Wheeling; got there at about 9 p.m.; got out, leaving Mrs. T. and the boys on their seats; train rolls away; I ask an Irishman to "change baggage;" Irishman, polite as the middle man of a minstrel show, informs me that baggage is not changed there but at Bellair, ten miles beyond; "Thunder!" says I. "Why?" says he. "Where's that train," says I. "Gone," says he.

At this point I find that I quit keeping further notes in my diary, for I presume I was too much exhausted to write; but I remember I swore so that the poor Irishman thought I was a lunatic. One hour after I followed on a freight train, and found my charge and baggage in the depot at Bellair. I learned that the train did not again connect until the next day at 12. So getting the sick woman and those poor, peevish, worn-out children on board a dray, we went to the hotel, (oh Lord, what a hotel!) and remained all night. The next morning I transferred both my semi-animate and inanimate baggage — by dray and bus — to the Baltimore and Ohio depot, located far above the roofs of town on immense stone arches. It was still raining, and the train being again behind time, we remained until one in the afternoon, when again we started; but, oh heavens! gentle and patient reader, after rolling slowly over the bridge, the train halted and the brakeman stuck his head into the car and shouted: "Passengers will all get out and change baggage."

And again, once more, sick, disgusted, and weary, I crawled out and pulled that wet, sea-sick, desponding triangle, including bag and baggage, into a dirty, dingy, smoky little depot to await the arrival of another train at 3 o'clock. I was moody, deeply devilish, and didn't talk any. I don't remember how Mrs. Tompkins acted, or whether she could act; but I know this: In due time we again started and arrived at Moundsville shortly. That was the end of Mrs. T. and her children. But lo and behold! not of my troubles; for I had to remain there until 7 that evening. Then I started and rode all night long, sandwiched, bolt upright, in a seat with an Irishman, who smelled like a gravel train, and so until we stopped at the junction, at the Relay House, at 10 a.m. But we arrived too late for the connecting train, and in consequence had to stay until one in the afternoon, when I, for the ninth time, "changed baggage," and at 3 1/2 o'clock, with my eyes full of cinders, hair full of dust, beard full of sand, soul full of disgust, with weary limbs and soiled clothing, I rolled into Washington.

BEAU HICKMAN
CA SEPT. 7, 1873

"Beau Hickman had no friends, but he died without enemies." — *The Evening Star*

His quarters for jesting hereafter
Will be pitched in the land of no mirth,
The jester who moved us to laughter,
At a quarter apiece upon earth.

But he'll shamble around and not mind it,
In spite of his bunions and cramps;
Quaint business I reckon he'll find it,
While dunning the angels for stamps.

He will pun on the key of Saint Peter,
And the trumpet of Gabriel he'll toot,
And bore them in rhyme or in meter,
And tax them a quarter to boot —

That is, if they charge him for lodging,
But there they ne'er dicker nor trade;
So Beau will be done with his dodging,
Since the debt he owed Nature is paid.

And his face, that was tanned into leather,
I suspect will its freshness regain,
For the airs of that beautiful weather
Will woo away wrinkles and pain.

I have heard that poor Beau was dishonest,
A statement I scorn to believe,
For he paid every cent — if he promis't —
Doing neither he did not deceive.

He professed to subsist without labor,
A wag, and a dead beat, it is true,
But they say he ne'er slander'd his neighbor,
Which is more than his neighbor can do.

Of his faults I have mentioned a sample,
They were many, and barren of love;
But the good I have written is ample
To secure him a corner above.

And I bid him good-night, without feeling,
Poor Beau! with a vagueness of tears,
So stopp'd have the wheels of his being,
And the weights have run down with the years.

THE RAZOR GRINDER
CA Nov. 16, 1873; HH June 5, 1875

[The 1875 version did not include the final two stanzas. — Ed.]

His lathe he rolls around the streets,
A shambling sharper, day by day,
As with a signal bell he keeps

The tinkling tenor of his way.

And when an edge to grind he finds,
He halts and rigs his wriggling wheel,
And promptly proves for whom he grinds,
A grinder worthy of their steel —

As knee akimbo and aflex,
And foot upon the pedal laid,
He spins agleam the sparks that vex
The temper of the tempered blade —
Until its jagged gaps to smooth,
He deftly checks the whirling stone,
And then proceeds its ire to soothe,
Upon an oil-anointed hone.

And with an handy hand he draws
The testy edge, with sure avail,
And tests the same for lurking flaws
Across his index-finger nail.

Until 'tis duly sharp, when he
Still round the dull routine of years
Re-rolls for something dull, may be
A blunted knife or pair of shears.

Yet notwithstanding, he is but
At best, a luckless child of chance,
In short, his luck is shortly cut
Upon the edge of circumstance.

Yet still he shambling grinds for bread,
Nor for an helping hand doth wait,
And so till life's unraveling thread
Is severed by the shears of fate.

P.S.

Since putting this in type we learn,
His ill-bred wife, a type of sin,
To dough has caused his cake to turn
And pi'd him with a rolling-pin!
LATER

The telegraph has brought us word,
That while he ground a carving knife,
It slipped and cut a vital cord,
Acquitting rolling-pin and wife.

Washington, D.C.

Tulkinghorn's Offense
CA Nov. 30, 1873

A Ballad of Baltimore

That Jim is cute and clever
Are facts which none deny,
And his jolly face is jeweled
With a glass abnormal eye,

And a nose inclined to Roman,
With a hook and graceful bend,
While a blushing whisky blossom
Amply justifies its end.

And his trade it was an artist's,
Which the same he now conceals,
But the proof we read around us
On the signs and wagon wheels.
But at length he grew ambitious
When his pot of paint he dropped,
And upon the Thespian ladder
He ascended — till he stopped.

Stopped and ran the "Holliday,"
As well the public know,
And will furthermore remember
That it was not long ago;
And the incident was told me
Of the arson and of Jim
By Johnson's late successor,
Mr. Manager McKim.

Now the stock of Johnson's company,
From comedian to page,
Was the quaintest set of roosters
That ever walked the stage;
And a gamey sort of actor
By the name of Tulkinghorn
Was often found a roosting
In the station-house at morn.

So returning late one evening,
Just as usual, from the play,
He partook of double-triggered,
Forty-rod upon the way;
And the fiery demon in him
Kept arising high and higher,
Till Tulkinghorn went raving
And set the house on fire.

Of course you know what followed:
Mr. Tulkinghorn was lugged
By four or five policemen
To the station-house and jugged;
But Jim knew nothing of it
Till rehearsal came next morn
When he asked "What in the devil
Had become of Tulkinghorn?"

Out spake the high comedian:
"Why, Tulkinghorn was tight,
And the fool committed arson
On his homeward way last night;
And I understand he's lying
At the station, and no doubt
He is patiently awaiting
For you to bail him out."

Then a shadow darkened Johnson
And his heart it hove a sigh,
While a squint was quite apparent
In the said abnormal eye;

And he smacked his fists and ranted,
And he swore with might and lung,
"That every drunken arsonist
Should then and there be hung."

"What! Bail him, blast him; ball him
For committing arson? No?
He may languish in that station
Till his hair's as white as snow!
Me, bail a main for arson!
No, I hope, although I'm riled,
That the gal they'll make him marry,
Or else support the child."

Washington

THE WINDOW-PANE TINKER
CA DEC. 7, 1873

The window-pane tinker don't cavil
Though pained for a pane to put in,
But itinerates on in his travail,
An itinerant tinker — for "tin,"

But the riddle is, how to keep tally
Of the every-day tinker you meet;
Is the straggler who straggles the alley
The same whom you see in the street?

Though you never can see one with another —
For together no two ever hitch —
And you always take one for the other,
And the two for the devil knows which!

Moreover, I'll add, as I'm giving
The tinker a notice, I'll give
My note to the oldest man living,
If he know where a tinker doth live.

For I meet him benighted and groggy
In ways that are crooked, alas!
And straightened when mornings are foggy,
With a diamond, and box full of glass —

A fugitive, vagabond, rover,
Leaving tracks in his life-running sands,
As he runs the town over and over,
In a pair of run-over brogans —

And a light-looking coat that looks tattered,
Yet he's on the look-out, for all that,
For the light of a window that's shattered,
And plugg'd — with a broken plug hat.

And he not only drinks and carouses,
But the truth of the adage disowns:
"That people who live in glass houses
Should be careful to never throw stones."

So it happened, one day, when faultfinding,

That a chap interposed, to combat him,
Who to make the conclusion more binding,
A cobble-stone grabbed, and threw at him;

So direct, that it practically laid him,
Pain-racked, in the wreck of his glass;
While a stone on his head is what made him
Lodge under a stone in the grass.

Washington

THE OLD UMBRELLA MAN
CA JAN. 18, 1874; <HH MAY 8, 1875>

[Irvine constructed much of this poem from "Ye Umbrella Mann." — Ed.]

If the morning rain you meet him,
With a face of saddle-tan,
This weather-beaten vagabond,
Th' old umbrella man.

But never in the afternoons,
In either mist or fog,
For then th' old umbrella man
Is overcome with grog.

And so he shoves his earnings
At the "local option" folks,

While his fun at "Jonadabers"
Like an old umbrell he pokes.

Till his broken ribs he shoulders
And walks devoid of pain,
As a second-handed handle
He handles for a cane.

For it rectifies his wobblings
And proves a propping friend
As at intervals he hollows:
"Umber-ell-er-ers to mend."

Till he meets with one that's crippled,
When he squats him to the ground
And gouges with a pegging-awl,
And bindeth 'round and 'round.

With wire the dislocations
Of whalebone and rattan,
This eccentricest of mortals —
The old umbrella man.

But since with awl his gouging
His bill, it bores you too,
For the tink'ring charge exceedeth
The price when it was new.

One morn this old curmudgeon
Was a-tink'ring in a fog,
When something snapped and bit him,

Which the same it was a dog!

A bob-tail'd brindle mongrel
Of cur and rat and tan,
But he'll never bite another,
Not an old umbrella man.

For behold this old curmudgeon,
(Who was groggy then on grog)
In dogg'rel swore as follows:
"Dog-on the cuss-ed dog."

When he grabbed an old umbrell,
(Accompanying the remark)
And jabbed it down his throttle
When he op'ed his mouth to bark

And hoisted it, which rather
Caused his hide <skin> to stretch and swell
Like a gum-elastic scabbard
O'er an opened-up umbrell.

But the dog was old Dogberry's,
And Dogberry had a gun,
Hence the old umbrella man
And the dog became as one.

So a jury sat upon him
And found a "double charge"
Of buck-shot in his abdomen,
And scattered 'round at large.

And his ribs were also broken,
Which a doctor whose desire
Was panting <*yearning*> for a skeleton
Proposed to bind <*splice*> with wire.

But the verdict bound him over,
In a true dogmatic way —
Since aforesaid old Dogberry
Was entitled to his day —

To the final court which tried him,
And condemned him to the cells
Of a prison where he's tink'ring
Out his crime on old umbrells.

ICHABOD
CA MAR. 15, 1874

It is far from my wish to inveigle
Fond faith, from top-loftical things,
But a length of the tail of the eagle,
Should, in short, be curtailed from his wings.

For soaring, he alights (without joking)
On the monument's top — as you know —
And because it's unfinished, sits croaking
"Nevermore," like the Raven of Poe!

Since truth is the prophecy spoken,

Then the typical bird who can blame?
For the pledge of the nation is broken,
And her gratitude branded with shame.

Like the castle confounded at Babel,
So it stands a derisive reproof,
With a weather-warped, clap-boarded gable,
And a derrick-like thing on the roof.

And crumbling, the ill-tempered mortar,
Is dusting the cob-webs and bats,
While the inner walls make a safe quarter,
For stampeded neighborhood rats.

Better then on the door stick a knob
That will lock with a bolt, and thereon,
As of old, write the word "Ichabod"
Which means that the glory has gone.

Washington, D.C.

A Brace of Canary Birds
CA July 5, 1874

The Male

T. Simmons Fitz Noodle is attached to a cane —
(That pun needs explaining, I mean as a friend of it) —
Of his love of a dear little, sweet little cane,

With the leg of a woman stuck tilt on the end of it.

T. Simmons Fitz Nood. wears a languishing air,
And a ring on his neckerchief, just for the tie of it;
In the middle he parts both his love and his hair
And the glass on his nose, with a string at the eye of it.

On the oroide chain of his watch there's a head
Of an owl or a gander, but a fig for the name of it,
Since but little it boots, as it serves in its stead
To emphasize his when comparing the brain of it.

Then his narrow-toed, oval-shaped, sled-runner shoes,
His left little finger with the very long nail on it,
And his very long ears, and his barber-pole hose,
And the latest-cut coat, with a very brief tail on it.

Saying naught of his very cheap wit and his talk,
With its drive and slang, and billiards, and drink of him,
And his women and conquests of virtue, and walk,
Is the make-up of Noodle, and just what I think of him.

THE FEMALE

Miss Gussie Van Goosie is a delicate blonde
With a chignon that woos by the grace of the hang of it,
Then add, if you will, to this beautiful blonde,
The hair on her intellect and the sweet bang of it.

Miss Gussie Van Goosie has a wasp of a waist
And the fullest of eyes, but so short is the breath of her,

Since her liver is pinched and her lungs are displaced
I'm afraid that tight lacing will soon be the death of her.

But her pannier's not pinched — you can make up your mind,
While she favors inflation — as you'll see by the swing of it,
While among its department of news you will find
A file of *The Capital* strung on the string of it.

Moreover, Miss Gussie takes arsenic, and paints,
Chews gum, (on the sly,) and she thinks you don't know of it,
Laughs sweetly by note, flirts, waltzes and faints,
Wears a shoe with the heel but an inch from the toe of it.

Then the puffings and bows, and the style of her hat,
And Fannie — a poodle — the dear little pink of her,
And a spread-eagle fan and her trail, and all that
Is the make-up of Gussie, and just what I think of her.

THINE AND MINE
CA JULY 26, 1874

DEDICATED TO MR. AND MRS. JOHN JAMES PLATT, THE BEREAVED PARENTS OF LITTLE ALFRED VICTOR.

Touch thou my hand no major string,

Nor chord the mirthful ear to please,
For lo! the hearts to whom I sing,
Are tuned in sorrow's minor keys.

Two poet-hearts to whom belong
The air and alto of the pen —
Those sad and silken threads of song
That woo to tears our fellow men.

Ah! thine and mine are one and one
By night and day I sit and cry,
I watch the stars and watch the sun,
And wonder if my child is nigh.

My dainty darling who like thine
Was snatched away in one fleet breath,
Dear Victor thine, and Lizzie mine —
Sweet angel-loves of life and death.

Into the dark we stretch our hands
And cry a cry as in the night,
Whereas the mystic bridge that spans
The far between is filled with light.

Yet though they ne'er shall cross again,
We'll wait and touch the garment hem,
Till Faith shall heal our longing pain,
And lead us o'er the bridge to them.

Washington

SONG OF THANKSGIVING — NOVEMBER 26
CA Nov. 22, 1874

[This poem shares several lines with "Hymn of Thanksgiving." — Ed.]

Oh! dear beloved King of kings,
Wilt roll thy chariot low and list?
The regal earth exults and sings,
And seas are hazed in amethyst;
The joyful hills and mountains view
The gold and crimson skirted dales,
And silver waters glinting through
The purple raiment of the vales.

With fragrant hay the farms are sweet,
And thrifty herds the granger drives;
The mows are filled with amber wheat,
And limpid honey drips from hives,
While every wayside vineyard yields
Its vintage with the blush of wine,
And homeward lowing from the fields
With burdened udders file the kine.

So heavenly Father, gracious King,
With banners of our faith unfurled,
And rapturous tongues to Thee we sing
The gladness of the rolling world;
For hills and vales to Thee belong,
The mounts and deep abundant sea,

The fullness of our gift of song,
And life and love we lift to Thee.

SMITH SANDERSON
CA MAR. 14, 1875

A BALLAD

I
Where winds the way of Vernon Run
Around a spur of wood,
The smithy of Smith Sanderson
Begrimed and humble stood

II
Behind, in somber majesty,
The mountain summit loomed,
In seeming like a thunder-cloud,
Fleece-cap'd and tempest-plum'd.

III
Before, a thousand valley-farms
In lazy languor lay;
The ample barns were filled with grain,
The mows were sweet with hay.

IV
The while, as supple Vernon Run,
Away through mead and lea,

With glint of nimble silver trout,
Went gliding to the sea.

V
The dappled turnpike, white and gray,
From shell and broken stone,
Had crossing tuned the limpid ford
In ceaseless monotone;

VI
Which, flowing near the smithy-door,
Had babbled in the ears,
And timed the stroke of Sanderson
For nearly forty years.

VII
For nearly forty changing years
His anvil rang in rhyme,
As beat by beat his hammer seemed
To time the pulse of Time.

VIII
A grim and grizzly Tubal-Cain
Of tireless might and zeal,
Who fanned aglow the flaming forge
Till scarlet blushed the steel;

IX
And redder still, in time of war,
As loud his bellows roared;
The pruning-hook became a spear;

The plowing-share a sword.

X
And then anon, in time of peace,
The idle sword he took,
And beat it to a plowing-share,
The spear a pruning-hook.

XI
Likewise, all vagrant odds and ends,
And links of broken chains,
He welded well, and shod the teams
And set the tire of wains.

XII
So thus, beside a smithy forge,
Right leal he wrought his part;
Yet all the neighbors swore that he
Possessed an iron heart;

XIII
Was rude and rough, and had not learned
The dark of grieving ways,
Nor burthen of a rain of tears,
Nor clouds of sorry days.

XIV
Ah, me! they did not know of whom
They spake in wanton strife,
Forsooth, the dream-land gates were barred
Where dwelt his inner life.

XV
Still oft he oped those gates to me,
With neither fret nor frown;
Sometimes the rain was in the clouds,
Sometimes 'twas falling down.

XVI
And thus the man of "iron heart"
I found of sorrow proved,
And on his cheek a gentle smile
That little children loved.

XVII
I knew that he had learned to grieve
At Leonora's birth,
The night his wife her angel-hood
Put on and left the earth.

XVIII
To me he seemed a bruise-ed reed,
Yet kneeling by her side,
He sobbed into the ear of Death
"That Christ was crucified."

XIX
While underneath his window-sole,
Out in the dark and chill,
All lonely, like a 'boding call,
I heard the whip-poor-will.

XX
But Spring at length, with bobolinks
And swallows, came, and gave
The daintiest of violets
To blow upon her grave.
XXI
While baby Leonora grew
In beauty day by day,
Till like a Balm of Gilead
She wooed his wounds away.

XXII
Moreover, ceased the rain to fall,
For clouds had left his skies,
And his bitter life was sweetened
With the love of azure eyes.

XXIII
Until one autumn evening late,
Out in the gloom and chill,
Again I heard that 'boding sound,
The calling whip-poor-will.

XXIV
For lo! the cot of Sanderson
Was darkness all about,
Though lamps were trimmed and burning, still
The light of home was out.

XXV
Hard by the window, on a couch
She lay so mute and low,
Enshrouded in her burial clothes,
As white as drifted snow.

XXVI
As one in dreamless slumber lies,
She seemed at peaceful rest;
The saintly hands, as if in prayer,
Enclasped upon her breast.

XXVII
Her airy curls of amber hair
Were from the temples thrown;
The faint, fine lacing of the veins
In solemn mock'ry shone.

XXVIII
Meanwhile the father, who his grief
No longer could restrain,
Would cry a cry, as in the night
One cries a cry of pain:

XXIX
"Oh! Leonora, sainted child,
My life, my love, my all,
God takes thee, only leaving me
The shadow on the wall.

XXX
"No more, my dear, when noon shall come,
Wilt thou in patience wait,
A watcher for my weary steps
Beside the open gate.

XXXI
"Nay, nay, on earth thou ne'er cans't run
With open arms to me,
But some day I will cross the dark,
My angel-child, to thee.

XXXII
"Twill not be long, for I am old,
And weary-worn beside,
And then I know that God is good
And Christ was crucified."

Washington, D.C.

"Peace, Be Still"
CA Oct. 31, 1875; <AX Mar. 13, 1891; GL May 1891>

<Title: *The Bells of Kirkwood*>

'Tis the twilight of eve, and the going <*It is eve, and the coming and going*>
Of the cares that encumbered the morn <*Of cares, since the gray of the morn*>

Are at rest, and a harmony flowing
From the village comes over the corn;

As a song o'er the sea when the breakers
Are acalm from their turbulent swells,
And so, <*Soft-winged*> o'er the manifold acres
Flows the sound of the beautiful bells.

And behold, as I list, my behavior
Is softened, as come unto me
Sweet thoughts of an Infinite Savior,
On Eternity's deep Galilee.

Of the evening my life-time is bringing,
With a calm that shall woo and enfold
As a garment, and the bells that are ringing <*As a garment of peace, of the ringing*>
Far away in the City of Gold. <*Of bells in the city of gold.*>

Kirkwood, Ill.

CONCERNING WASHINGTON AND HIS MONUMENT
Dec. 1875

[This poem was published as a chapbook. Alfred Downing illustrated Irvine's words, which were an expansion of his earlier poem "The Washington Monument." — Ed.]

I
I've just been gazing on it, George,
From yonder hillock green
And wondering if your spirit-eyes
The thing had ever seen;
Mount Vernon isn't far away,
And then I know, you see,
That ghosts are very often moved
With curiosity.

II
I truly hope you hav'nt, George,
For if you ar'nt tough
A patriot posterity,
Have bored you quite enough
For ever since the day whereon
Your sands of life ran out,
They've been a tinkering memory up
And changing things about.

III
E'en from the ancient family vault,
Where first you lay entombed,
Your lengthy-limp anatomy
Was long ago exhumed,
And laid within a wider house —
The narrow one instead —
The solemn front is built of bricks
And painted flaring red!

IV
While down in old Westmoreland, George,
Where you were born — they say —
The stump your little hatchet hacked
Is grub'd and hook'd away,
And turned in whirligigs and spoons —
A fact which none deny —
And many a queer tobacco box
For snuff and cut-and-dry.

V
All in the Patent Office, George,
Your gods of other days,
And camp and kitchen furniture,
Are placed for public gaze,
With Martha's dainty handicraft
Of needle, quaint and old,
Your semi-buckskin uniform
With epaulets of gold.

VI
For many a year Mount Vernon ran
To ruin and to seed,
But now she runs a Regency,
Right royally indeed;
The grounds are wound with winding walks,
The house veneered with pine,
And well preserved from weather tan
With paint and turpentine.

VII
The monument's unfinished, George,
I grieve to tell you so,
According to the plans devised
Some forty years ago;
A grand and stately marble shaft —
A type of thee and wars —
Its base amid the columned states,
Its top amid the stars.

VIII
And furthermore, I'll here remark —
I blush to tell you — George
Of funds within the treasury
There wasn't such a gorge,
And e're 'twas half way builded up —
According to the plans —
The funds and glory petered out,
And there, by George, it stands!

IX
It looks so like a Chimney-wreck,
Or lime-kiln on the main,
Or wind-mill, Sancho Panza thought
A giant on the plain;
The mortar's crumbling from the joints —
A hint of time's reproof —
And a thing they call a derrick is
A rotting from the roof.

X
The inner-walls are laced and hung
With spider-webs and bats,
The flooring ratified into
A rendezvous for rats;
While 'neath its shadow ruminate
The couchant cows in peace,
The park's a common pasture-ground
For filthy goats and geese.

XI
The country's rife with gratitude,
But Uncle Samuel grieves
Because of reckless habits
So peculiar unto thieves,
For there's been a million dollars,
If there's ever been a cent,
Of penny contributions paid
To build the monument.

XII
At all the public places, George,
Throughout the lavish land,
Were contribution boxes put
To reach the willing hand,
Where drop by drop, for years and years,
The jingling silver fell,
But where it's gone's a riddle which
No honest tongue can tell.

XIII
Now really to be honest, George,
I'll tell you what I think,
The monumental money has
Been mostly spent in drink,
Or stuck to nimble finger-tips —
Without regard to law —
Or trick'd away in faro banks,
Or poker known as "draw."

XIV
Of course there's a committee, George,
Whose pockets hold the keys —
All very worthy gentlemen
Of leisure and of ease
Whose bowels are filled with yearnings and
With patriotic cramps
For the tardiness of people
In coming down with "stamps."

XV
I know it's awful shabby, George,
And we regret it sore
For memory's just as green to-day
As e'er it grew of yore.
A thousand towns and villages
Abroad from sea to sea,
And patriot sons of valor are
In honor named for thee.

XVI
The pulse of War has ceased to throb —
The drums their last tattoo —
The age foretold of prophesy
Is rolling into view.
While winsome hymns of jubilee
Are swelling in our ears,
The noise of hammers beating in
The temple's hundred years.

XVII
Columbia's great Centennial —
Where countless as the leaves
Shall troop the nation's harvesters
Returning with their sheaves —
The reapers and the binders from
The mighty grange where blows
The golden grain of Liberty,
And blooms the Sharon rose.

XVIII
And then, I ween, 'twill finished be —
As I have said to Jones —
They will bring the mason's with them who
Shall cut and hew the stones
And thus the glorious monument
In beauty shall arise
Its base amid the columned states
Its summit in the skies.

Indian Summer

SB Nov. 1877; TR Nov. 1877; <GL May 1891; CH Sept. 12, 1891>

[*The Travelers Record*, published by the Travelers insurance company, aggregated and reprinted pieces from other magazines. — Ed.]

At last the toil-encumbered days are over,
And airs of noon are mellow as the morn;
The blooms are brown upon the seeding clover,
And brown the silks that plume the ripening corn.

All sounds are hushed of reaping and of mowing;
The winds are low; the waters lie uncurled;
Nor thistle-down nor gossamer is flowing,
So lull'd in languid indolence the world.

And vineyards wide and farms along the valley <*And mute the farms along the purple valley,*>
Are mute amid the vintage and the sheaves <*The full barns muffled to the beams with sheaves;*>
Save 'round the barns the noise of rout and rally <*You hear no more the noisy rout and rally*>
Amongst the tenant-masons of the eaves.

<*A single quail, upstarting from the stubble,*>
<*Darts whirring past and quick alighting down*>
<*Is lost, as breaks and disappears a bubble,*>
<*Amid the covert of the leafy brown.*>

The upland glades are flecked afar in dapples
By flocks of lambs a-gambol from the fold;
The orchards bend beneath the weight of apples,
And groves are bright in scarlet <*crimson*> and in gold.

But hark! I hear the pheasant's muffled drumming,
The [turtle's] water murmur from a distant dell;
A drowsy bee in mazy tangles humming;
The far, faint tinkling tenor of a bell.
And now from yonder beech trunk sheer and sterile,
The rat-tat <*rat-tat-tat*> of the yellow-hammer's <*woodpecker's*> bill;
The sharp staccato barking of a squirrel,
A dropping nut, and all again is still.

Two Towns
CA Nov. 25, 1877; <*GL May 1891*>

[The 1891 version ends with the three stanzas that don't appear in 1877. — Ed.]

My cottage crowns a knoll of land,
And peering upward through the green
Of maple boughs — on either hand
Its dormer-windows may be seen.

And there it is when looking down,
Through golden sun or silver rain <*The season long in sun or rain,*>

I <You> see a thrifty neighbor town
At either ending of the lane.

A narrow lane and travel-worn,
From lagging wheels and feet that tread
A-weary with the burdens borne
Between the Living and the Dead.

Though scarce a furlong either way,
In one the blithesome <I hear the> robins sing,
And in the other all the day
The anvil and the hammers ring; <The smitten anvil's measured ring,>

All day I hear the champ of drills,
The roll of trains and engine-booms;
The low, incessant grind of mills,
The muffled pounding of the looms.

<Meet whom ye will, there's none but seems
Pursuing some elusive quest,
Two fretful, counter-passing streams
That never know a moment's rest.

The streets may climb the rugged hill,
Or straggle outward to the plain,
But wind and wind the way they will
They lead at last unto the lane, —

The narrow way we all must pass —
How soon or late there's none may know,

Our quiet homes beneath the grass
Are always ready when we go.>

The tramp of teams, the wonted noise,
And babble where they buy and sell;
The rabble rout of shouting boys,
The ringing of the auction bell.

And so, where'er in crowded street,
Or dusky shop, or market-place,
I see the tired uneasy feet,
The lines of care in every face.

And still, I ween there's sweet repose
In yonder town — it is not far —
And there a Balm-in-Gilead grows,
And there the blithesome robins are.

And ere you enter in to wait
The shining raiment and the crown,
You pause beside the outer gate
And cast your cross of troubles down.

And there for aye there's naught of tears,
Nor pain of longing in the breast,
Nor dreams to vex in all the years,
The holy hush of perfect rest.

Illinois

LET US EDUCATE AGAINST THE DIME NOVEL
MA FEB. 15, 1878

While I have long known of the large quantity of light and trashy literature launched upon the country through weekly periodicals — known as "story papers," and printed in our great cities, I was not aware, until recently, of the prodigious increase, resulting, as I shall attempt to show, through other and more attractive forms of publication.

Whether such papers as the "New York Weekly," the "Ledger," "Saturday Night," "Police News," and hundreds of others which might be mentioned in the same category, are gaining ground, in simple point of circulation, I am unable to say, but you may be assured — good reader — the general demand for the sort of fiction they dole out is not decreasing, while the Dime and Nickel series have, within the past two or three years, put in an appearance, and because of their cheapness and pictorial embellishments, have more than proportionally increased the pernicious results.

Stories appearing in the hebdomadals mentioned above, are mostly long-drawn out serials, which bait the reader from week to week, with blood and thunder installments, each installment closing on the giddy verge of some awfully dramatic scene to be enacted in the next chapter, and so on, from one degree of horror to another — if possible, still more awful — until the intoxicated student of fiction comes to the end, and throws the nasty thing down much less wise than when he took it up.

In the first place, the Dime and Nickel abomination is printed in a form much more alluring to the youth than the story paper. There it is to be seen upon the cunningly tricked-out show-case or counter of the vendor; the cover is gorgeous in colored embellishment; there is the handsome, dashing, black mustached dare-devil hero in blue, begirt with a bloody belt stuck full of revolvers and [illegible] knives until he resembles a perambulating arsenal, his foot on the neck of some dead Indian or brigand, or infernal monster, which he has just cut and shot into holes. Of course no boy can long withstand this. The circus poster with rushing horses, stand-up riders, ring-streaked and speckled clowns, long-necked giraffes, monstrous elephants and royal Bengal tigers is not a whit the less alluring, so that he straightaway, "by hook or by crook," (sometimes by hook) gets hold of a nickel and buys a book. He reads with avidity. He is filled with wonder. He believes every word of it, admires and emulates the hero; and if over sixteen years old, is in love with the heroine. Does he stop here? No, indeed, he immediately proceeds to inform every boy in the neighborhood of the wonders of the book, and instead of throwing it away, as he would a story paper, he sells it to a chum, and with the proceeds goes directly to the news stall again. His appetite is sufficiently sharpened for "another of them books;" this time he buys a work on "Buccaneering!" The buccaneers are in green, armed to the teeth with maroon cimeters. There are two ships; the vessel carrying the buccaneers is bristling with cannon as red as so many Babcock fire extinguishers, and they — the buccaneers, not the cannon — are boarding the other ship and from general appearances, there is a thundering fight on hand. This is sweet intellectual gruel for the youthful mind isn't it? This the beginning, but where is the end? As the twig is bent the tree will incline, aptly applies. The mind of a boy is plastic, and as he reads so it is shaped, therefore as the sensational novel casts it in a sensational mold, there, alas, it will remain. It will never expand — not any more than a plaster-Paris image. In fact, there is not the least desire for expansion. No appetite for knowledge, so that the individual, who has been a constant reader of this trash, even at the age of forty-five or fifty, knows no more of history, science, or art than a child. It is a notorious fact that the patrons of light fiction read that and only that, and not occasionally, but almost constantly. The daily newspaper, with its record of stirring events — if perused at all — is made secondary to the sensational novel. Like a pampered thirst for strong drink, the habit grows, and the more they read the more they desire to read. The effect is peculiar, and instead of strengthening, as does the reading of standard literature, it blunts the conceptions and gradually weakens the mind. Ask a moderate reader of standard fiction regarding some particular character therein, and you will be answered fully and intelligently, but question your sensational disciple respecting any one hero of a thousand over whom the midnight kerosene has been wasted, and barrels of emotional tears shed, and the reply will be vague and uncertain. Why? The mind is in confusion, for heroes, heroines, names, dates, places, shooting and cutting scenes, courtships, elopements, hair-breadth escapes, and fifty other peculiar features are mentally jumbled. In nine cases out of ten, these lightning readers — for this class does read with marvelous rapidity — will have the hero of "The Great Red Scout, or Buck Skin Avenger, by Wild Bill," married, or murdered, as the case may be — to the heroine of the Blonde Butcher, or Weird Poet of Devil's Gulch, by Ned Buntline.

Yes, it's a fact, too, that this class reads more pages, and gains less knowledge, than any other readers on earth. I care not how studious, for readers of other books, whether of standard fiction, History, Poetry, or Science, read for information, and not only for the special teachings of its pages, but for the style, the diction of the author. The readers of light fiction read for one end only, namely, to get at the ending of the plot, to see how the thing comes out.

Some years since, while residing in Rockford, Ills., I induced a young lady, the daughter of a near neighbor, to quit Mrs. Southworth and Ned Buntline and try Dickens and Walter Scott. She accordingly came to my library and borrowed the first of fifty volumes of Scott's Waverly. At the end of two weeks she had finished the last! Of course I was amazed, and when I questioned her as to certain characters, I found that she had them mixed. She had Rebecca in Ivanhoe married to Old Mortality, and in fact, I suppose that today she has even forgotten the name of the author.

Alas! the extent to which trashy fiction is devoured by both young and old, is simply astounding. Look on the news stands of hotels, on the counters of more pretentious dealers, and the open stalls along the street, often in the arms of newsboys, saying nothing of the unseen current pouring unceasingly through the post office. Recently I made it my business to visit the book and stationery stores of the collegiate and moral town of Monmouth, and while I am glad to note the extent to which the standard magazines, such as *Scribner's*, *The Atlantic*, *Harper's*, &c. are patronized — by the more excellent class to be sure — I was grieved to learn, notwithstanding the Warren County Library with its six thousand volumes, that another class — tremendously in the majority — refuse to be comforted with any literary diet, short of the lascivious hell broth dished out by such precious caterers as those I have mentioned

And yet I have hardly touched the evil results attendant upon the reading of flash novels. They are many, and some of the more common have names unfit to be printed in a moral newspaper. However, I take it for granted that my reader is aware of what these bad fruits are, so that I may pass directly to the suggestion of a remedy.

This remedy, I believe, can be made effectual through the medium of the common school. Instead of instructing by means of stale lessons from the stereotyped readers, put the current issues of the daily newspaper and monthly magazine into the hands of the pupil. No fault can be found with the moral tone of the serial school reader, indeed it is most excellent, but the books lack in two very important features, which the newspaper and magazine would fill, namely: the lessons of the reader are read and re-read, day after day and week after week, in the hearing of the assembled school until they become old stories, so old, so stale, so familiar, that many an urchin nearly reads his lesson by rote, not in the least fascinated or interested in the context for the simple reason that he knows just what is coming and exactly what the ending will be. To repeat: first he can nearly anticipate the words of the lesson, and second, the story, incident or moral thereof. In the newspaper, (I mean of course a non-partisan journal of pure morals, and in case the schools demanded [illegible] this fresh newspaper would contain the events of the day in good, clear-cut English, while the magazine — such as "Scribner's" and "St. Nicholas," would supply the more substantial literature, the former for the more advanced, and the latter for the younger pupils.

I am not the champion for any special periodical, but I mention the above for their peculiar excellencies. They are both illustrated by the very best artists and engravers in the country. It is a fact, too, beyond dispute, that pictures invite perusal of the subject they illustrate. *Scribner's* is conducted by Dr. J. G. Holland, a gentleman who has endeared himself to every moral, intelligent home circle in the land, through the lessons of his pen — a pen which has not seen an idle year in a quarter of a century — one that has consistently labored for the bettering of humanity and one that still writes in a riper experience and with none the less conscientious motives.

St. Nicholas undoubtedly leads in juvenile literature,

more talent, skill, labor and money being expended on it than any youth's paper in the world. It possesses features for all grades of years from twenty to the little people in pinafores. I have examined every article that has ever appeared within its covers, not one of which would prove unworthy in the instruction of youth in our common schools. In fact those papers on astronomy, which have appeared during the past year, by Prof. Proctor would be invaluable.

But I find my pen has run beyond the limits of editorial courtesy and I must close.

Kirkwood, Ill.

MUSTERED OUT <MAY 30TH>
MA JUNE 7, 1878; <CA JUNE 9, 1878> [NO INTRODUCTION]

[The D.C. version cut the four stanzas bookended with **bold lines**. The final six stanzas appear in Irvine's book as part of "The Fond Heart's Benediction." — Ed.]

Read by the author at the decoration of loyal graves in the cemetery of Kirkwood, Ills., May 30th, 1878.

To-day we hear across the years
The drums of mem'ry beat,
The fifers fifing martial airs,
The tramp of must'ring feet.

Again the neighing charger snuffs
The battle from afar
The clarion trumpet sounds aloud
The wild alarms of war!

And standing here, in retrospect
Beyond the vale is seen
The weary sentry on his rounds,
The <*white*> tents upon the green;

The lines of march, the skirmishing,
The army battle-formed,
The charge, the lightning of the guns,
The fort in thunder stormed!

The lifting cloud unveiling slow
The field of carnage lain
With thrice a thousand wounded men
And twice a thousand slain!

The valiant dead! How sweet they sleep!
And better for it seems
Than wounded life with painful days
And nights of fitful dreams.

Aye, dreamless is the soldier's rest,
Though in the foeman's land,
He dies without a woman near
To hold him by the hand.

And who can tell how deep the pangs

Of pain are hid beneath
The wan white face where patience waits
The welcome call of death.

And wheresoe'er sweet Patience is
There Mercy bears the shield;
Two meek-eyed nuns beside the coach,
Two graces on the field.
But <Yet> blood alone in battle shed
Did not the debt suffice,
And every hour its off'ring brought <*came*>
Unto the sacrifice.

And far along the beaten trail
Of march — at every mile
A weary soldier dropt behind
His comrade in the file.

Mayhap he lay in parching thirst
A mountain spring anear
Whose liquid silver babblings fell
Upon his famished ear.

And one, perchance, was shot and left
Behind the forage train;
And one in sore distress all night
Lay wounded in the rain.

And one on furlough going home
Died where no warrings be,
Another from a gunboat dropt <*fell*>

And sank beneath the sea.

And one by one their names were missed
From roll-call and parade,
So went and went they on their way
From Bastille and stockade,

From field, and barracks, and from camp,
From trenches and redoubt,
For Death recruits his ranks for aye
But musters no one out.

Yet though they went, and went so far,
I ween they're here to-day —
The Blue, who loved the Union so,
In mem'ry green — the Gray.

And thus in mute accord we come,
To meet, as met we last,
And as we call the roll, they file
In solemn silence past.

We come with songs in minor keys,
We come with eyelids wet,
We come with lilies of the vale,
We bring the violet.

We come with wreaths of Sharon's rose,
With fragrant heliotrope;
We come with loyal steadfast hearts,
With golden anchored hope.

We come in time of bees and bloom —
In airy halcyon hours;
We come in faith, and love as sweet
And tender as the flowers;

When oriole and bobolink
From every mound and tree,
And robin-red-breast flute their notes
Of dulcet melody.

And thus we give to them the best
We have in heart and words,
And leave them sleeping sweetly with
The blossoms and the birds.

1880-1889

AT THE PASTURE BARS
CA Apr. 18, 1880; MR July 30, 1880; <*GL May 1891*>

Returning lonely from the field,
She met me at the pasture bars;
The moon was like a golden shield,
The firmament was lit with stars.

As morning dawn her face was mild,
As evening, so her limpid eyes
God never gave a sweeter child
For weary man to idolize.

So winsome seemed her artless mirth,
Her soft caress and ardent kiss;
I thought of all delights of earth
The angels surely <*sure will*> covet this.

I know they mean to do no ill,
But whom they love they lure away;
Good angels, love her as ye will.

But leave her with me while I stay. —

Just as she is, for I would set
The hand of time behind an hour,
If that would stay a little yet
The bud from blooming <*blowing*> to the flower.

And <*But*> when at length we homeward went,
The fragrant azure shone so clear,
The great familiar firmament,
I thought, had never seemed so near.

So near, the moon above the trees
An airy globe of silver swung;
And in the dewy tops of these
The stars in mellow clusters hung.

So near, that I could scarce forego
The thought that one who longing waits,
Might hear a whisper <*them singing*> sweet and low,
Across the golden-portalled gates. <*Of love beyond the golden gates.*>

Moses W. Allen
MR Sept. 9, 1881

[Allen was the father of Henry, the friend to whom Irvine dedicated his only book of poems. Leigh Hunt wrote the poem quoted in full at the end. — Ed.]

Last week the decease of this worthy gentleman was briefly announced in these columns, and the writer well knows that he desired no further notice, in fact, he intimated as much during his last hours, saying that he wished neither show nor publicity, but that the obsequies should be few and simple.

Thus he died, as he had lived, but in view of his long life — and the good deeds that mark every mile of its progress — deeds done almost in secret — is it not fitting that his example should be [illegible] record, not that it may benefit him — for he is receiving a reward above all that earth can give — but for the emulation of the living.

Born March 20th, 1815, in Northampton, Mass., he was sixty-six years old at his death. At the age of twenty he was employed in a store at Alton, this State, which shows his youthful enterprise, for at that time — before the days of railroads — Illinois was considered the Far West, the very frontier of civilization. From Alton he went to Rockford, where he opened a store of his own, and in June 1845, married Miss Minerva C. Fletcher, who still survives and mourns his loss. Sometime after he removed to the village of Rockton, located in the same county, thirteen miles north. Here he ran a saw mill and manufactured in wood, until 1864, when we find him with his family in Young America. It will be remembered that he bought out the store and business of a Mr. Thatcher — and from that day forward carried on a large trade, being [illegible] town and community.

It is not our purpose to speak other than the simple truth touching Mr. Allen's character. Those who were not intimately acquainted, regarded him as somewhat eccentric. But is this not true of any man of independent and decided views? Perhaps it was because he was aggressive in argument. Generally from habit — of which he was doubtless unconscious — and often from sheer amusement, he opposed the popular side of every day questions, always using a free lance, and from his ability and store of information, was able to successfully cope with the best and combat opposition. Yet concerning the weightier matters of the law wherein did he err? Upon the contrary, where can we find another who, when weighed in the balance of immutable justice, will be found as little wanting? He was a man of the nicest honor, and the strictest integrity. He was a stranger to falsehood, and an oath or obscene word, or even the slightest hint of a vulgarism never tarnished his lips. Who ever heard him say aught against a neighbor, or engage in the idle gossip of the [illegible] of the neighborhood? But more than all, he was charitable in the strictest sense of the word. In some way or other he was continually assisting the [illegible] saying to the one he helped, "I guess this is coming to you," or "Here is a trifle of a gift" — and invariably with the injunction, say nothing about this. Even his own family were unknown to [illegible] of his good [illegible] defendant in a trial at law, and notwithstanding the large retail business transacted in his store, and in all the years thereof — a large share of the sales being on credit — no delinquent was ever, with his consent, sued or unduly harassed for payment.

Like all self-made men, Mr. Allen was intelligent

and especially versable. It seemed as though he had investigated everything — even the sciences. Well-read in history, an excellent practical grammarian, he wrote terse and concise English. He was thoroughly posted in the Pension laws, an was quite an expert in drawing legal business papers.

He was not a poet, and neither professed to be, but he was certainly an acute and apt versifier, as his numerous recent pieces in the Atlas will supply witness. They were written to break the monotony of hours and hours of weary confinement, thrown off hastily, many of them at one sitting, they evince a well-tuned ear and [illegible] and reticent in his charities, never speaking or hinting of them himself [illegible] with the generality of his neighbors. If any reader questions this, let him inquire of the poor of the village. That will settle it.

He died with disease of the kidneys, and for the past six years suffered extremely [illegible] weeks he would be confined to the house. Then he would be about again. Then down, and so on till the last illness. Yes, he died as he lived, and what a beautiful, even-tenored life it was, and how gentle and resigned he passed away. No shadow upon his home, his unbroken family, grown to the estate of man and womanhood about him, death steals in — just as [illegible] wing.

Put Mr. Allen in the place of Abou Ben Adhem, and you may judge of his reward.

"About Ben Adhem — may his tribe increase —
Awoke one night from a deep dream of peace,
And saw, within the moonlight in his room

Making it rich, and like a lily in bloom,
An angel writing in a book of gold,
Exceeding peace had made Ben Adhem bold,
And to the presence in the room he said,
"What writest thou?" The vision raised its head,
And with a look made of all sweet accord,
Answered, "The names of those who love the Lord."
"And is mine one?" said Abou. "Nay, not so."
Replied the Angel. Abou spoke more low
But cheerly still; and said, "I pray thee, then,
Write me as one that loves his fellow men."
The angel wrote, and vanished. The next night
It came again, with a great awakening light,
And show'd the names whom love of God had blessed,
And Lo! Ben Adhem's name led all the rest!"

J.P.I.

Summer Drought
CY Oct. 1882; <GL May 1891>

When winter came the land was lean and sere:
There fell no snow, and oft from wild and field
In famished tameness came the drooping deer,
And licked the waste about the troughs congealed.

And though at spring we plowed and proffered seed,
It lay ungermed, a pillage for the birds:
And unto one low dam, in urgent need,

We daily drove the suppliant, lowing herds.

But now the fields to barren waste have run,
The dam a pool of oozing greenery lies,
Where knots of gnats hang reeling in the sun
Till early dusk, when tilt the dragonflies.

All night the craw-fish deeper digs <*deepens out*> her wells,
As shows the clay that freshly curbs them round;
And many a random upheaved tunnel tells
Where ran the mole across the fallow ground.

But ah! the stone-dumb dullness of the dawn,
When e'en the cocks too listless are to crow,
And lies the world as from all life withdrawn,
Unheeding and outworn and swooning low!

There is no dew on any greenness shed,
The hard-baked earth is split along <*cracked across*> the walks;
The very burrs in stunted clumps are dead
And mullein leaves drop withered from the stalks.

Yet, ere the noon, as brass the heaven turns,
The cruel sun smites with unerring aim,
The sight and touch of all things blinds and burns,
And bare, hot hills seem shimmering into flame!

On either side the shoe-deep dusted lane
The meager wisps of fennel scorch to wire;

Slow lags a team that drags an empty wain,
And, creaking dry, a wheel runs off its tire.

No flock upon the naked pasture feeds,
No blithesome "Bob-White" whistles from the fence
<*The sheep with prone heads huddle near the fence;*>
A gust runs crackling through the brittle weeds,
And heat and silence seem the more intense! <*And then the heat still waxes more intense.*>

On outspread wings a hawk, far poised on high,
Quick swooping screams, and then is heard no more:
The strident shrilling of a locust nigh
Breaks forth, and dies in silence as before.

No transient cloud o'erskims with flakes of shade
The landscape hazed in dizzy gleams of heat;
A dove's wing glances like a parried blade,
And western walls the beams in torrents beat.

So burning low, and lower still the sun,
In fierce white fervor, sinks anon from sight,
And so the dread, despairing day is done,
And dumbly broods again the haggard night.

THE RESURRECTION MORNING
HC MAY 31, 1883

[Part I starts with lines that become Irvine's poem "A

Winter Morning Still Life." Part II starts with lines that end up in "An April Morning." Parts III and IV turn into some of "The Judgment Morning." — Ed.]

The following poem was written by, and delivered in Oquawka, Memorial Day, May 30th, '83, by Maj. J.P. Irvine, of Kirkwood.

I
You have seen a winter morning, the horizon dull and low,
When the earth and all belonging lay a level waste of snow;

In the bleak and empty distance there was naught of all we knew,
Save the gaunt and lonely poplars, to arrest the wandering view.

It was as a stretch of desert, with no sign of life thereon,
The familiar hills and hollows, and the fields and fences gone.

Every road and lane and by-way, far and near were blotted out;
Hushed the sound of bells, and silent were the huntsman's gun and shout;
E'en the axes of the choppers were unheard amid the wood,
And in drifts the "horse of iron" with his train imprisoned stood.

Thus it was, as from my window once I gazed in dumb despair
Far across the wintry vastness, melancholy, bleak and bare,

That I said, "Oh heart, as hopeless as the scene that lies before,
So will stretch the earth in nothingness when time shall be no more;

For the mortal is but mortal, and in vain has been our trust,
The dust of countless myriad dead will still remain as dust."

II
You have seen an April morning when the clouds and winds were lain,
And the gladsome world was smiling, as in sunbeams after rain.

When the uplands and the lowlands and the woodlands far and wide,
From the bonds of icy fetters, had been loosed and glorified.
Wheresoe'er the eye would wander there was naught but what was fair;
There was scent of balm and balsam in the clear refreshing air;

Every germ with life was quick'ning into green above

the mold,
Every bud a leaf and blossom was beginning to unfold;

There was promise in the furrow, in the hatching of the brood,
In the heifer growing clumsy from approaching motherhood;

E'en the aged were feeling younger, with a brighter hope in view,
And the happy-hearted robin sang the song forever new.

Then it was I read the lesson, heretofore so dark and strange,
Of decay and reproduction in their round of mystic change,

And my tongue broke into rapture, as before my clearer eyes,
All the purple distance opened like a vale in Paradise.

And I said, "Oh heart, be hopeful, there's another life than this,
Now I know we are immortal, and beyond us there is bliss!"

III
Who may reckon of the coming of the solemn judgment day,
When the sea shall roll no longer and the earth shall

melt away!

But we know the spinning planets through their wonted measures run,
As upon the natal morning when elanced around the sun,

And the ages unremembered came and went, and others came,
And grew old and were forgotten, so to-day it is the same;

And so will remain to-morrow — men will buy and sell and sow,
March and countermarch in armies, storm the fortress, charge the foe

Flash the lightning through the ocean, o'er the isthmus wheel the ships,
Delve the mountain, build the city, calculate the sun's eclipse;

Till at last shall come an evening — just as other evenings come —
But a spell of deeper silence shall arrest the busy hum;

And the sun shall e'er his setting pause and turn a ling'ring view —
Fondly backwards, as if bidding earth and time a last adieu;

And at midnight all the army of the stars in bright array,
With the moon, adown the heavens will forever go their way;

And I fancy all the living will in heavy sleep be lain
And a hush of awful stillness till the waiting dawn shall reign.

IV
'Twill be startling — in a moment — in the twinkling of an eye,
Swift and loud a herald-trumpet-sound shall break athwart the sky,

And a host of shouting angels shall on gleaming wings descend,
White and vivid as the lightnings, when in wrath they strike and rend!

'Twill be such a sound as never echoed since creation's birth,
'Twill reverberate throughout the length and breadth and height of earth,

And shall quicken and awaken all the dead that lie beneath,
Who shall rise, as He of old arose triumphant over death!

Oh, my fellow men, my comrades, what a gathering there will stand!

Such a host as none can number, far and wide on every hand!

There they'll be in countless myriads from the mighty ages past,
Though their dust a thousand summers may have winnowed to the blast:

They will rise from arid deserts, from the everglades and woods,
From prairies vast and lonely, and from mountain solitudes.

There will be no sea so fathomless, so wide and tempest-tossed
But will cease its restless roaring and give up the lov'd and lost.

We are told the sainted company in the happy realms above
With each other hold communion, as on earth, in conscious love.

So will we not meet and mingle? Is our little grave yard wide?
See, in every lot the family sleeping sweetly side by side.

Yet although they may be scattered, as are leaves by winds of fall,
There will no one there be absent but united one and all.

Meetings! aye, I know there will be — meetings there to part no more.
Bosom close to bosom claspings, thrills of joy unfelt before.

With what fondness will a father look into a daughter's face,
With what ecstasy a mother will her tender child embrace!

It may be the blue-eyed darling who was lost and never found,
It may be the little fellow who went swimming and was drown'd,

Or perchance, the boy who left her and enlisted in the war,
And was killed and lay unburied in a thicket dark and far.

Will the soldier not be foremost, not the promptest to obey,
When upon his quickened hearing breaks the judgment reveille?

He may sleep at Chickamauga, on the height of Mission Ridge,
In a trench with crowded hundreds, by a ford or by a bridge!

He may lie beneath the waters of a river swift and deep.

Or where falling, may have clutched and hung and died upon the steep;

With a squad of half a dozen who were sent to guard the train,
And surrounded by guerrillas fought till every man was slain;

With the foe he may be lying where the struggle there had been,
He may moulder where he famished — in a rebel prison-pen;

He may rest beside a comrade in a little nook of green,
On the hill his skull may white, and his bones in the ravine;

In some great silent city 'neath the rose and myrtle groups,
In an humble country grave-yard where the weeping-willow droops.

For by hundreds and by thousands went and went they on their way
In all seasons, in all weather, in the night-time and the day

When the lightning and the thunder of the guns were quick and loud,
And the armies rushed together like the tempests in a cloud;

In the charge upon the battery, where to do was but to die,
In the throes of mortal struggle, hand-to-hand and hip-and-thigh.

Aye, by the hundreds and by thousands they have gone — and others go,
Year by year the men we muster less and less in numbers grow;

And the young that marched so lightly and were sunny, blithe and bold,
Now are shoulder-bent and weary and we all are growing old.

Yet, it is of God's appointing, it is well, and we shall meet
Every comrade, friend and neighbor when the end shall be complete.

But 'twill not be as we left them, ere was closed the burial case,
Sunken-eyed and worn and pallid and the death damp on the face

But in perfect form and beauty with no care of earth oppressed
For the long and dreamless slumber of the grave will heal and rest.

May Thirtieth
MA June 5, 1885; <GL May 1891>

O comrades though in thick'ning green,
Your lowly graves the grasses screen;
And years are long since last we met,
With all the change that years beget,
There's naught of life or time between
To woo away remembrance yet;
Nor naught that is, nor is to be
Hereafter, shall your valor stain;
For all abundant as the sea,
And steadfast as her broad domain,
So is the Nation's love for thee.

And lo! upon this hallowed day —
The sweetest e'er to sorrow born —
We seem to wake afar away,
In field and camp <*As oft we woke*> at early morn
And spring to arms <*In other years,*> again to hear
The gath'ring sounds of battle near;
The stormy drum's redoubling beat,
The bugle's swift, defiant peal;
The sharp commands, the hurrying feet
Of must'ring squadrons, as they wheel
And league themselves in stern <*grim*> array,
To storm the valiant hosts of Gray!
The word to charge, that breaks the pause
Of dread suspense, the wild huzzahs,
As forth the phalanx springs and runs
Full front upon the flaming guns!

As when against a headland steep
A billow strikes and strews the deep
With warring breakers, even so,
The column breaks against the foe,
When man and man in all the heat
And might of fiery fervor meet,
And hand to hand with naked blade
And bayonet, fight undismayed,
The weaker yielding only when
Have fallen half their valiant men;
Their cannon gone, their colors lost,
They smite for every inch they yield,
Until, alas! at fearful cost
The stronger win the sanguine field.

And so a grateful people come,
With martial step to fife and drum,
And cornets sounding silver strains,
Along a thousand crowded lanes;
We come when spring in fullness breathes
The wooing airs of summer's dawn;
With plumes of fir and cedar wreaths
Dark green, that smell like Lebanon;
We come with roses and the bells
Of lilies and with asphodels,
And fleur-de-lis <*flower-de-luce*> in beauty blown,
And violets so frail and dear,
That each beseems a blossomed tear
That God had cherished for His own.

We bring them fresh of tint and hue,

And all aglint with sun-lit dew
And lay them in their sweet perfume
With tender touch on every tomb;
And in lagoons and water-ways,
In lakes and harbors and in bays,
From every fortress on the steep,
And stately ship where cannon frown
We let a fragrant garland down
For all who slumber in the deep.

Aye, in the deep or on the land, <*Sleep, comrade, sleep, on sea or land,*>
There's not a palm-full of your clay,
So hidden, but a blossomed spray
Is drop't by some remembering hand.

And so beloved and near [illegible] <*For thee the healing rains of spring*>
The best of all the earth we bring, <*Fall earlier that the grass may grow;*>
The sweetest songs the tongue can sing, <*The flowers in daintier fullness blow,*>
The fondest treasures of the heart. <*The robin redbreasts sweeter sing.*>

For thee we lift the granite high,
The graven urns of marble set;
Their silver lutes the poets fret
To dulcet strains that never die,

Sleep, comrade, sleep, there lurk about

No ambush'd foe to fear or shun,
The Blue and Gray are one and one,
And all the fires of camp are out,

Sleep, comrade, sleep, nor dream again
The vague uneasy dreams of life,
Sleep all forgetful of the strife
The sleep that lulls away your pain.

Sleep, comrade, sleep the sleep <*and dream*> of bliss,
The night of death is calm and deep,
The war is over, sleep the sleep
That wakes no more to weariness.

Sleep, comrade, sleep in earth's green breast,
There's none to trouble, fear no ill,
The night of death is sweet and still,
Sleep on in the eternal rest.

Kirkwood, Ill.

A VOICE FROM KIRKWOOD
MR Nov. 13, 1885

No. XII

The Delights of Humbuggery — The Despotism of Illusion — The Patronage of Quack Nostrums — Alarming Increase, Extortionate Price, Etc.

People delight in being humbugged. They love to hear of the marvelous. Barnum's What-is-it (an ape with its tail chopped off) was of more value to the showman in a financial sense, than were the shining talents of Wendell Phillips to the lecture Bureau. Curiosity develops with infancy, which accounts for the invention of toys and explains the youngsters' propensity for digging inside to see what causes the rattle.

Is it any wonder, then that children of a larger growth are prone to believe in hoop snakes and yearn to be comforted with cock and bull stories? We all love to abandon ourselves to the sweets of illusion.

Macauley, in speaking of this, illustrated by pointing out how a little girl becomes affected by the story of poor "Red Riding Hood." She knows that it is all false, that wolves cannot speak, yet in spite of her knowledge she believes, she weeps, she trembles and dares not enter a dark room alone lest she be eaten up. Ordinarily intelligent people cannot sleep after partaking of a hearthstone repast of ghosts and hobgoblins before retiring, all of which proves the despotism of imagination over the mind. But the more we give over to this desire the more the habit grows. Curiosity, the love of illusion, the witchery of humbug, are all sweet.

Taking in addition to this the promptings of disease, whether real or imaginary, and we have a reason for the immense patronage given to quack nostrums. Of course a diseased person will seek a remedy. It is also safe to say that every nineteen out of twenty is in some way out of fix; and if the twentieth were carefully looked over you would probably find a loose screw or worn gudgeon somewhere about him. However, it doesn't follow that all are in need of medicine. Most of the ills to which flesh is heir result from a sheer violation of nature's laws, and the remedy lies in simple reform. If you drink whiskey, stop it. If you run gadding about o' nights, stop it. If you stuff yourself with mince pie and gorge you inner man with devil-crabs before bedtime, you will have an interview with the nightmare. It's all easily understood. Then again, a large number out of the above twenty are of the imaginary sort; they imagine a deadly ache where there is hardly a suggestion of a pain, and are sure of a consuming malady where there is scarcely a symptom of disorder.

Again, there are those who anticipate disease and treat themselves against its coming. It is safe to say, then, that every one of the nineteen out of the above twenty is a patron of quack remedies, and I am not sure that I ought to except the twentieth.

The manufacture and sales are astounding. They are on the increase, too. The more respectable of family newspapers advertise but a few of the best, or of those that from long standing have become well known. I suppose, in reason, there is not one of these mixtures out of two hundred that possesses the qualities and merits claimed for it. Yet they all sell, and the proprietors get rich just the same.

It is a wonder how they keep up the extortionate prices on them. The competition is great, while there seems to be several hundred different decoctions for each disease. And yet, a compound only costing the proprietor a few cents, sells readily at almost as many dollars. You may expect a change in price of sugars, or calicoes, but no reduction in quack medicines.

Next week I shall try and continue this subject.

J.P.I.

Special from Kirkwood
MA Nov. 13, 1885

An elegant oyster supper was given the members of Prof. Pletscher's band by Mr. and Mrs. Henry W. Allen on Friday evening last. Those of the band present, were: Prof. Pletscher, B.D, Sotield, R.D. Irvine, Mr. Betzinger, Mr. Gilbert, Mr. Robbins, Willard Tubbs, Mr. Eden, and Leon Flowers. The guard of honor, or the ornamental gentlemen of the evening, were presented in the persons of Mr. Sam Allen, Mr. Chas. Bradshaw of the *Leader*; Mr. Ed Herndon, one of the most promising amateur violinists in the country; Mr. Chas. Kaiser, of the 1st National Bank; Mr. Cal. Howard, artist in photography, and J.P. Irvine.

After the band had played a few pieces in front of the gate, the company were welcomed into the beautiful parlors of the host, where all hands fell to playing at social games of cards until supper, which proved both elegant and bountiful.

After the feast, Mr. Cal. Howard entertained the

crowd with a number of tricks known only to the most accomplished prestidigitator. He is only an amateur, and claims nothing beyond what he has picked up, yet he is proficient enough to elude the sight of the closest watcher.

Henry W. Allen also came forward with a piece of mathematical legerdemain quite bewildering. A certain number, unbeknown to the juggler, was chosen and multiplied and remultiplied, by any sum whatever, the process ending by cutting off the extreme right hand figure of the result. They mystery consisted in his naming this number. I am convinced, however, of some secret rascality in the business! The company broke up about midnight, and went home in the best of humor.

There were no ladies present other than Mrs. Allen, Miss Anna Johnston and Mrs. Morgan L. Ryder. Miss Libbie Hamsher, accompanied by Mr. Milt Robinson, of Monmouth, were expected, but for some reason did not arrive.

The band under the labor of Prof. Pletscher, has come to be an excellent one, at least above the average of non-professionals, and if the rest of our people were as liberal as Henry W. Allen, in encouragement and patronage, the organization would hold together and be an honor to the town.

A VOICE FROM KIRKWOOD
MR Nov. 13, 1885

No. XIII

Quack Nostrums — Enormous Prices and Big Sales — Some Standard Remedies Used by Good Physicians — Extensively and Shrewdly Advertised — How Constantly Some People Use Them, Etc., Etc.

I closed my paper of last week, the theme being on the humbugging of patent medicines, by speaking of the continuance of the enormous prices at which they are sold. A decoction only costing a few cents goes at a dollar or a dollar and a half. I could name a certain mixture for hog cholera — which doesn't cure it — that sells for five dollars per package — you might as well throw your money into the grass. Of all impositions on earth, the hog cholera cure is the worst. An inhaling preparation, put up by a firm in Philadelphia, taxes the poor victim of weak lungs fifteen dollars for a supply of three months, saying nothing of express charges. A second supply comes at a dollar less. The original cost is probably below ten dollars. Nevertheless, its sales are enormous, although it is not without its merits.

It is well enough to be just. The "cure all" lie on their face and have had their day. Special remedies is the style of advertising now-a-days. "Our remedies don't cure everything." "We only claim to relieve the patient of the malady for which our great discovery is intended." "We are not 'cure alls,'" is about the style they keep the thing before the public.

However, it would be unjust to assert, as many of our physicians do, that all patent medicines are worthless. Doubtless it would be well if about ninety-five percent of them were wiped from the face of the earth, and their proprietors banished to the Dry Tortugas. It will be admitted I think, that the remaining five percent could not well be spared. Certain vegetable pills, whose brands I might name, have become valuable and are used with excellent results not only in thousands of families, but by numerous physicians of good standing (on the sly, of course) everywhere. There are patent medicines that will cure ague; others will prevent the effects of malaria, and there are some good liniments. In face of the testimony of so many it would be hardly wise to deny, in toto, the efficacy of certain extensively sold remedy for "Bright's Disease."

Quack nostrums, of course, live only through shrewd and persistent advertising. The more extensively advertised, just in proportion run the sales. The surest test of a good remedy is the continuance of its use after the advertising has ceased. It then lives on its own merits. Doubtless the reader can recall some of these.

The advertising of patent mixtures [illegible] been reduced to an art. The compositions are the shrewdest and most cunningly devised to be met with. For example, there is a proprietor in Buffalo, N.Y., who invests his circulars and papers with a quiet grace and seeming learning that is winning, in spite of one's prejudice. In fact they all read well. The writers seem to understand what they are talking about, so that the invalid into whose hands one of these documents falls is usually won over, and becomes a victim to the use of nostrums. The most cunningly devised part of these advertisements is the apparent correctness of the diagnosis; the seemingly minute description of one's malady. You are warned, reasoned with, solicited, asked to read testimonials, told if you only buy and [illegible] directions, until [illegible] bottles, that a cure [illegible].

I can name a [illegible] months past had [illegible] pints of a villainous [illegible] to be a permanent [illegible] consumption. It retails at a dollar per pint, but by taking an installment of thirty bottles he paid but twenty-five dollars. I think he is now on the second installment. Does it help you? I asked the other day, in amazement. "Well," he replied, "I can't tell yet, I've not taken enough to know!" One thing is certain, if the disease don't fetch him the remedy (?) will.

I might also name two other men of whom, apparently, there is nothing wrong, yet they imbibe quack mixtures as old topers quaff rot-gut. The first thing they do when getting into town is to make for the drug store. Within a few weeks I heard one of them inquiring of a druggist if there was anything new in the way of patent remedies. In a half hour after I left him absorbed in the perusal of a new almanac setting forth the benefits of some great discovery for the cure of liver complaint. You can bet he bought a bottle or two before leaving.

I have never believed that the distillation and sale of whiskey can be stopped so long as the human appetite demands it, which of course will always be. Therefore, patent medicines will find patrons just as long as disease lasts.

Next week I may have something to say of itinerant quack doctors.

J.P.I.

A VOICE FROM KIRKWOOD
MR DEC. 18, 1885

No. XIV

The Itinerant Quack Doctor — Their Methods of Catching Patients — Their Abuse of Local Physicians — How One of Them Fleeced the Sick of Kirkwood, Etc., Etc.

Of all the learned professions — so called — that of medicine affords the best opportunities for practice of deception, and a long suffering public need hardly be told of how the advantage is abused. Once in a while a patent or proprietary medicine proves of some force as a remedy (the rule, of course, being the exception), but the "doctor" who perambulates from town to town on the hunt of chance patients is always a fraud. Many of them are libertines and real mountebanks, and deserve to be treated to a coat of tar and feathers when first entering the village. Those who "deliver" lectures (?) are the most pronounced villains of the class. Who of my readers have not seen the town running wild after the "professor" who "hires a hall" and hangs the walls with the "heads" of distinguished persons, authors, orators, philosophers, artisans, painters, etc., in crayon, (caricatures, of every one of them). In one collection I saw the name of Darwin written under what I took to be the "head" of Jonathan Edwards. It might have been the face of Cotton Mather — it was anybody else than that of Darwin. He examines craniums free ($1 for a chart). After being "delivered" of one or two open lectures, generally on the laws of health, in which he roundly abuses the local physicians and affirms his ability to cure all the ailments of the place, especially those of a chronic nature. He announces that on a certain night he will lecture to the men, and on the evening following the "lecture" will be for the women alone. Here is where he gets down to business and strikes it rich. If there is a woman in town who don't go it is simply because the fates keep her at home, and if there is a woman, of all those who do go, in health before going, she will come away firmly impressed that she is diseased and needs a course of medicine. This mountebank has by sheer cheek and gab talked the notion into them! The men are but little better, and the result is that he succeeds in pocketing an exorbitant fee all round without curing the well or sick.

Last winter one of those fellows lit down on Kirkwood. I don't think he hung his hall with "crayon heads," but he made it up in one of the most stunning "lay-outs" ever seen by a chronic patient. The display was in his room or office at his hotel. Skulls, retorts, shin-bones, syringes, stuffed birds, nippers, sea shells, odds and ends of dental and surgical instruments, and a spread of bottles, with silver mountings, that would have made a druggist green with envy. When the doctor appeared on the street he wore a long velvet overcoat trimmed with mink fur; kid gloves, diamonds and gold-headed cane were adjuncts. I had in former years known "the doctor" in another town, in this state, where he still resides. He had grown distinguished since our former knowledge of each other — some ten years having passed. He told me the story of his trip around the world; how he had saved the lives of scions of royalty; of a certain duke whom he had doctored from the point of death back to life; these diamonds were a gift from the duke; they were valued at £10,000! (I think they were cut from the bottom of a lager beer mug.) He showed me the diplomas from five or six of the principal medical universities of Europe, and as far as I was able to see they were genuine; also from Philadelphia, and I don't know how many more. How the nation he had accomplished all this since I knew him was what bothered me. But I was charmed, and although I knew him to be the most infernal liar I had ever met, I could not but admire his sublime cheek. Of course he won, and in two weeks carried nearly $600 out of the little town. His charges were enormous, but his cures were few and far between, and yet if he should again make his appearance he will carry off a larger sum.

Same subject continued next week.

A Voice From Kirkwood
MR Jan. 1, 1886

No. XIV

Again continuing the subject of quack doctors I may remark that his days are about numbered. However he will continue to travel, for in these times of laws and diplomas he will not be permitted to local practice. Our State laws regulating this matter are both direct and stringent. He who would "doctor" must produce his parchment — his collegiate evidence of qualification — or in the absence of this he shall have been a regular and bona fide practitioner for at least ten years, etc.

We have three excellent physicians here in Kirkwood, between whom there is neither jealousy nor rivalry. This of itself shows what kind of stuff they are made of — honest, Christian gentlemen. Heretofore it was not so; we were infested with our quacks. In 1876, or thereabouts, there suddenly turned up in our midst a "professor, late of the Eclectic Medical College of St. Louis." The announcement caused Armstrong and McClanahan to turn pale, and the citizens to retire to their closets and meditate. The "professor" was a portly, good looking man, apparently some fifty years old, but with a husky voice and an eye that betokened a lack of frankness, or rather a betrayal of perfect integrity. He opened an office and hung out a shingle, besides he played the violin; in fact, he was a jam-up country fiddler; he could just everlastingly jerk a hornpipe crazy and knock off jigs by the hour. He mingled freely with the boys, and doctored any little thing the matter with them. He played at dances, got in with the editor of our paper and had himself announced on all occasions. He joined the temperance society and the Methodist church, and the Lord only knows what he didn't join and didn't attempt to do. Of course such a fellow would get practice; a good deal of it was worthless, but on the whole he was always busy. "Professor M. has been called to another part of the state as consulting physician in a very critical case of surgery," would appear in the locals of the *Leader*, or perhaps he would be announced as being absent at the bedside of some big bug in Iowa. One I particularly recall: "Professor M. started yesterday for St. Louis, to examine the class preparatory to graduation in the medical college of that city. He will not return for some days." In the meantime a reply to a letter of inquiry had been received by one of our regular doctors, stating that no such man had ever been heard of in the college. It was written by one of the faculty, and of course settled the question. In due time the professor returned, and you may imagine the surprise it created, when his diploma appeared hung in one of our drug stores. A diploma from the St. Louis medical college, bearing a date not a week old, certifying (in the usual manner) to the graduation of "the Prof." himself (in the same class he went to examine), and with his own name signed to three chairs of the faculty, namely, Materia Medica, Obstetrics and Surgery!

Now the fellow's cheek was lean in comparison to his impudent presumption of the people's ignorance.

He must have thought us a pack of fools. This diploma hung in his office up to the time he went away, which was about a year since. He was no graduate and no physician, and the riddle is, how or where he got that diploma, for in everything save his own name it appeared genuine.

The professor had a partner a while, of whom it is well to speak. An adventurer from nowhere in particular and everywhere in general; a hatchet-faced, thin nosed, keen, black eyed sharper; an embodied exclamation point, always on the alert and forever on the inquiry, "What might I call your name? Smith? Ah yes; are you not in ill health, Mr. Smith? You have fever in your hand, let me see your tongue;" and so he went. I saw him in a drug store the second week after his advent in town. He said, so all could hear him, that he was almost worn out with riding. It was true that he did ride; he would be seen going out of town on the full gallop at all hours, the "Prof." one way and Dr. "S." another, but where in the deuce they went no one ever knew.

He had a way of baiting gudgeons that was unique. One day a poor fellow showed him his hand (he had the itch) and asked him what was the matter with it. Dr. S. took one quick glance, snatched from his medical case a glass and squinted through it, shook his head deprecatingly, looked grave and said, "come upstairs; my God! sir, your case is serious." It was on the street corner, with a crowd gawking around. He got the poor devil in his office and scared him nearly to death with big words, ending by telling him that there was but one chance of recovery, and that was by a medicine he could get in New York. Twenty dollars would do to commence on, which he (the doctor), would have to pay in order to secure it in time to do any good. The victim asked until the next morning to raise the cash. The Dr. warned him to keep the case to himself, for if it got out the whole town would stampede for the disease was contagious (all of which was Greek to the patient). With a heavy heart, the victim betook himself towards home, when in passing the office of old Doctor Stewart he called and tremblingly showed his hand, asking what it was. "That? why Dan, that's the 'eetch,' where in the devil have you been?" Could he cure it? What would it cost? "Oh shucks! Nothing. Go and get some mercurial ointment and rub on," was the plain old doctor's reply.

J.P.I.

A VOICE FROM KIRKWOOD
MR JAN. 15, 1886

No. XVI

Again resuming the thread of my last theme concerning that pair of precious quacks, "Prof." M and "Dr." S., late of our town, it is worthy of mention that the partnership didn't last long. Dr. S. was a more cunning financier than the Prof. In fact Prof. M. was not as shrewdly impudent as Dr. S., yet what he lacked in this direction he made up in egotism — in sheer pretentiousness. I one day heard him assert that when a student in college he was in the habit of conversing in Latin and Greek to the Profs. A graduate indeed! He never was in a college, and he knew no more of the classics than a mule of the comic sections. He was not a loud braggart, but low, confiding and complacent. There was no knowledge too abstruse for him, and nothing he did not attempt to perform. He was present and conspicuous on all occasions. The next night after fiddling "Dan Tucker" and "Leather Breeches" at a hoe-down he was "delivered" of a lecture (he called it a lecture) in one of our churches. It was soon after his advent into town, so he had a fair audience at commencement, which however, disappeared in a series of dissolving views as he proceeded. He always "spoke" someplace on the 4th of July, also at all political meetings. He said he did it in order to re-elect Cousin "Ben" (Marsh) to congress. He badgered applicants for pensions by promising "his influence with Ben!" Indeed he acted as attorney in a number of cases, which were either rejected or perhaps never placed on the files of the office for want of proper prosecution.

He wrote poetry (?) by the yard and pronounced eulogies on the eminent dead of the land. That on Garfield, before the lodge of odd fellows, is said to have been unique. But enough. I will only refer to the arrangement of his office, and drop him. I am not certain, yet almost so, that he was in partnership at one time with our friend Denny Walker, a whilom tooth-carpenter of the village. Anyhow, the Prof. and Denny occupied rooms adjoining. The front office opened into three other apartments, over the doors or entrance to which were placed placards thus: Over one, "Operating Department;" over another, "Consultation Chamber;" and above the third, "Lecture Rooms." Of course this naturally took the breath out of the rural rooster who came within reading distance.

As to Dr. S., he did not spread quite so broadly in office show (that is, after the dissolution of partnership), although he wrote weekly medical articles for the *Leader*. They read well enough; had something of the medical almanac flavor about them, and served to advertise the doctor. His plan was to look up people who were seized with money as well as disease. He was successful. A woman down towards Raritan is said to have advanced him $60 for aggravating her malady. A poor devil here in town paid him $15 for tinkering at his kidneys and doing them no good. Another fellow living a few miles north was ornamented with an off eye that had an eccentric habit of squinting across the bridge of his nose. The doctor tied him down and cut the puckering string, only to yank the orb as far round the other direction. Only the other day I heard of a victim from the vicinity of Salter's Grove who purposes in case of ever meeting him to "lick" an advanced fee of $15 or $20 out of him. He managed to manipulate one of our capitalists out of several hundred dollars, which I believe was to be invested in eye water or some wonderful dope, the returns of which was to be enormous.

What has become of him? I don't know. I don't know where either of them are. The Professor I think went East, and the probably the Doctor is skinning victims in the West.

The doctor found it necessary to skip on account of his health. I can't say just what took the professor off; he still had practice, or seemed to have, although many had ceased to employ him. He was in debt, and had just sense enough to comprehend that he had been weighed in the balance of public opinion and found wanting. Still, the witchery of humbug is so potent that many wish him back, declaring that he was the best doctor ever in these parts.

J.P.I.

A Voice From Kirkwood
MR May 21, 1886

No. XIX

Hemp Rope and Lamp Posts

It was the evening following the battle of Germantown that Washington is reported to have said "Put none but Americans on guard to-night." I doubt if he said anything of the sort, but that don't detract a whit from the wisdom of the sentiment.

In view of the recent troubles in Chicago and Milwaukee, its caution becomes at least suggestive. The fact is, we have been singing too long and too loud the refrain of the "Star Spangled Banner" — the "Land of the free and the home of the brave." Our boast of being the asylum for the oppressed of all nations has gotten us into trouble.

When a foreign minister at Washington was asked if any Simon-pure aristocracy of the old world ever settled over here, he answered in a roar of laughter, "Heavens, no! They are quite able to remain at home. No sir! Not even the ordinary well-to-do ever emigrate from Europe." He need not have troubled himself with telling us something we all knew.

Did any of my readers ever stand on the wharf in New York and witness the unloading of one of those great emigrant steamers, say at Castle Garden? Ignorance, squalor, lice and dirt are the predominant factors in one's thoughts as he looks on. Thousands of such cattle pour into New York every day! The small percent we see going west on the emigrant trains are of the better class. They are in pursuit of land and a home; in time they naturalize and become the best of citizens — a credit to any country. The women become domestics in families, and many of the men make the best of farm hands. However, the larger percent are without families and remain in the cities. This is the class to be feared. They come over here with highly exaggerated notions. They expect to be received with open arms, to be paid big wages for little work — if they have to work at all. They have an idea that liberty means license in crime; freedom to bawl and blab all sorts of incendiary doctrines; in brief, they are the offscourings of all the discontented, crowded, poverty-stricken, despotic regions of the old world, the scabs and scum from the festering pest-holes of ancient cities, vagabonds in-bred through generations of vice and squalor.

Out of this rotten dung-heap is spawned your anarchist, saying nothing of thieves and murders, and all that saved Chicago the other day from being sacked and burnt to the ground was the lack of a bold, defiant leader. Their acknowledged head, the creature Most, has proved himself to be nothing but a weak, bloated coward. Though in truth they are all cowards, as men lacking in moral principle are sure to be. But you must remember on the other hand that when once a coward gets into a fight there is no stopping him; he plunges into the fray in sheer desperation, with head down and tail up like a rampant bullock in a field of corn, he goes through utterly regardless of consequences.

The liquor traffic, the labor trouble, the Chinese difficulty, and all other kindred problems, it seems to me, dwindle into insignificance before this socialistic question. Great in numbers as are these we already have amongst us, we can take care of them, but what of the constant increase? Every day brings it ship loads. New York is the dumping ground for all the scavenger gatherings of Europe — yes, and the whole world. We have been for the past two hundred years constantly inviting emigration, and now that it has got the upper hand what are we going to do about it? In ten years the public domain will all be taken up by the only foreigners — save skilled mechanics — that are fit to live anywhere; those who make good citizens, we mean. But why ask a conundrum that no one can solve, not even the one that asks it? I'll tell you what we can do with those we have — the leaders I mean — hang them; if not on the gallows by due process of law, then to lamp posts, by good citizens behind masks. Mob law is not to be generally tolerated, but its lessons are at least salutary. I believe that "Judge Lynch" to-day is more feared by murderers and ravishers of women than the most extreme penal statutes in the land. As for justice, how often does this swift and terrible judge err? Probably not more often than does a jury.

The trouble seems to be with the law, that it delays execution too long. Don't lock the stable door until the horse has been stolen. For instance, the papers now state that the police of New York know of three or four halls in the city over lager beer saloons where the anarchists are meeting for company drill three or four nights in the week. Well if so, why do they not break the thing up at once. Why do they not hang Most and a half dozen of the leaders, anyway, and not wait until they get a good ready and before they can be stopped murder a dozen or so? And if they succeed in getting a leader, some of these days they will level the metropolis. One city is all they will ever succeed in burning. When that happens you will see the boys who put down the rebellion getting into line. But why burn even one city when hanging will stop it for the time being, at least.

I would not by any means be understood as condemning all foreigners. I refer only to the lazy, vicious element which is despised worse in the old country than it is hated here.

THE FOND HEART'S BENEDICTION — DECORATION DAY
MA June 4, 1886; <GL *May 1891*>

[Irvine took about half of this poem from an earlier piece, "Mustered Out." — Ed.]

Again we file into the camp
Wherein they bivouacked last
And as we call the roll they file
In solemn silence past.

We come with songs in minor keys,
We come with eye-lids wet,
We come with lilies of the vale
We bring the violet.

We come with wreaths of Sharon's rose,
With fragrant heliotrope;
We come with steadfast, loyal hearts,
With golden-anchored hope.

We come with snowflakes in our beards,
With winter in our hair;
Yet still the flag in hallowed trust
With valiant hands we bear.

And when we're gone our sons and theirs,
Heroic, strong and proud,
Will in the vanguard <*step*> stop and lift
Its folds above the cloud! <*And lift it flowing to the cloud.*>

We come with those they <we> left as babes —
Fair women now are they —
Who wove the dewy garlands lain
Upon their <your> graves to-day.

We come with fathers, hoar and frail,
With mothers, bent and low,
And little children in whose hands
The bluebells overflow.

Aye, old and young — in sun and shade —
From sea to sea we come;
The plow stands idle in the field,
The doors are shut at home.

We come from hamlets and from towns,
In hosts along the lanes;
From factories in great cities
Where a Sabbath's stillness reigns.

We come in Summer's rosy dawn —
The green woods darkening near —
When orchards drop their bloom and round
The young fruit into sphere.

We come when bees are on the wing,
In airy halcyon hours;
We come with faith, and love as sweet
And tender as the flowers;

When oriole and bobolink

From every mound and tree,
And robin-redbreast flute their notes
In dulcet melody.

We come rejoicing and in tears,
In fondness and in trust,
We kneel above their hallowed mounds
And kiss the very dust.

And so we give to them the best
We have in heart and words,
And leave them sleeping sweetly
With the blossoms and the birds.

A VOICE FROM KIRKWOOD
MR JUNE 25, 1886

No. XX

The Drouth — The Crops — The Grasshoppers — A New-fangled Bug — And Racket All Along the Line

Not since the cool, dry summer of 1862, the year in which we had frost every month, has the country needed rain as now. We have experienced many longer drouths with hotter days; drouths which dried up the streams and left no water in the wells, but they came later in the season, after the small fruits had matured; when the meadows had been mown and the corn was in ear; not in June, when everything grown upon the farm is in the green state, but a few degrees removed from the germ.

The hay crop is already greatly shortened, and unless we have immediate and copious rains the forthcoming hoard of grasshoppers will strip what is left of the meadows so clean that the granger may leave his scythe rusting in the apple tree and his mower unused in the barn.

The same is also true of the oats prospect. The straw at best will be short — an object to be desired, provided the head is well filled — but I doubt if there will be either head or straw unless we are relieved by a big rain, for little showers will do but little good.

The "stand" of corn is excellent, especially of the earlier plant, and up to this time has grown well, the weeds being easily kept down; but never have fields been so cloddy. Some pieces of ground, mostly on low lands, are literally covered with them, ranging in size from that of a hen's egg to a cocoa nut, and as solid, almost, as stones, which, when plowing roll over and break the young shoots.

Now as to the grasshoppers, be not deceived; they are now hatching, millions to the square rod! Three days since I carefully examined a meadow, or pasture, where they had been very thick last year. In order to discover their presence I had to get down and look closely. The grass seemed to be alive with them — little fellows the size of a pin head, but now probably a half inch in length. Some say they are not the 'hopper. There may be another kind of thing of the half-and-half grasshopper order coming on deck, as many affirm, but what I have seen is the 'hopper in color, legs, appetite and general cut; the same infernal pest we had last season. But who can answer this question? Last season, as we all remember, the hoard was always accompanied with a large sprinkling of young, even up to the time frost caught them. When an old one disappeared a young recruit always stood ready to hop into file and business going. Now where did this supply of small fry come from; from eggs the year before, or from eggs lain by the present insect? In other words, will an egg lain this season hatch a 'hopper before the season ends, or does that egg lie in the ground until the year following before incubating? Who can answer? I am of the opinion that they lay the egg and reproduce the same season, and only those deposited late in the fall are the ones that remain over, yet I am not certain. Sometimes, however, the insects do not remain in the locality where produced, but up and fly to another quite distant. Let us be selfish enough to wish this may be the case; still we might as well feed the 'hopper native to the manor born as to exchange with some other region. If we are to be cleaned out it makes little difference who or what does it.

The ground squirrel, consisting of three branches of his family, namely: the big gray, resembling in color and size a gopher; the common, prairie fellow and the little chipmunk, are doubtless on the increase, the damage to young corn being serious. Some fields along the ends and edges have been left naked. The dry weather has given them an advantage. The same is also true of the moles. Some farmers down this way have killed the former by the fifty and hundred. Some strew corn, but this seems only to increase and court their presence. If you poison this corn you kill off the birds — little friends we cannot get along without. I believe they can be exterminated by letting the small boy at them; by paying him a bounty of two cents for every dead squirrel he fetches in, the farmer owning the field footing the bill. I am sure it will pay the granger and amply compensate the boys, besides furnishing them rare good sport in shooting, trapping, drowning out, digging, etc.

As to the drouth, we suffer more as the country grows old or the soil becomes reduced by long farming. The poorer a piece of land is the more moisture it demands. The tilling and draining of the land also makes a demand for more showers. The clearing away of our groves and forests likewise causes us a proportionate loss of rain-producing agents, so that we are continually in need of an occasional deluge from the watering-pot of old Aquarius.

In case of a year of failure the farmers will realize great disappointment and the country a serious setback, for while we have never really had a total loss of crops they have been gradually on the decrease as to the average production for the past ten years or more. Every season records a new insect to be fed. The corn had no enemies until the past two or three summers, and it would be hard to name anything that grows on the farm without its parasite. All we had to do a few seasons back in the raising of cucumbers and cantaloupes was to protect them a day or two from the little yellow striped bugs. One night last week a great, hard-shelled, offensively smelling insect, as large as your thumb nail, fell foul of my cucumbers (in blossom) and destroyed them — ate them off close to the ground! All my neighbors are cussing the same bug — a bug we have never seen before. When you discover your melon vines beginning to look sickly and backward, pull a plant up and you will find the fibers and main branches of the root completely grooved and honey-combed by some infernal little worm or other pest, I know not what for I have no more patience to investigate.

I have written enough — sufficient, I should think, to give my readers the blues until my next.

J.P.I.

A Voice From Kirkwood
MR July 16, 1886

No. XX

Concerning the Proposed Revision of the Revenue Laws of the State of Illinois

During the session of the 34th General Assembly at Springfield, a joint resolution of both Houses was passed directing the Governor to appoint a commission whose duty it should be to amend and revise the revenue laws of the state of Illinois, and to propose and form a code thereof which should be just to all classes of property, and in keeping with our complicated system of business as well as that of our individual and corporate avocations.

In due time the committee was accordingly appointed, consisting of the twelve following names:

Horatio C. Burchard, of Stephenson County
Andrew D. Duff, Jackson County
W. Selden Gale, Knox County
E. B. Green, Wabash County
Charles D. Waller, Cook County
Charles A. Ewing, Macon County
Wm. C. Wilson, Crawford County
Frank P. Crandon, of Cook County
Charles W. Thomas, St. Clair County
Benj. Warren, Sr., Hancock County
Geo. Trumbull, Cook County
Milton Hay, Sangamon county.

Suffice it to say they went duly into session, and on the 1st of March last completed their labors — which much have been both critical and perplexing — by filing with the secretary of state a drafted bill for an act, covering over seventy closely printed pages of pamphlet, the same being accompanied by a learned and explanatory address.

Great numbers of this report in pamphlet form have very properly been sent broadcast over the state. Yet how many of them have been read or studied?

Probably not one out of every hundred of our most intelligent people have more than glanced at the title page. Of all printed matter on earth a "public document" — as such they are called — is read the least. However, it is the people's duty to read this one. Knowing, therefore, that it will not be read, I take this opportunity to place a somewhat condensed report of its meaning and provisions before the public, believing it will become a law by the sanction of the next legislature of Illinois.

The work of this committee has doubtless been ably and thoroughly performed. Their inquiry into the defects of the existing law seems to have been patient and careful, and in order to be fully informed on all causes of complaint they not only consulted other members of the legislature who had made revenue matters a study, but bro't to their aid the experience and criticism of county officers and other experts familiar with the practical workings thereof. The following are the principal defects pointed out:

First — The gross inequality in the assessments of different pieces of property of the same kind, owned by different individuals in the same community, and of different kinds of property, regardless of ownership; as for instance, real estate and personalty — a large proportion of the personalty escaping all taxes.

Secondly — The arbitrary and unjust operation upon individual assessments of equalization between counties by the State board.

Thirdly — The low rate of assessments.

Fourthly — The high rate of taxation permitted by

law.

Fifthly — The inadequacy of existing methods to discover and estimate the valuable interests which have grown out of the inventions and refinements of modern commerce.

Sixthly — The want of a central and efficient supervision of the administration of the revenue laws throughout the State.

The evils and abuses of the first of these, namely, the inequality of assessments, are so great and widespread as to have become the subject of general condemnation. Everybody, especially those of ordinary means, or the average taxable citizen, complain of the injustice entailed by the operation of the present system. It is a generally conceded fact that thereby the poorer or middle classes are too heavily and the richer too lightly assessed. It is the theory of the law that the burden of taxation shall rest equally upon the citizens and tax-payers of the community in proportion to their property. No man, no good citizen, would ever think of finding fault or objecting to cheerfully conform to such a just principle, paying their share of expenses of good government, even though they should be heavy, without complaint. But the practice is altogether different from the theory. The realty of one man is assessed at one-third, one-half, two-thirds, or often at the full measure of the actual value; while that of his neighbor is put at one-sixth, one-tenth, one-twentieth. I quote the above rates from the report, so that it may not be gainsaid. The board also quotes further, showing that in one instance a property of considerable magnitude was assessed at just one twenty-fifth its full value. The owner of the one pays, on his annual tax, five or six percent of the whole capital invested, while the owner of the other pays one-fourth or one-fifth of one percent. Is it not about time to rectify these evils? The discriminations in favor of personal property and against realty are glaring and unjust, amounting in some species of the former class to almost total escape from taxation. In proof of the above the pamphlet says:

Take for instance, the year 1884, the total valuation of Cook county, containing the great and wealthy city of Chicago: Credits of bank, banker, broker, etc., was $98,615; credits of other than bank, banker, etc., $209,466; bonds and stocks, $75,830; shares of capital stock of corporations not of this state, $100.

Can any fail to see fraud in such a showing?

The second objection quoted to the operation of the present law is shown to be a very grave one, the board stating that it was reiterated and condemned by nearly every officer and expert who appeared before them. For the same year, 1884, the valuation of credits, other than those of bank, banker, etc., was shown by printing the listed values of fourteen different counties of our state. The reader can judge by the four or five following:

Cook...$209,446
Knox...793,819
Winnebago...725,218
LaSalle...632,618
Morgan...461,730

Metropolitan Cook probably don't pay on the one-twentieth; nay, perhaps not on the one-fiftieth of her real valuation. A blind can discover injustice here. More next week.

J.P.I.

A VOICE FROM KIRKWOOD
MR JULY 23, 1886

No. XXI

Continuance of the Proposed Revision of the Revenue Laws of Illinois — A Word Concerning Drouth

Continuing the revenue question from last week, let me say that while equalization seems necessary its practical workings under the present system are far from satisfactory.

The commission says, in substance, that the State Board deals with the aggregate assessments of lands, lots and personal property, adding or subtracting from each class a fixed and arbitrary percentage, which of course has the effect of raising or lowering the property of such class in equal proportion. Here is the injustice that follows: A piece of property already assessed at a large fraction of its value is "equalized" by an addition of the arbitrary percentage, which brings it up to its real or full value; hence the owner pays something like 66 percent or over more taxes than his share.

By way of illustration the pamphlet cites one instance in Cook county, as follows:

A block of real estate worth one hundred thousand dollars was assessed at ninety thousand dollars. The Board of Equalization added sixty-seven percent, making the equalized assessment of that property one hundred fifty thousand and three hundred dollars. If a scrupulous owner of credits in Cook county should return them at their value, he would be ruined by an equalization that would bring the county to its full equalized value, in this particular, with other counties. Similar instances, more or less extreme, occur every year.

The third evil to be considered is the low rate of assessments. All property, real as well as personal, is assumed to be assessed at one-third its actual or cash value. But how is it regarding the facts? The assessors are sworn to closely follow the letter of the law. Some are capable of doing it and others are not. Like other men, they differ in capacity as well as morality. It is hard to find two men who exactly agree as to any laid down rule or principle. One of these assessors may be a man so "set" in his way that in his opinion he "knows it all." He listens to no reason and absolutely follows his own judgment and not the law. Such a man is unfit for any public trust. Perhaps in the next township is an officer of exactly the opposite characteristics. He has no mind of his own. He listens to the importunate and complaining property holder, sympathizes with him, (probably wants his vote) and having lost sight of the standard of law assesses his belongings at the taxpayer's own figures. Again, the old assessor goes out of office and a new one comes in. He is of course inexperienced and naturally enough takes as guide the books and plats of his predecessor, so that one follows the other in a groove, the same farm year after year being assessed at the same figures, although in the meantime it may have been improved to double its original value. The Board states that if there was uniformity in this low rating but little harm would result, but there is not. The assessors having once forsaken the standard of the law follow their own varying judgments, subject to the pressure of the tax payers who are always pulling steadily downward. The desire of each locality to avoid the payment of any undue proportion of the state tax would of itself be sufficient to explain this tendency to low assessments, while the same is intensified by the impression, everywhere prevalent, that low assessments stand for a low rate of taxation; and on the other hand, that full assessments will increase the amount of tax to be paid.

The reader will understand that the greater part of the whole trouble, namely, the liability to inequitable assessments, is chargeable to this system of low valuation; and that his low and uncertain valuation — under the present law — superinduces a higher rate of taxation. It arises, as I have shown, from the use of a fixed and arbitrary percentage by the Board of Equalization, simply because there is no other method by which equalization can be effected.

The commissioners state that the only course of

correction seemingly possible for this vexed system of undervaluation, lies in a divorcement of the collection of the state and local revenues. They claim that without such a separation no provision of law, however stringent, and no penalty however severe, could produce the desired result. Hence this separation of the state and local taxes became the fundamental proposition with the Board and the system framed and to be submitted to the next legislature was constructed on that theory.

The acts authorizing taxation, exclusive of state, library, park and a few other things, are about as follows:

County purposes on $100...$.75
School...5.00
Road and bridge...2.00
City and village...2.00

Seven dollars and seventy-five cents on every hundred dollars of his assessment! And this, remember, is exclusive of state and other matters. It may also be increased by a vote of the locality interested, and further augmented by old municipal indebtedness, etc. A man may be taxed over eight percent of the value of his property, the resident of a city being in still greater peril; all of which I deduce from the report of the Board.

Another difficulty is met in estimating the vast aggregations of capital employed in the great business enterprises of the state. Such values cannot be measured by the same methods employed in other kinds of property. Millions and millions of dollars are invested in railroads and other corporate business, much of its value being intangible, consisting in the exercises of special franchises. Our present system, say the commissioners, endeavors to separate the tangible property of the corporation from the intangible, and commits the assessment of one in part to the local assessor, the remainder of that part and the whole of the other to the State Board of Equalization, and compels the State Board to consider them dissevered. They claim that this separation cannot rationally be made, because the two elements of value belong together. A railroad company should be treated for taxation as a whole at least within the state limits, the same being true with relation to the telegraph, telephone, express and insurance companies.

Up to this point I have taken the pamphlet and carefully endeavored to give my readers a condensed report of the errors in the practical working of our present system of revenues. That such errors — glaring ones — exist, no one has ever doubted; and since reading the above I am confident they will still be more confirmed in the belief. Next week I shall endeavor to give you a synopsis of the remedy proposed, together with the reasons given, pro and con, of the commission.

J.P.I.

The attentive reader will remember that some weeks ago I spoke of the festive grasshopper, of the millions that were then being hatched out; of a little giggermaree that seemed to be about half 'hopper and half something else, with wings, and all that sort of thing. I predicted that in due time they would clean us out, but they didn't do it, and the reason was that the drouth cleaned them out. I have an esteemed neighbor in the person of Mr. J.P. Firoved, a close and practical observer, whose suggestions in this regard are worth repeating. Recently he called my attention to the fact that everything green raised on the farm or in the garden had its parasite, all of which was not so until within the past few years. He believed the 'hoppers had perished from lack of succulent roots and juices in the grass, from the fact that they still existed in considerable numbers along the streams and partly damp places, where vegetation was still somewhat green. This year's crop of corn had escaped the ants and blue lice, so that it looked as if the drouth might in the end prove a blessing. Let us hope so.

I.

A VOICE FROM KIRKWOOD
MR JULY 30, 1886

No. XXII

A Remedy for the Assessment and Collection of the State Revenue
Continuing from last week: Among the more

important deficiencies pointed out by the commission is the want of some competent body having a general oversight of the whole business, of both the assessment and collection of the revenues throughout the entire state. In round figures, the revenue of Illinois is some thirty millions of dollars, and a sense of common business principles would seem to dictate that it should be subject to the vigilant supervision of some efficient control. There being now no such supervision the board recommend:

That the office of the township assessor be abolished and a county assessor be substituted therefor; that such county assessor be elected at the regular fall elections for the period of four years, and be ineligible for re-election; that they be provided with offices at the county seat, and accessible there throughout the year; that they shall, with the approval of the county board, appoint their deputies throughout the county, and be responsible for them; that they shall begin the work of assessment on the 1st day of January, instead of May, and that they shall receive pay commensurate with the importance of their duties, and sufficient to command the services of competent and reliable men, and we require of the assessor an oath that he has not valued property at other than its cash value, and that he has not knowingly omitted any property from assessments; and adequate penalties are provided for breach of duty in these particulars.

They further recommend the division of the county into small assessment districts, and the preparation of a map showing plainly the limits of such districts; also of detailed plots of such districts containing each piece of property; that the assessment of each tract be marked on its face in such plot; and that such maps, plots and assessments be kept in the assessor's office, at all times exposed to public view, and open to the convenient inspection of taxpayers — a simple, intelligible picture of his own assessment and that of his neighbor.

The Board very pertinently remarks: It will be easily practicable for the most ignorant of unsophisticated taxpayer to ascertain what valuation has been placed upon his property, while efficient and adequate means have been provided for any injustice that may arise, either from the prejudice or erroneous judgment of the assessing officer.

The rules recommended for the assessment of corporations local in their character, are somewhat varied, but still under the control of the county assessor.

In assessing, the oath heretofore required to the schedule is to be done away with. The members of the commission say they believe the requirement to be debauching to the conscience and subversive of the public morals — a school for perjury, promoted by law! With the unscrupulous the oath simply amounts to nothing, hence works an evil to the honest taxpayer insomuch as he is compelled to take upon his conscience an obligation which he well knows is disregarded by others. It is claimed that this oath has nowhere been found effective in the disclosure of property that the assessor could not have discovered. In place of the oath there is to be substituted a substantial penalty for a false schedule, the state's attorney to be given ample fees for the conviction of the assessor or tax-payer of dishonest assessment or dishonest returns.

As heretofore intimated the day of valuation is to be changed from the first of May until the first of January, being the beginning of the business year.

The Board believe that the county assessor will be free from township jealousy, since he will act for the whole county. His term will be longer, being four years in duration; he will be better paid, will have more time to devote to his duties, will be better equipped for finding and valuing property, will be more under the public eye, and will have every motive possible to administer his office with fidelity. Moreover, there will be a competent board of review for each county, which will meet on the first Monday in July to sit not less than three nor more than thirty days, to hear all complaints as to assessments.

One, or rather the fundamental principle upon which the proposed reform is made, is, as I have before frequently mentioned, the separation of the collection of the state from the local, or county revenue. This the Board proposes to bring about in this way: The tax on railroad, telegraph, telephone, express and insurance companies is to be paid directly into the state treasury and applied only to state purposes, and in case of there being a surplus it is to be distributed among the counties. Should there be a deficiency the counties will ratably be called upon to make it up. The pamphlet says the annual state budget is something less than three millions of dollars. The income from the Illinois Central Railroad is not far from $400,000; from the other railroads the would be derived, from this mode of taxation, from $2,300,000 to $2,400,000. The other interests relied upon, such as the telegraph, telephone, etc., will yield enough to make up the deficiency. The pamphlet remarks that whether the assessment of a county is high or low will be of no importance to citizens of other counties, the work of equalization being obviated and the Board thereof abolished. And with the removal of the selfish rivalry between counties to bear as small a portion of the burden of state taxes as possible, the tendency to low assessments will, in the opinion of the commission, be greatly diminished.

Next week I shall explain the proposed law in detail.

J.P.I.

A Voice From Kirkwood
MR Aug. 6, 1886

No. XXIII

How Railroads are to be Taxed — The Main Points of the Proposed New Law Recapitulated, etc., etc.

Great difficulties are experienced under the present system of our revenues in assessing correctly and justly the property of railroad companies, hence the Board has framed and recommended a provision which we think will operate fairly to the owners of railways as well as to the owners of other values, it being a rule of taxation bearing on a fixed, definite, and equitable relation to the rates levied on other property. It is claimed that the ordinary rules of valuation have but little application to railroad property, the true criterion of the value and the best basis for the taxation being framed in the gross receipts. In brief the commission say:

That a rate of taxation equal to the average rate throughout the state imposed upon five times the amount of the gross receipts of an Illinois road, or upon the Illinois portion of the gross receipts of an inter-state road, would be just and more flexible than the arbitrary percentage, provided, however, that such rate of taxation should not exceed five per centum of such gross receipts. We have proposed that method. It is simple; bears lighter than the present mode on the weak roads, and heavier on the prosperous ones, and takes the assessment of that great property out of the range of caprice or corruption. The mode of thus assessing railroad property may be further illustrated and commended by the considerations following:

For want of space we will condense the language: The amount of gross railroad receipts returned is fifty-six millions of dollars; multiplying this by five gives a result of two hundred and eighty millions, as the fair taxable value of all the roads in Illinois. On this sum the net earnings returned at twenty millions amounts to seven percent. The proposition of the commission, then amounts to this: Seven dollars of net earnings shall be considered the equivalent of one hundred dollars capital. Seven percent is very near the average on money loaned in this state. Let it be kept in mind, too, that in taxing the earnings of a railroad you reach all their property.

The commission, then, having determined the rule of comparison between gross receipts and assessed values, proceed to fix the rates of taxation on the railroad valuation, which is five per centum, the rate adopted being the average rate of taxation throughout the state, which was obtained by the Board adding together all the taxes levied in state and dividing the amount of tax by the total assessed value of all the property of the state. This seems fair, does it not? Fair and just it must be, since all the property in the state is to be assessed at its full cash value.

The Board then say they feel it incumbent upon them to provide protection to the tax-payers from the rapacity of unprincipled tax-consumers, and recommend taxation limited, so as not to exceed on the one hundred dollars, as follows:

For county purposes, other than road and bridge...$0.25
For city, incorporation, town and village purposes, except school...0.50
For educational purposes...0.50
For school building...0.75
For roads and bridges, for ordinary purposes...0.20

For all other purposes one-third the present rates, and for park rates one-fourth. The power of municipalities to incur indebtedness is limited to two percent of the assessed value instead of five, as now.

I had intended to give a synopsis of the bill drawn by the Board for an act which doubtless will become a law by the next legislature, but find I have no room; however, before closing, in order that the reader may refresh his memory and keep in mind the main points I will briefly recapitulate.

The faults of the present system, then, may be enumerated as follows: The gross inequality of assessments of different pieces of property of the same kind owned by individuals. The arbitrary and unjust operation upon individual assessments of equalization between counties by the state board. The low rate of assessments, and the high taxation permitted by law.

The faults are to be met and corrected by a divorcement or separation of the collection of the state and county revenues, the local revenues alone to go to county, school, road, bridge and village purposes, the tax from railroad, telegraph, insurance companies, etc., to the demands of the state.

An assessor is to be elected over the whole county who does the work by deputies. He keeps an open office the year round, where a large map will hang in full view at all times. It will be made up of detailed plots of each piece of land, with the owner's name and value marked on it. All property is to be assessed at its real or full cash value instead of at one-third, as now.

A competent Board of Review will meet and sit not less than three nor more than thirty days, in each county, to hear and settle all complaints, etc.

As I said in starting, the pamphlet has been widely circulated and should be read and studied by every taxpayer in the county. Knowing this to be an impossibility I have done my best to give its contents to the many readers of the REVIEW in the four columns of the last four issues. The provisions I believe to be wise, timely and judicious. There is no doubt, whatever, that the present law regarding the assessment and collection of our state revenue is lame and hence unjust in its workings, as the pamphlet fully shows. It is not at all a party measure, and all good citizens are alike interested in its success before the legislature to meet next winter.

J.P.I.

Reunion Address
DR Aug. 30, 1888; MR Aug. 31, 1888

Delivered by J.P. Irvine Before the Old Settlers Association of Warren and Henderson Counties, at Kirkwood Mineral Spring, July 30, 1888

Sweep the face of the country clean of its buildings, hedges, fences, orchards, groves, and grazing herds; obliterate the lanes, roads, bridges and railways, letting every feature lapse to a state of primitive wildness, emptiness, vastness, loneliness, broken only at intervals by the yell of an Indian, or the howl of a wolf, and you have the territory of Warren and Henderson counties as it existed prior to the beginning of settlement sixty years ago.

Thus it was in 1827, when an old-fashioned, long-coupled, high-bedded covered wagon, drawn by a yoke of oxen, came crawling in, from the far horizon — like a schooner on a lone ocean — and stopped at or near where Monmouth now stands. This was Mrs. Talbott with her family, the eldest of whom was her son John B. Mrs. Talbott died in Monmouth, in the year 1849, aged 80. Jno. B. removed to Oregon in 1850. With the Talbotts came Allen G. Andrews, an educated man, who settled on Cedar creek.

The next year 1828, brought Jas. B. Atwood, who pitched his tent in Kelly; also, Peter Peckenpaugh, who settled on Cold Brook. Almost immediately after him came Peter Butler and Jeremiah McFarland, from Kentucky. In this same year of 1828, Adam Ritchey, Sr., with a family of nine children, and a Mr. Craig, moved in, driving stakes in Hale.

The next year, 1829, brought Solomon Perkins and Solomon Kaiser, to the vicinity of Berwick and soon after them Peter Scott, a Mr. Smith, and Jonathan Tipton, and about the same time came three brothers of Sol Perkins, namely, Isaac, Daniel, and Elisha. Isaac was killed, a few years later, in the Black Hawk war. In this same year (1829), William and Josiah Whitman settled in Cold Brook. William was a preacher, and perhaps preached the first sermon ever heard in these wilds. He was an earnest man, and died in 1838. His brother Josiah, died in Monmouth, in 1865. The echoes of Nigger creek, Ellison, were awakened this same year by the incoming of a perfect giant in height, a fine rifle shot, and famous bee hunter, Field Jarvis. William and James Armstrong stopped in the neighborhood of Floyd, David Findley and Thomas Campbell halted their ox teams in Hale, and Andrew Robinson and family of wife and six children, came to Kelly, while Abram Swartz and wife struck the first licks of a new house where Monmouth was to stand. Perhaps one or two others also arrived this same year, 1829. Anyhow, the next half dozen years brought an increase in the families of such sterling people, as the Lewises, Cables, Hayles, Sheltons, Wallaces, Rusts, Birdsalls, Rays, Thompsons, Laffertys, Phelps, Davidsons, Bonds, Simmons, Kendalls, Gibsons, Colwells, Paxtons, Maleys, Rodgers, Turnbulls, Adcocks, Browns, Mitchells, Terpennings, Riggs, Baldwins, Parkhursts, Pierces, Lockwoods, Carrs, Millers, Frantz, Smiths, McCoys, Rockwells, Martins, Ritchies, Pollocks, Tinkhams, Creswells, Oaks, Hannas, and many others too tedious to mention.

Such people would not be long without the school and church, and as early as 1830, we find Miss Martha Jenkins teaching a small knot of urchins in Hale. In 1835 Miss Jane Allen — afterward the first wife of Judge Ivory Quinby — taught in Berwick, being followed by Miss Sarah Cable. Seth C. Murphy presided over the first birch that was wielded in Cold Brook, and Peter Terpenning also taught in 1837. I think, too, that Mr. Andrews taught at an early day in the vicinity of Sugar Tree Grove.

In 1833 Baptist and Methodist churches were organized in Berwick, but even in 1830, the Associate church, then known as seceders, was started in Hale, and continued to prosper until it became the largest in all the region.

The speaker then spoke of the early building of mills, the first being put up by Thomas Wallace, on Cold Brook. It was a saw mill, with a small stone added for grinding corn. A little after this, small mills were also built on Cedar and Henderson, by Calvin Glass and Rockwells. In about 1834, Chester Potter built what is since known as the Olmstead mill, but it was burned in 1837, and rebuilt by Wm. S. Paxton, soon after. Some, however, claim that Adam Ritchey built this mill and sold it to Aniel Rodgers. It is now owned by Peter Oswald.

The first child born in the county was Henderson Ritchey, December 1828. Margaret Ann Robison, born November, 1829, was probably the second. In May 1852, she was married to James Gardner, and I believe is still living — a woman of 58.

The first death was that of a child of Roland Simmons. The first marriage was solemnized between David B. Findley and Jane Ritchey, in 1829. Instead of a license, three notices were posted.

In 1831 groceries were started by Elijah Davidson and Jacob Rust in Monmouth, S. S. Phelps opening trade the same year at the Yellow Banks, since Oquawka.

This, then, was the beginning of settlement in Warren county, and at this distant day, how little we realize of the hardships and suffering this handful of brave people underwent. Even we of middle age, who came here as children, in the forties and early fifties, when the country for the most part was still wild and primitive, and therefore endured great privations ourselves, fail to fully realize what toil and want they passed through, all for the sake of their little ones, and those who were to follow after.

As we look steadfastly back, we see a white sail crawling in from the horizon. It is the wagon of the first pioneer. It halts, perhaps, near a grove and water. The worn-down oxen are unyoked, the poor wife and children climb out of the wagon that holds all of their earthly belongings. What a pathetic group! They stand as in a dream, half dazed, half lost! To the eye of sentiment the outlook might seem poetical, but not so to them. The standpoint is practical. They gaze away to the east, and the empty prairie rolls on and still on; to the north, over a vast expanse of nothingness; to the south, and the eye finds naught to rest upon; and to the west, where there is either line nor limit this side the land of sunset. yet they gaze but a moment, when they clear the deck for action. They all worked, man, woman and children. Timber is fallen, and the four walls of a cabin of round logs is lain up. It is roofed with clapboards, rived with a frow, and if unable in the hurry to build a chimney of sticks and mud, a hole is left for the egress of smoke. The great cracks are imperfectly chinked and daubed. If a floor were lain, it was of puncheons. Open holes, perhaps covered with greased paper, served for windows. The door was also of puncheons, hung on wooden hinges, and when opening and shutting creaked and complained like the rasping grating of an old-fashioned cider mill. The latch was lifted with a string, and according to popular saying, "was always out." When I describe one of these cabins, I describe all. They had but one apartment, sometimes no loft. The rain dripped through the roof, and the snow sifted through the cracks. Stoves were unknown, and the "fire places" generally smoked. The family huddled spoon fashion in the night, and may be slept warm enough, while the winds moaned a requiem, and the wolves howled in concert. The supply of wild meat was abundant, but wheat flour was hardly known, and corn meal — often cracked in a mortar or ground in a coffee mill, was the chief stand by. Everything was done by hard knocks. The wolves were so thick and aggressive that the sheep, upon whose clip solely depended the supply of frocks, wamuses, blankets and socks, had to be guarded in daylight and shut under cover at night. Ah, what do the women of this age know of toil? This wool was first clipt, then washed, picked, carded between hand cards into rolls, then laboriously spun on the "big wheel" into yarn, and then dyed — not with diamond dyes, mind you, but with sumac, butternut bark, and often with madder, then this yarn was "doubled and twisted," reeled into "cuts" and "hanks," then run onto "swifts," and thus prepared for the loom whereon it was woven. I well remember how proud we boys used to be of our new red "wamuses," and little wonder. Oh, ye mothers of the early years, little wonder your poor old hands are clumsy and wrinkled and drawn. And ye fathers, something more than the burden of years has bent your backs and rounded your shoulders.

The winter of 1830-31, was long and cold, the cabins were far apart, an early snow covered the ungathered corn, so it had to be dug out. Feet and hands were frozen, and suffering was the rule. This winter brought John Smith (of course the pioneers had to have their John Smith,) and Sheldon Lockwood to the vicinity of Roseville. They encamped in the timber, and while Lockwood worked on the cabin, Smith went with an ox team to town for provisions. The town was Springfield, and he was gone over a month.

Here the speaker narrated how Mrs. David Robinson and her sister-in-law, Fannie Birdsall, being left along in the winter, let the fire die out, and how they yoked up an ox team and drove four miles to the cabin of Dikeman Shook, Sr., Mrs. Robinson carrying a young child — where they got fire and took back in a big iron wash kettle.

For several years after the commencement, the privations of many families must have bordered on penury, but ere long the prospects grew brighter. Oquawka being on the river, became a real emporium, and as early as 1837, kept a good supply of everything needed. It commanded the trade of Galesburg, Knoxville, and all the region. The road between Monmouth and Oquawka was a sort of grand trunk for all the other roads leading in from three points of the compass, north, south and east.

My father came here in 1843, and although the cabins were still few and far between, and not a human habitation to be seen between Centre Grove and

Monmouth, that road was smooth and hard beaten, and in a few years later, was lined daily with passing and repassing teams, for people had begun to build, and the sound of hammers and the crash of saws could be heard everywhere, and I fancy if one had lain an ear to the earth he might have caught the footfalls of the coming millions. These teams were drawing the product of the new farms, grain, corn, butchered hogs, hoop-poles, &c., pouring in, and great loads of lumber, salt, groceries, and dry goods, pouring out, not only to supply the vast region of country settlements, but for a half dozen new towns and villages beyond. I don't think I exaggerate when I say that as high as 100, perhaps 150, and may be 200 teams, drawing loaded wagons, came into and left Oquawka per day, especially in the winter. S. S. Phelps employed from six to eight clerks, McKinney & Adams nearly as many, saying nothing of Moirs, the Simpsons, John Edwards and others. These were not dry good stores alone, for beside groceries, they ran large warehouses and lumber yards, and some of them large slaughter houses, and many a time teams had to turn aside from roads that were crowded with droves of fat hogs that were being driven thither.

And who doesn't remember the old red four-horse stage coach, that neither turned to the right nor left, but would knock a wheel off if you didn't? It was driven by a little old man by the name of Monteith, who savored of rum and talked "hoss," and whose eyes looked as if bound with red tape. When the shadow of the old cotton wood tree was lengthening athwart the Monmouth square in the late afternoon, who has not heard

Monteith's horn, setting the echoes wild by sounding his coming down the street leading north — sounding shrill and defiant as the blast of a battle trumpet? The resurrection amongst the ancient landmarks was sudden. The supper bells of each of the opposite taverns broke loose. Old Mr. Seaton adjusted his gold-rimmed spectacles, and came forward to the front door of his harness shop. The thin, elongated form of Cap. Denman stood fixed on the steps of his tailoring establishment. E.C. Babcock, with a pen behind his ear, appeared at the raised windows near his desk where he stood for more than forty years. Wm. F. Smith even took time to take a look from his drug store, and Col. Jas. W. Davidson paused with a volume of the law under his arm in front of the courthouse, while all the boys, Bill Grant, Jim Baldwin, Ran Webster, and a dozen others, were promptly on hand. The fellow in the circus who handles the reins over two rampant, galloping horses under his feet, two beneath his straddled legs and four in front, was not a whit less a hero in our eyes than this same stage coachman, as he sat upon that high seat manipulating the lines of the four plunging nags, as the whole establishment rushed circling around the square by way of the post office, stopping at last with lumbering flourish, in front of Claycomb's tavern.

The most conspicuous individual in Monmouth was "Ran" Webster. He was not at all a vicious boy, but his habit of being everlastingly everywhere present, and never anywhere in particular, knowing everybody, and sparing no one with his ready tongue, he became a terror to all other boys, and especially to those coming in from the country. He won all their marbles, playing for keeps, and always had a bag full with him. But his main forte was the orchard and watermelon patch. Old Mr. Hodgins, catching him in one of his apple trees, sung out: "You young rascal, what are you doing up there?" "Trying to get down," yelled Ran. But you can't always tell; that boy became one of the most distinguished physicians in all the country.

The Wolf Hunt

Longest to be remembered and doubtless one of the largest ever held in the state came off on the 22d of February, 1846. The wolves that winter had been terribly aggressive, and had slain the sheep at our very doors, so something had to be done.

The place of centering was marked by a pole bearing aloft the stripes and stars, planted on the farm of Lewis Olmstead on the road leading from Oquawka to Monmouth. The chief marshal of the day was Ira A. Butler. The south line formed on a course running between Monmouth and Lancaster was directed by Col. Jas. W. Davidson. That from Lancaster to Olena by Daniel Leecock. That from Olena to Oquawka by Preston Martin. That from Oquawka to the mouth of Cedar Creek by S. S. Phelps. That from the mouth of Cedar to Rockwell's Mills by David Turnbull, and from Rockwell's Mills to Monmouth, thus completing the circuit, by Jno. H. Mitchell. All these men were known as assistant marshals. I am persuaded if all the wolves in that scope of country had been run in there would have been enough to have turned and eaten their pursuers up.

There were only about four sources from which pleasure was derived in those days, namely: The wolf hunt, the coon hunt, playing bull pen (a game of ball,) and scratching for the itch, and if any of us were ever deprived of that pleasure, I don't remember it.

In a word, the scarcity of fun and recreation — as well as the common duty in driving out the destroyers of our flocks — kept none at home. It is safe to say that every able bodied man and boy in the region was in line that day.

Hardly had the gray dawn lightened into the clearer blue of the morning, ere the sounds of preparation could be heard in all directions — for the whole country was on the move and like mustering cavalry marching to fall in ranks on their respective lines. In a few hours these lines were advancing and gradually shortening and thickening into columns. To the barking of dogs and the blowing of horns, every field, grove, brake and thicket is explored and beaten over. Here a rabbit springs into view and scuds out of sight. Now a covey of quail shoots up and vanishes like a gust.

A little further, and a great multitude of prairie chickens whir with a sound of muffled thunder from the bleached stubble and skim away to the far horizon. An old horse fumbling about the nooks for a taste of new grass, lifts his head, stares intently, lets a furious snort and strikes out for fresh fields and pastures new. The brutes about the stable yards are nearly all stricken with a desire to get away, but the movement sweeps on. That supple bounding deer yonder if seen an hour later will be dejectedly seeking safety in a herd of fifty. There goes a tandem team of three, tail up and bounding swiftly forward but only to meet the opposing column and be driven back, and so on until finding themselves baffled at every point, will fall in with others and wearily run here, and there and everywhere. Now and then a single wolf may be observed loping up the depression of a slough or gliding like a shadow into the hazed thicket where he will remain until routed again for he will make no attempt to break back until the lines grow closer.

It is now two o'clock in the afternoon and the opposite columns are approaching in sight of each other.

No hunting seen on earth was ever more exciting. The noises which have been incessant all day are now gathering into an uproar simply alarming. I can compare it to nothing save the din and turmoil of a hundred combined charivaris, for the same ear splitting instruments employed in one are used in the other; the lacerating blasts of tin horns, the rub-a-dub of drums, the sharp snapping racket of rattle traps, the yelping of dogs, the yelling of the multitude, saying nothing of the occasional whickerings of an anxious mule, and you have an idea of the din raised that day.

In the meanwhile the columns moving in solid phalanx are bending until at last their respective flanks meet and unite around the centre pole in a great circle.

The prairie is as level as a floor and covered with a limp, tawny grass just thick enough to hide what few wolves may be in, but not the deer. To kill them is not only against the law, but contrary to the express rules of the hunt, yet many of them have been overtaken and inhumanly clubbed down. Grouped in great herds they are wearily and heavily running from point to point, and as they approach momentarily, and in utter consternation near the lines, their sore distress becomes painfully apparent. Their sides are heaving and palpitating. Their nostrils distended and dripping with perspiration, and their tongues lolling from their mouths. The does are "in fawn" and as the whole herd gaze at you with their great, tender, dilated eyes the mute appeal for mercy is so touching, so piteous, I wonder, boy as I am — or was then — what heart could be hard as not to grant it. Just then however, a tall marshal with a red sash at his waist rode up, ordered the lines opened and away the poor liberated creatures went to their native wilds. That marshal was David Turnbull — father of our Capt. John M. — and a nobler man never lived; brave, yet tender; strong, yet full of sweet humanity. It is pleasant to recall his memory. It is claimed that five wolves came to grief in the arena. The killing of a wolf, however, when run down is a very tame affair; giving up he ignobly allows his pursuer to dismount and dispatch him with a club, but while he is fleeing he is game. Of extraordinary fleetness and endurance, he veers to the right, evading the hoofs of an incoming horse. Again he darts to the left, snapping viciously at a pack of worthless curs — not one of which dare seize him. But as the onset thickens he makes a dash and in spite of all efforts goes through the ring with the velocity of a bullet. And now that he is clear of flank movements he keeps straight forward, and no chase on earth ever rivaled it in excitement. There is a movement at every point in the great circle. Hundreds persist in pushing at full speed after, while as many others are adding consternation to confusion by leaving their places and trying to restore order and hold the ring intact. In the meantime a hundred horsemen are thundering with the rush of a tornado after, yet the fugitive is still game. Stretched to the utmost he lies close to the earth and flees as if shod with the feet of the wind. His pursuers sweeping backwards, are mounted on nags of every age, gait and condition, while an equal number of curs with as many variations and degrees of "cussedness" are scrabbling along, yelping and bellowing under their feet. The pluck and game of the wolf by this time has won the admiration and sympathy of us all, when he gains the depression of a miry slough and escapes.

So ended the hunt, which only had the effect to destroy and drive out the deer, while our neighboring county of Mercer got the benefit of the few wolves ran off — the females arriving in time to whelp in the spring, thus adding to the original stock already on hand.

But we had lots of fun all the same.

Here, Mr. Irvine spoke at some length of the advantages and disadvantages of early times, describing how they broke the prairie, the enormous crops grown, of how plentiful the game was, of the abundance of blackberries, grapes and plums. He spoke of how the cattle and wagons mired in the sloughs, followed by a graphic portrayal of a prairie on fire, and how it was fought and conquered. He described the old fashioned way of planting corn by hand and said the fellow who invented the 3-row marker was considered a genius, and that the boy Wm. S. Weir had not yet dreamed of the cultivator. Everybody shook with ague, and was dosed with calomel, quinine, boneset, gamboge, and ipecac. When a tooth was pulled it was yanked out with "cant-hooks" — and if the molar didn't come the top of the head did — at least the victim thought so. He described the game of bull-pen — a game of ball. Mr. Barnum, the president, came in for a little of the speaker's fun. Irvine told how he first met Barnum and scared him out of the blackberry patch by telling him that a panther was about. He said that "O. S." at that day wore a big, long, painted slanting, linen collar, and a coon skin cap, and played ball in gloves. Then turn 'round he added: "But we grew to be the best of friends and are still so to this day. All of you know what a success O. S. Barnum has made of life."

The following was well merited eulogy was pronounced on the Rev. Richard Haney:

Here is the grand, old, Uncle "Dick" Haney — whom all delight in honoring who never turned aside — for man or the devil — when in pursuit of duty. His was the voice that earliest proclaimed the gospel to the hungering and thirsting ones in the pioneer cabins. He may have preached the terrors of the law, but the burden of his message was concerning the sweet and all-abiding love of the Savior. He was as loyal to his country as to his God.

In the same strain the speaker also eulogized the memory of old Capt. McClanahan, and spoke touchingly as follows:

And there are so many dear old mothers, mostly dead and gone who toiled in obscurity, raising sons whom they afterwards brought forward and bound upon their country's altar, as offerings in the great sacrifice made in behalf of the Union. I cannot call the names of them all — for the list is too long, and why need I? For we know they are enrolled in letters of gold, in the great books of immortality.

Doubtless, none of us are satisfied with our lives, but the fifty years just past are more than a hundred of the aforetime, and better than a cycle of the medieval age. Ah we should be thankful for what our eyes have seen and our ears heard. The coming millions — the echoes of whose footfalls we caught long ago have come, and we have met them face to face on equal terms, and are now one mighty people. What progress! What change! Our cattle are abroad on a thousand hills. The green-walled lanes are flanked with fields of deep, abundant corn. Palace homes arise on every hand. Great trains of gleaming chariots roll in splendor from city to city, and sea to sea, across the continent. The harvester, marvelous as a thing of life, clicks a ditty across the fields of grain and drops the sheaves, bound, into the stubble.

The poor seamstress no longer sings: "I am sewing at once with a double thread, a shroud as well as a shirt," for the swift needle of the sewing machine has made it possible for her to live a little above "Poverty, hunger and dirt," of the past.

Ariel, indeed, has put a girdle around the earth, and the lightnings flash messages to and fro under the sea. The telegraph and telephone have outrun time and annihilated distance.

Aye, glorious things have come to pass. We have lived to knock the shackles of bondage from 4,000,000 slaves, transforming them from the condition of chattels to freemen. We have taught enemies at home and kings abroad that a republic — founded like ours — is not to be overthrown, but to live forever. We have sent the Bible into every corner of the earth, and our missionaries have gone forth under the white banner of King Jesus bearing the good news and glad tidings of salvation to every unconverted people under heaven.

Therefore, we should be thankfully content, each of us singing:

"Bless, oh my soul, the Lord thy God,
And not forgetful be
Of all his gracious benefits
He hath bestowed on thee."

THE LIGHTNING EXPRESS

BF Nov. 1889; <GL MAY 1891>

Swift as the wind's untrammeled speed,
A train of chariots, all a length

Of splendor rolls behind a steed
With loins of iron and the strength
A legion horses; and as breaks
The noise of trampling hoofs, and shakes
The solid earth, he thunders past,
Outpouring on the riven blast
His notes of warning, shrill and loud,
Through vapors rolling cloud on cloud,
In purple-bordered volumes; yea,
In storm and darkness, night and day,
Through mountain gorge or level way,
With lightning<*tightening*> rein and might unspent,
And head erect in scorn of space,
Holds, neck-and-neck, with time a race,
Flame-girt across a continent.

Think not of danger, every wheel
Of all that clank and roll below,
Rang singing answers, steel for steel,
Beneath the hammer's testing blow:
And what, though fields go swirling round,
And backward swims the mazy ground,
So swift the herds seem standing still —
As scared they run <*dash*> from hill to hill;
And though the brakes may grind to fire,
The gravel as they grip the tire,
And holding, strike a quick'ning <*startling*> vein
Of tremor through the surging train,
The hand of him who guides the rein,
Is all controlling and intent:
Fear not, although the race you ride

Is on the whirlwind, side by side
With time across a continent.

1890-1892

THE EVENING OF THE YEAR
AX Jan. 17, 1891;

[The first four stanzas become part I and the next four stanzas become part V of Irvine's poem "November" in his book. — Ed.]

The longer days no more appear,
The shorter fly on quicker wings,
Night cometh and the poet sings,
It is the evening of the year.

Sings of the sundown, with a sigh
Of pity for the tender call
Of yonder quail — the last of all
The scattered covey left to cry.

Sings, as abroad the waning light,
The shadows into darkness creep,
As from the uplands troop the sheep
To safer folds against the night.

Sings, as the cows come lowing near,
The sweet bell tinkling down the path —
The frost has nipped the aftermath,
It is the evening of the year.

The fields are naked, and the wood
The burthen of the leaf has cast,
The low-hung sky is but a vast
Expanse of black infinitude.

The trail of smoke the engine made,
Hard panting past, an hour ago,
Unbroken still and hanging low
Along the length of heavy grade.

The dullness brooding as a pall
Alike at morning and at noon,
The wan-like rim that girts the moon
From night to night, betoken fall.

"There'll be a snow," the farmer says;
Up-taking reins, and pulling down
His muffled cap, drives out of town
Fast homeward by the nearest ways.

Kirkwood, Ill.

Prelude
GL May 1891

In the spring when leaves are green,
And the bud unfolds and blushes,
And I from my window lean
Out into the blue serene,
List'ning to a pair of thrushes,
Pouring forth their witching strains,
Sweet as tingling silver chains
At the breaking of the morning,
I forget the restless night;
And, half tipsy with delight,
Linger long and turn again,
Wistful, just to catch a note,
But I lack the sylvan tongue,
Far too fine for words, and hung
Tuneful in a golden throat:
Still, it is not all in vain —
All for naught my bosom swells;
And within me all the bells
Of rapture take the time and swing,
Till I cannot choose but sing;
And that sweeter strains, I know,
Tinkling through my numbers run,
And from sun-lit zephyrs spun
Brighter threads of color glow:
And, I may have caught, perchance,
From the rhythm of the dance
Of airy dapples on the grass
A lighter measure; still, the voice

Is not the thrushes' — not, alas,
The hymn that makes the vale rejoice;
But, when leaves are green in spring,
And delight is on the wing,
Somehow, one is prone to sing.

Be it so, will any hear —
Any pause upon their way,
Turning an arrested ear?
Is there aught of love and cheer
In the green leaf of my lay?
If so, in the singer's throng
There will still be room for me;
Rhyme has run its way too long,
Fond hearts never tire of song
Nor the world of poesy.

In the fall when leaves are gray,
Winds are lain, and vales and hollows
Flanked with hills in blue array,
Seem to drift in dreams away,
And the barns are mute from swallows,
Distance mellows, and you hear
Through the drowsy atmosphere,
Sounds as soft as murmurs are —
As of waters falling far
In the lonely mountain glen,
And at times, the pheasant's drum
Rolling muffled, once, and then
All the woods around are dumb.
Howe'er, when the sun is low,

And the shadows lengthen tall
In the evening of the year,
And the gray leaves turning sere
From the boughs begin to fall;
Steals a voice unto my ear,
Oft repeating one low strain,
Subtly plaintive; and although,
Just a voice and nothing more —
Just a still and small refrain,
Without words, that one may hear
All the day long in the rain,
Somehow, it becomes the key
That awakens memory,
Till she joins and sings of yore —
Sings so of the long ago —
Chords responding heart to heart,
Till my themes are but a part
And an echo; and if tears
'Twixt my lines have left a trace,
Eyes were wet in other years
For a loved one's absent face;
For the playthings left in place
Of a darling gone its way —
Flow'ret of a summer's day;
For a sash hung in the hall —
Dim with dust of twenty years —
Yet the rent made by the ball
Through the darker stain appears.
Thus it is, whate'er is mine,
Oh, my friend, I know is thine;
Fate is common, though unseen,

Walk we all the self-same way;
In the spring the leaves are green,
In the fall they're just as gray.
Yet, will any cease their quest,
Turn and listen from their road?
As the dove a coveret nest,
In some warmly welcome breast,
Will my gray leaf find abode?
If so, in the singers' throng
There will still be room for me;
Rhyme has run its way too long,
Fond hearts never tire of song,
Nor the world of poesy.

A Shining One
GL May 1891

Stay, oh stay, sweet dove of heaven,
Yet a little, let me be
At thy feet a yearning suppliant,
Let me kneel and question thee:
For I know thou art enraptured
By the glory of thine eyes,
And the whiteness of thy raiment,
Thou art here from Paradise.

Hast thou seen the daintiest angel
In all heaven? Is she fair?
Has she grown in radiant beauty,

Are her foot-falls light as air?
Did she smiling run to meet thee,
Were her kisses sweet and bland?
Through the open gates of jasper
Did she lead thee by the hand?

Has the flash of time between us
Quickened darkness? does she know
Of the cruel grief that smote us
When our hope was changed to woe?
Is it true that the Immortal
Is unshadowed by the Past,
That the burthen of remembrance
At the door of Death is cast?

There was one of twenty summers —
More than twenty years ago —
In the vanguard of the battle,
Fell with face unto the foe;
He was truthful, he was tuneful,
And he wore the blush of spring;
In his sanctified perfection
I should love to hear him sing.

Is the rapture born of heaven
So complete, there's naught remains
Of the earth-life's bitter sweetness,
Of its pleasures or its pains?
Are you touched with our emotions?
Are the dear old voices dumb?
Do you ever long to meet us?

Would you love to have us come?

Draw near me now, make answer;
Let me touch thee, feel thy breath;
Reach thy hand and I will clasp it
Half across the dark of death:
Just a moment, and no longer,
Would I lure thee, if I could,
Though we grieved so when you left us
And put on your angel-hood.

'Tis enough that I have seen thee,
Gentle spirit, heavenly dove;
And I know thy silent presence
Is to tell me of thy love:
Yet I would not have thee linger;
Stay no longer, rise and go,
Lest a touch of earth should tarnish
Thy unsullied wings of snow.

FEVER
GL May 1891

Stay near me, sweetheart, clasp, caress
My hand thy soft white palms between,
Stay all the night, that I may lean
On thee my whole weight's weariness.

Fold, fold me close unto thy breast,

I am so tired; sing sweet and low
Your love-songs of the long-ago;
O sing away the night's unrest.

Sing soft, and ope the window full
On yon great woodland, white and still
In pallid moonlight on the hill,
It is so deep and dim and cool.

But God is good, my dear, and when,
Across the dewy fields of corn
Shall blow the healings of the morn,
I shall not be so weary then.

Two Kids
GL May 1891

[In a copy of his book that Irvine signed to Henry Allen's sister Ina, handwritten marginalia, presumably from her, indicates that Irvine dedicated this poem to her in 1885. — Ed.]

I know of a home in the village near,
Where two little children are treasured dear.

A sweet little girl who betrays her grace
In the delicate lines of a Raphael face;

And a rogue of a boy, who can barely walk

By pushing a chair, and they say he can talk.

Set square on his feet and firm at the knees,
He stands like a sturdy young Hercules!

God grant that he grow to manly estate,
And the path he may climb be narrow and straight.

But the girl is a daisy — a mischiev'us lass,
Who tosses me kisses whenever I pass, —

Tosses them laughing, and standing alert,
Tempts me to chase her — the gay little flirt;

Catch a weasel asleep — why, she flashes away
If I move but a hand, like a mirrored ray.

And wouldn't I scamper, if I were she,
From a great, big bearded fellow like me!

God grant that howe'er in that fullness of time.
She bloom into womanhood's beautiful prime.

And yet, little friends, I utter my prayer
With a falt'ring regret for the ills you must bear.

For the loss of the sweetness of innocent trust,
For the truth without guile and the love without lust;

For the laughter that ripples and runs and is glad,
In exchange for the smile from a heart that is sad.

But pardon, sweet children, I fear I do wrong,
For the sigh that I drop with the notes of my song.

Play on and laugh loud, we rejoice in the sound;
You're the gayest young kids in the neighborhood round.

REST
GL May 1891

Deep broods the night on land and sea,
As bent and lame I homeward creep,
And fondly lay me down to sleep,
Through all the night-of-years to be.

It is the sleep that lasts for aye,
The balm that heals the hurts of all:
My heavy eye-lids droop and fall,
And all my being swoons away.

O friend, come grant me one request,
Make wide the confines of my tomb,
I am so weary, give me room
To lie full length in blissful rest. —

Full length, as on a folded fleece
Around by curtained darkness hung,
Till healed forever and made young
For that new world where all is peace.

Thanksgiving
GL May 1891

He is of all the gracious Lord,
Before His throne we bend the knee
And lift our voice in grand accord,
As swells an anthem of the sea:
We praise Him for His mercies done,
The crystal fountain from the springs,
The life reviving, shining sun,
The winds with healing on their wings.

Our cup is full: a thousand scents
From hampered garners fill the land;
Like countless towns of golden tents
The stacks of wheat in clusters stand;
The meadows glow with aftermath,
In heaps the gathered apples shine,
And lowing homeward down the path
With burdened udders file the kine.

Thus unto Him, our gracious king,
With banners of our faith unfurled,
Ten thousand times ten thousand sing
The fullness of a gladdened world;
For Him our souls in fervor burn,
Our life, our love and all are His,
At best, alas, a poor return,
So boundless His abundance is.

THE JUDGMENT MORNING
GL May 1891

[Irvine included several stanzas here in "The Resurrection Morning." — Ed.]

Who may reckon of the coming
Of the solemn Judgment Day,
When the sea shall roll no longer
And the earth shall melt away?
But we know the spinning planets
Through their wonted measures run,
Just as on the natal morning
When elanced around the sun;
And when we have been forgotten
And the things we know are gone,
Through a hundred future ages
They will still roll on and on;
Till at last shall come an evening —
Just as other evenings come —
But a spell of deeper silence
Shall arrest the busy hum;
And the sun, before his setting,
Pause and turn a ling'ring view,
Fondly backward, as if bidding
Earth and time a last adieu;
And at midnight all the army,
Of the stars in bright array,
With the moon adown the heavens,
Will forever go their way;
And I fancy all the living

Will in heavy sleep be lain
And a hush of awful stillness
Till the coming dawn shall reign.

'Twill be startling, in a moment,
In the twinkling of an eye,
Swift and loud a herald-trumpet sound
Shall break athwart the sky,
And a host of shouting angels
Shall on gleaming wings descend,
White and vivid as the lightnings,
When in wrath they strike and rend.
'Twill be such a sound as never
Echoed since creation's birth,
'Twill reverberate throughout the length
And breadth and height of earth,
And shall quicken and awaken
All the dead that lie beneath,
Who shall rise, as He of old arose
Triumphant over Death.
Oh, my fellow men — my brothers,
Count the sands upon the main,
Count the waves that break between them,
Tell the drops of summer rain —
But a host no man can number,
Far and wide on every hand,
With the grave's dust shaken from them
Shall the risen myriads stand.
There they'll be in countless numbers
From the mighty centuries past
Though their dust a thousand summers

May have winnowed to the blast:
They shall rise from arid deserts,
From the everglades and woods,
From prairies vast and lonely
And from mountain solitudes:
There will be no sea so fathomless,
Nor wide nor tempest toss'd
But shall cease its restless roaring
And give up the loved and lost.

Meetings, aye, I know there will be,
Though mayhap you have lain alone
In the potter's field a stranger,
You will stand amid your own;
How within his arms a daughter
Shall a yearning father press,
How a mother in her rapture
Will a tender child caress.
It may be the blue-eyed darling
Who was lost and never found,
It may be the little truant
Who went swimming and was drowned;
And of mine, a precious idol
Who, when taken, broke my heart,
Yet I know that I shall meet her
Though a thousand miles apart;
It must just be as I left her
In her old-time childish grace,
Ere the heavenly radiance touch her
I must look into her face:
Yes, it must just be as we left them —

Ere the death-damp on them lay —
For the grave's sweet Balm of Gilead
Shall have healed their hurts away:
Yes, it must be that we shall greet them —
As of yore in love again —
Elsewise, heav'n would not be heaven
And the hopes of earth be vain:
That the old love in its fondness
Still will linger, is not strange;
It may be the new is stronger,
But the old will never change,
Till transfigured with the dawning
Of the new, we shall arise
To the home of many mansions
In the mount of Paradise.

THE MAYFLOWER — DEC. 11, 1620
GL MAY 1891

I see her on yon boundless world —
Gray-winged and tempest tossed,
The foam-plumed breakers beating in
And thund'ring on the coast;
The Indian yells, the eagle screams
And breaks the wild repose,
A light is on the wilderness,
'Twill blossom like a rose!

A hardy handful land ashore —

A hundred, age and youth —
A band of Christian Alchemists
To test the gold of truth; —

The vanguard of a mighty host
The coming years should bring,
Who should kneel before no master
Save to God, their sovereign King!

MY TWO WHITE DOVES
GL May 1891

Somewhere between the great extremes
Of mortal life, to-day I stand,
And muse and wonder — as in dreams —
A white dove clinging to my hand, —

A wee white dove with azure eyes,
Yet still, I wonder through my tears,
How far it is to Paradise, —
I know the past is forty years.

For lo, in Paradise have I
Another dainty dove like this,
Who some day in the by-and-by
Will greet me with a seraph's kiss.

How far the great Beyond may be,
I know not, there's no hint nor sign;

Will I first 'tempt it, or will she,
This wee white, nestling dove of mine?

If first for me the still, small voice
Of death should call, I'll humbly go;
Between my doves I make no choice
For Oh, my God, I love them so!

But fleet the years that roll on earth,
A little while and she will come,
And she who gave my white doves birth,
Till all the loved are safe at home.

FOR THE BACK OF A PHOTOGRAPH
GL May 1891

The brush may err but not the art
That paints with sunbeams; here you trace
The very thoughts upon your face,
So clearly cut in every part
And well defined in every grace
The subtlest feature, unconcealed,
Your living presence stands revealed.

A PSALM OF TRUST
GL May 1891

Be near me when I die and lean,
Your head above my bosom low,
Remembering dear, the long ago
And all the golden years between.

For arm and arm through cloud and sun,
As lovers long, we hither came, —
In life and death we are the same,
And humbly pray His will be done.

For well we know his mercies are
As sweet and all-abundant now,
As when at first we made the vow
To trust Him truly, near or far.

Nor would we change our destiny,
Nay, even though we had the power:
Our parting will be scarce an hour
Compared with all the years to be —

But scarce an hour, then why forlorn,
'Twill be as though my way I took
At night across a silent brook,
And you came over in the morn.

MYRRH AND FRANKINCENSE — DEC. 25
GL MAY 1891

There's morn in the land when, from lake unto lake,
And from ocean to ocean, the people awake
To the pealing of bells, and the hills all ashake
From the shots of great cannon: 'Tis Columbia's voice
To come forth and lift banners, beat drums and rejoice
In a heritage dear to the sons of the free.

And again, there's a day when, on suppliant knee
Bowing low, we give thanks, and arising, outpour
Sweet hymns and grand anthems for a bountiful store
Of the cluster and sheaf, for the herds on the plain,
For the dews and the balms, and the sun and the rain.

But the day when all peoples in all of earth's climes
In glad exultation sing psalms and ring chimes,
Wreathe their homes in green holly, give gifts and make mirth,
Is the glorified one of our Lord's lowly birth,—

The day that brought peace and good will unto earth, —
Brought peace and glad tidings song-winged, and a light
To relume the deep darkness of Error's long night, —
Brought healings for anguish, and a balm for all woes,
From a fountain so brimm'd with sweet love it o'erflows
In a hundred full streams.

Oh, then let us pray,
Giving thanks, let us sing, let us dance, blessed day!
Let us meet and clasp hands and rejoice that we live,
And if aught have estranged us, forget and forgive,
And our gifts, let them come from the heart's proffered store;
Let us go through the land and unlatch every door
To the huts and the hovels where dull squalor pines,
And where Want never laughs and the sun never shines;
Let us climb to lone attics, go down to low dives
And the dark slums of death in the tenement hives,
So dark that one needs light his way through the halls,
There is slime on the floors and mildew on the walls;
There are women so haggard and with faces so gray
One fears to gaze on them, and in pain turns away.
There are mothers with infants that hang uncaressed
Like limp and forgotten wet rags on the breast;
An e'en the half-grown are so shrunk and so lean,
And with hands so like claws, they look old and unclean!

But enough, they are legion — these hungry and gaunt
Hapless wretches in tatters — these children of want
And of vice and distress — 'tis enough, let us go
And relight with our smiles their dark hour, and bestow
The white loaf and rich cluster, place beneath the sick head,
With a touch, the soft pillow, and ease the straw bed;
Stir aglow the dead embers, bar out the sharp cold,
And enwrap the frail forms of the helpless and old, —
If for e'en but a day, that they may not forget
There are hearts that still beat with warm charity yet, —

Just to ease but one moment the chastening rod,
Just a taste of the sweets of the goodness of God.

O, thus it is well we're akin unto all,
And alert to respond to distress at her call;
And well we are touched with the grace that is kind,
For there so many lame and there so many blind,
There are so many waifs, little-bodied and thin,
Standing out in the cold, looking wistfully in;
Aye, so many wee forms that are naked and chilled,
So many wee stockings that are hung and unfilled:
There are so many wives waiting late in dull homes
For a step that is weak and outworn when it comes:
And there so many friendless and lone in the land
Who but want a kind word or the clasp of a hand.

O, it's easy to bind the bruis'd reed, and to bow,
Pressing soft the cool palm on the pain-smitten brow;
And it costs but a farthing to pause and to feed
The poor, little, starved mouths that are gaping in need;
And still less to take hold an unsteady man's arm —
Though mayhap he's been drinking, 'twill do you no harm,
So it's easy to help, and withal, we are told
That the blessings, rained down in reward, are ten-fold;
And thus it is well we are touched with a chord
Of the love reaching forth from the heart of our Lord.

A June Morning
GL May 1891

Aye, sing I must, ecstatic June,
Such morns the charms of Eden bring,
Untouched the bells of rapture swing
And all my being breaks in tune.

As well restrain the roundelay
Of yonder golden-throated thrush,
Keep still the wren, or seek to hush
The hymning waters on their way.

I know the world is tired of rhyme,
But melody is ever new
When heard amid the plashing dew —
The subtle scent of mountain thyme.

Ah me, I fear a breeze may blow,
Or cloud may cast a passing screen;
O winsome morn of bloom and green,
I would that thou might never go.

Before the Rain
GL May 1891

When yestermorn upon my early route
To fetch the cows — far up the hollows found,
I knew 'twould rain; a myriad frogs were out

And all the marsh a sheet of crackling sound.

The sky was naught but one blank waste of gray,
The rank skunk-cabbage clumps were dull'd to blurs,
And on the knolls, a furlong's length away,
A gorge of gloom arose the silent firs.

Dim lines of moisture all the night had crept
Out-wid'ning from the edgings of low sloughs,*
And wheresoe'er a passing hoof had stept
There lay a seeping puddle of dark ooze.

The clumsy cows grazed lagging as they went,
The bell, trailed muffled, struck a dull refrain,
And ere we knew, the misty world was blent
In one dark lowering raiment of gray rain.

* I give this word the western pronunciation.

A Sultry Night
GL May 1891

He night swooned in a sultry lull,
And as we drowsed around the doors,
We heard away across the moors,
A lonesome dog bark faint and dull.

Then all was dumb: bats swirled about,
Glimpsed through the dusk; mosquitoes bit—

The smudge of chips against them lit
Flamed wanly once and nickered out.

Above the aspen tops entwirled
The vapory moon hung half concealed;
The flame-lit cloud at times revealed
The darker borders of the world.

Retiring then we slept till morn —
It thundered deep — the curtain stirred,
The big drops fell, and then we heard
The deluge breaking on the corn.

A Winter Morning Still Life
GL May 1891

[Irvine included several stanzas here in "The Resurrection Morning." — Ed.]

You have seen a winter morning,
The horizon dull and low,
When the earth and all belonging
Lay a level waste of snow.
In the drear and empty distance
There was naught of all we knew,
Save the gaunt and naked poplars
To arrest the wand'ring view.
It was as a stretch of desert
With no sign of life thereon —

The familiar hills and hollows
And the fields and fences gone;
Every road and lane and by-way,
Far and near were blotted out,
Hushed the sound of bells and silent
Were the huntsman's gun and shout;
E'en the axes of the choppers
Were unheard amid the wood,
And in drifts the horse of iron,
With his train imprisoned stood.
Save but once across the heavens,
When there flew a single crow,
Not a motion broke the blankness
Of the muffled world of snow.

An April Morning
GL May 1891

[Irvine included several stanzas here in "The Resurrection Morning." — Ed.]

I have seen an April morning
When the ling'ring winds were lain,
And the day arose triumphant
From a sun-lit gush of rain!

When the uplands and the lowlands,
And the woodlands far and wide,
From the bonds of icy fetters

Were unloosed and glorified.

Wheresoe'er the eye would wander
There was naught but what was fair;
There was scent of balm and balsam
In the clear, refreshing air.

There were rivulets of silver
In the valleys; there were gleams
Through the soft empurpled distance
From the dash of mountain streams.

I could hear the new wine beading
In the saplings, and I knew
There was jubilee in elf-land,
From the horns the fairies blew.

Every germ with life was quick'ning
Into green above the mold,
Every bud a leaf and blossom
Was beginning to unfold.

There was promise in the furrow,
In the hatching of the brood,
In the heifer growing clumsy
From approaching motherhood.

E'en the old were feeling younger
With a brighter hope in view,
As the happy-hearted robin
Sang the song forever new.

Just as when it broke in concert
With the brooklet as it purled
Through the dewy blooms of Eden
On the morning of the world.

An August Afternoon On the Farm
GL May 1891

In stifling mows the men became oppressed,
And hastened forth hard breathing and o'rcome;
The hatching hen stood panting in her nest,
The sick earth swooned in languor and was dumb.

The dust-dull'd crickets lay in heedless ease
Of trampling hoofs along the beaten drives,
And from the fields the home-returning bees,
Limp wing'd and tired, lit short before their hives.

The drooping dog moped aimlessly around;
Lop'd down, got up, snapt at the gnats; in pits
Knee deep, the tethered horses stamped the ground,
And switched at bot-flies dabbing yellow nits.

With heads held prone the sheep in huddles stood
Through fear of gads — the lambs, too, ceased to romp;
The cows were wise to seek the covert wood,
Or belly deep stand hidden in the swamp.

So dragged the day, but when the dusk grew deep

The stagnant heat increased; we lit no light,
But sat out-doors, too faint and sick for sleep;
Such was the stupor of that August night.

BEFORE HARVEST
GL May 1891

On my good steed, at early morn,
Along the green-walled lanes I ride,
The land is dark on either side
With fields of deep, abundant corn.

From end to end the plowman wades
Breast high between the mile-long rows,
As through the sea, behind him flows
A flashing wake of two-edged blades.

And still beyond the darker range
A fairer sight mine eyes behold,
From lighter green to glimpsing gold,
The heaving wheat begins to change.

And farther on, where lands are low,
The timothy is all amist
Of airy bloom in amethyst;
The amplest mows will overflow.

NOVEMBER — QUATRAINS
GL MAY 1891

[Parts I and V comprise the entirety of Irvine's poem "The Evening of the Year." — Ed.]

I
The longer days no more appear,
The shorter fly on quicker wings,
Night cometh, and the poet sings,
It is the evening of the year.

Sings of the sundown, with a sigh
Of pity for the tender call
Of yonder quail — the last of all
The scattered covey left to cry.

Sings, as abroad the waning light,
The shadows into darkness creep,
As from the uplands troop the sheep
To safer folds against the night.

Sings, as the cows come lowing near,
The sweet bell tinkling down the path
The frost has nipped the aftermath,
It is the evening of the year.

II
November is not all a shrew,
She hath her noons of mellow airs,
Her limpid mornings; and she wears

Of all the months the deepest blue.

So calmly deep, a leaflet caught
Hangs dead, but loosened round and round,
Floats slowly eddying to the ground,
As noiseless as unspoken thought.

The halos, too, belong to her
Of glittering sunsets, clear and keen;
The fields aflowing far between
With film of silvery gossamer.

The gold-touch'd purpling hills, the hush,
The hazel thicket and the glow
Of scarlet sumac, deep'ning so,
I think me of the burning bush!

III
The farmers haul their grain to town
In jolting wagons — driving slow
They talk of prices — say they're low,
When every tree has shaken down

Its mellow fruit in sixty fold,
And every acre of their fields
Where sickles clicked, have proffered yields
The thrashing engines beat to gold.

Yet, still they talk, as loads appear
So great, their teams can hardly pull;
To-day I counted, plump and full,

A thousand kernels to the ear!

A thousand kernels! why not lift
A song of trust and triumph then,
Hast thou not reap'd — my fellow-men,
As thou hast sown — in peace and thrift?

IV
The season hath her churlish moods,
But yesterday the air was bland,
A hazy languor wrapt the land,
A purple raiment veiled the woods.

But in the night an eastern gale,
With freezing rain, arose and beat
The roofs and window panes with sleet,
Till all the world was clad in mail.—

So glassylike, at morn I found
If one but touch'd a twig, its case
Of ice fell shelling, like a vase
Of fragile crystal, to the ground.

There came a snapping from the stalks
Where cattle fed; if there but hopped
A blue-jay in the pines, there dropped
A shower of needles to the walks.

V
The fields are naked, and the wood
The burthen of the leaf has cast;

The low-hung sky is but a vast
Expanse of bleak infinitude.

The trail of smoke the engine made,
Hard panting past, an hour ago,
Unbroken still and hanging low
Along the length of heavy grade; —

The dullness brooding as a pall,
Alike at morning and at noon,
The wan-like rim that girts the moon
From night to night, betoken fall.

There'll be a snow, the farmer says;
Uptaking reins, and pulling down
His muffled cap, drives out of town
Fast homeward by the nearest ways.

VI
The dark, wet earth begins to freeze,
That now the fog so long adrip
From every eave and pendant tip,
Is clearing in the nipping breeze.

The roads are gripped, as in a vise,
The hoof-prints lipping to the brim,
Like swollen pools, from rim to rim,
Are shot with javelins of ice; —

That closing fast will prove to be
Deceptive pits that split and break,

At every step the horses take,
Up-spurting mire unto the knee.

The load at best is hard to pull,
Say naught when lab'ring up the steep
The clogged wheels drag half-axle deep!
Nay, spare the lash, be merciful.

Untitled
GL May 1891

[These stanzas appear without a title at the beginning of the War Echoes section in Irvine's book. — Ed.]

Though o'er them rolls the restless main,
And lichens lace their tombs in green,
And though we call the roll in vain
Across the years that crowd between,

Immortal memory, strong and true,
Will keep their deeds, and as the sun
In golden lustre lights the blue,
So shine will they till earth is done.

THE DRUMS
GL MAY 1891

O with pomp of plumes and banners,
Ye may blow your cornets sweet,
But the airs that moved a nation
Were the tunes the drummers beat.

You remember how they thrilled us,
As we heard in other years,
When Rebellion smote the Union,
And she called her volunteers?

How "The Gates of Edinboro,"
For the feet a rhythm played,
And "The Girl I Left Behind Me"
In the heart a swelling made?

How the smith with lifted hammer
Heard a moment, caught the time
Struck his anvil into chorus,
As a ringer rings a chime?

How the mower paused and pondered —
He so young and leal and lithe —
As he tapped a martial ditty,
With his whetstone on the scythe?

And the mason scarce had caught them,
From the keystone on the arch,
Ere he dropped his line and plummet,

And took up his line of march.

Not a loyal ear but hearkened,
Not a soul afraid to dare;
There were pale lads from the counters,
Brave hearts from everywhere.

There were choppers from the timber,
Leaving half unhewn the sill;
There were plowmen from the furrow,
There were grinders from the mill.

There were fathers, poor and needy,
Brought the help of their old age;
There were sweethearts bade their lovers
Write their names on glory's page.

And among them all a widow
With her eldest and her stay,
How she kissed him as she bless'd him;
And with wet eyes went her way?

Till at length the full battalions
Stood aligned in shining blue,
When the "forward march" was spoken
And the fifes struck up anew

With "The Girl I Left Behind Me" —
And as when the tempest comes —
With rattling hail and thunder-booms
In broke the doubling drums.

Every footfall caught the rhythm,
Every heart in valor beat,
As the column swept unbroken
Like a flood-tide through the street, —

Swept unbroken and beyond us,
With the drums still throbbing far,
For the harvest must be gathered
In the scarlet fields of war.

The Halt
GL May 1891; HP Jan. 1892

The day was lost, and we were sent
In haste to guard the baggage train,
And all the night through gloom and rain
Across a land of ruin went.

But halting once, and only then
We turned aside to let the corps
Of ambulances pass before,
That hauled a thousand wounded men!

And leaning, drowsy and oppressed,
Upon my gun I wondered where
The comrade was I helped to bear,
Slow rearward, wounded in the breast.

When lo! I heard a fainting cry —

As wheels drew near and stopped aside:
"The man in here with me has died,
Oh, lift him out, or I shall die!"

"All right," the one-armed driver said,
"The horse can hardly pull the load,
We leave them all along the road,
It does no good to haul the dead!"

And so we turned by lantern light
And laid him in a gloom of pines,
When came an order down the lines,
"Push on, and halt no more to-night!"

FRANKLIN, TENN. — NOVEMBER 30, 1864
GL May 1891

[Irvine read a version of this poem aloud in Monmouth at the Military Tract Reunion for soldiers and sailors on Sept. 25, 1890. — Ed.]

Hard pressed, we fell back upon Franklin, called a halt
And broke ground in hot haste, to withstand the assault
That we knew would be swift as a whirlwind, and fought
Without quarter.

Howe'er, we were vet'rans, and wrought
As for life; fences were leveled, bridges seized, aids
Sent with sharp orders, trains hurried forward,

brigades
Double-quick'd to the trenches where batteries were set
With the guns loaded plumb to the muzzles, and yet,
Not a moment too soon!

For the foe had been massed
And were dark'ning the hills, and although we had passed
Through a hundred encounters, a hush as profound
As the silence of death brooded ominously 'round,
As we stood in amaze and beheld the dark sweep
Of battalions, interleagued to battalions — six deep —
Aye, the whole rebel army, pouring forth from the wood,
Forty thousand, in battle array under Hood,
Forty thousand, a gray and grim steel-fronted host
Sweeping forward, as dark waters sweep to the coast
Ere dashed into breakers, until they, with a shout,
Like the noise of the sea in its fury, broke out
And leaped forward!
And yet, there we stood helpless, nor dared fire a shot:
Two brigades by a blunder misplaced had been caught
Right between the two fronts, nor were cleared from the way
Till hundreds fell captive, and the onsetting fray
Struck the works by the pike and poured through, when Opdycke
Caught a glance of the route, and flashing his blade
From the scabbard, called out to as game a brigade
As ever faced bullets, "Up and at them, my men!"
When the lightnings leaped forth, and it thundered, and then

To the bayonets bent, right forward we broke
Through the hail-whistling flame of their volleys and smoke,
Till we met with a clash in a hand-to-hand fight,
Beat them back foot by foot, through the breach, yet in spite
Of the might of our valor, and the roar and the rack
Of that tempest of death, they wheeled round in their track —
All afire from our cannon, — and again and again
Re-enforced with dark masses of oncoming men
Stormed the line of our works.
Why repeat? You have read of the deeds of that day
In the records of valor; how we held them at bay,
As the sea-walls the breakers; of how they were led
Till the sweeps of their charges were strewn with the dead;
Of the fronting platoons that were mown from their feet,
Of the gaps that were filled with no thought of retreat
Until corps after corps were bereft of the pride
Of their heroes: of how they were shot from astride
The embankments, cut down in the breach, in their raids
On the colors, 'round the guns, till their scattered brigades
Could be rallied no longer, and stricken and sore,
With their captains unhorsed and their swiftest no more,
Their banners in tatters, their standards in two,
Aye, whipped but not conquered, at last they withdrew,

And the slain of the Gray and the slain of the Blue,
Were as one as they lay under night's heavy pall
With the flag of the Union afloat over all.

A Golden Wedding
GL May 1891

Tonight we turn and feign would call
To mind the smiles and tears
That flecked with dappled light and shade
A life of fifty years —
A wedded life of willing hands
That drudged from sun to sun,
And each succeeding morn anew
Took up the work undone.

'Twas plow and plant and gather in,
Again to plow and sow;
The threaded shuttle through the loom
Went ever to and fro;
It was a constant treadmill tramp —
Around and still around;
And though the mill forever went,
The grist was never ground.

But this were well, for, as the times
And seasons kept their speed,
Came restless little feet to shoe,
And little mouths to feed —

Mouths craving bread, and busy hands
In every mischief thrust;
They made the usual pies of mud
And pattered in the dust.

To fall and stub the bootless toes
Was ever boyhood's fate,
And fingers just as sure were pinched
While swinging on the gate;
The smoothly polished cellar-door
Was proof beyond a doubt
Of how the pants were worn in holes
Below the roundabout.

Yet there was mother, deft and quick
To knit and darn and mend;
She soothed the ache and bound the bruise —
Her love was without end.
With constant care her faithful eye
Was never turned away
From watching o'er the truant feet
So prone to run astray.

The first one born was little Jim —
A most precious chick;
The classic precinct of his birth
Was down on "Shaver's Crick."
At times across his back and legs —
To cure the itch of sin —
Was lain the rod's corrective salt —
They must have rubbed it in!

But as he grew he often caught
A glimpse of sunny gleams,
And heard the pulsing silver sounds
Within the land of dreams;
And in the night, when all was still,
Lay musing late and long,
Until he caught the magic spell
And wove them into song.

The next on deck was wayward Bob,
The drollest of the crew.
How often! oh, how often
Has he pinched us black and blue!
He went in manhood to the war,
And fought as he had pinched,
And when a bullet pierced his thigh
He swore but never flinched.

And then poor John in order came,
Kindhearted, dashing, free;
I never knew of one so full
Of sanguine hope as he —
A hope that turned aside and smiled
At grim misfortune's frown,
Until, alas! in dark eclipse
His noon-day sun went down.

And there was David, who, when grown,
In manly beauty stood —
A type of rounded strength, as stands
A young oak in the wood.

His heart was glad, and when the drums
Were beating far and wide,
He marched — a soldier — to the front
And, fighting, fell and died.

The next was Edwin, who from birth
Walked in his Maker's ways,
And kept in simple, faithful trust
His precepts all his days;
And when at length a dread disease
Its fatal course began,
He met it — dying as he lived —
At peace with God and man.

Then Bell in turn — a laughing lass —
One summer's day was born
The light that lit her nature seemed
A reflex of the morn.
Consumption! dread destroyer!
Thou hast claimed her for thine own.
White souls there are; a whiter one
Than hers I've never known.

Then on one snowy New Year's eve
In came a gift from heaven;
'Twas little, brown-eyed Sara-Jane,
The best of all the seven.
A faithful daughter she has been,
A sister true and sweet;
Her feet were swift to run, her heart
In loyal kindness beat.

In mother's stead she sewed and baked,
And scoured and cleansed the cup;
In sickness bathed the fevered brow
The faint head lifted up.
And still she's here to-night to share
The burthens yet unborne —
The strength and stay of these old forms
So weary and outworn.

So weary with the dizzy whirl
The turmoil and the strife,
The aches, the longings and the cares
Of this uneasy life;
So weary trudging up the hill,
So weary plodding down,
So broken underneath the cross.
So anxious for the crown.

Ah, well! we know the crown's in store;
The rugged path you trod.
And, oh! it must be beautiful —
The city of our God.
Has life not sweets to lure you still?
The loved ones power to bless?
Long as we may for heavenly halls,
We love not earth the less.

Oh, then, dear heaven! hold not thy charms,
And let the sun benign
In Indian summer loveliness
Upon them softly shine;

Stay winter's coming, and when come
Keep back the fall of snow.
We'll love and bless them while they stay,
And bless them when they go.

An Easy Chair, For Dr. A. W. Armstrong
GL May 1891

Doctor take this easy chair;
Soft its cushion as a fleece;
For an hour forget thy care,
For an hour thy labor cease.
Let the sun of heaven shine
Still in love on thee and thine,
Staying long his going down,
Is the fond and fervent prayer
Of every heart that beats in town.

Thou art worthy, and hast been
To thy stricken fellow-men
Faithful all thy lengthened years —
Faithful to them in their tears
And unto the bed of pain
Thou wert never called in vain;
Never was the day too warm,
Nor the night too dark with rain,
Nor too wild the winter's storm,
Nor too deep the drifted snow,
But that thou didst willing go;

Never patient yet so poor
But was welcome at thy door.

Often have you been the stay
Of our dear ones as they lay
Struggling in the mortal throes —
Which alone a mother knows —
In the trying hour of birth;
Heard the first awak'ning cry
Of our children, new to earth.
You have seen them bright of eye,
Seen them at their nimble play,
Seen them grow and go their way,
Seen them fade and droop and die;
Cheered us all when faint and low;
Laid your hand on wrist and brow;
Timed the life-tide's ebb and flow,
Cooled the fever of the brain
With draughts of healing, as the rain,
Show'ring, woos the arid plain
Back to living green again.

Eighty years are thine, and, though
White thy head is as the snow,
And the days since first we met
Lengthened to the long ago,
Thou art true to duty yet,
Just as if you were not old; —
True to Him who guides the way
And shall call thee to the fold
Ere long when thy work is done

Peaceful at the set of sun.

Howsoe'er, sit down and rest;
Soft the chair is as a fleece;
Set thee down and rest in peace.
Golden is the languid west;
Indian summer round thee shine,
Health and wealth to thee and thine.
Sit thee down and rest in ease;
Let thy dreams be dreams of bliss;
Little children climb thy knees,
Archly giving kiss for kiss.
Doctor, thou art truly blessed!
Take the chair, sit down and rest.

JO LEEPER
GL MAY 1891

Forty years ago, or nigh,
Barefoot boys were Jo and I.
I a child and he a child,
Here, when all the grove was wild;
Played together every day —
In the straw rick, in the hay;
Hunted birds' eggs, went to school,
And a-swimming in the cool,
Deep, delicious willow pool,
Now dried up, with just the stumps
To show where grew the willow clumps.

There's change! The creek sinks in its bed;
I am tired and Jo is dead.
He so lithe and fleet and strong,
Built, we thought, for living long.
Better boy was never known,
Nor a better man when grown;
Kindly-hearted, boy-like still,
Thought no evil, spake no ill,
Peaceable — he knew no strife,
Even-tempered all his life.
Loved to romp and laugh and joke,
Uncomplaining took the yoke
When others fainted. Noble heart!
Well he filled a brother's part.
Lay him gently down to rest;
He deserves it; God knows best.

FROM THE ALBUM OF MISS INA ALLEN
GL MAY 1891

My friend! your life is in the May,
The wine of spring is in your veins;
And like this virgin page, I pray,
It e'er may be as free from stains.

Ah, me! but May is fleet of wing;
She is too sweet to go so soon, —
We hardly hear the robins sing
Before she hies away to June.

Though June is dear, we sigh withal
Amid her lavish sweets to know
That summer nimbly seeks the fall;
Then comes the winter with its snow.

Still, when the winter of your years
Shall come, 'twill sweeter be than spring;
'Tis peaceful age alone that hears
From earth the bells of heaven ring.

FROM THE ALBUM OF MISS LIBBIE HAMSHIRE
GL MAY 1891

My dear young friend! your life is sweet,
Your virtue spotless as the snow;
Your hands are deft, and swift your feet;
I wish that God would keep you so.

Howe'er, we may not bind the years,
Nor from our course the shadows bar,
But Age forgets his pains and tears
When hope becomes the guiding star.

And as it shown in times of old,
And led the shepherds glad and wise,
For you it streams a rain of gold
Across the hills of Paradise.

And — trust me, friend — I wish that you

With willing feet may hither tend,
And keep as they the star in view
Till Jesus meets you at the end.

JOSIE
GL May 1891

Ah, Josie! We're weary with sighing
O'er the thought that you'll come nevermore,
But rejoice that the sweetness of dying
Was a balm for the suff'ring you bore.
For we knew by the saintly behavior,
When approaching the dark river's strand,
And in the light in your face, that the Saviour
Was holding your poor little hand.

It is rapture to know you're together,
That you'll never grow weary again
In the airs of that beautiful weather
That woo away sickness and pain.
Yet, withal, it is human to weep you,
And to see you, oh, what would we give!
But, my dear little girl, we will keep you
In memory as long as we live.

Tossings
GL May 1891

Not a wink all night. Toss? I should say so!
Turned fifty times, more or less; counted sheep —
A great flock disappearing, leap by leap,
Over a fence into dreamland; watch'd th' flow
Of dim waters; thought myself in a show
Riding the merry-go-round with a sweep
And swirl that made me dizzy; still no sleep.
Then I fell to thinking whether or no
There were crumbs in the bed, laughed, blamed the seams
In the sheets; got up and turned them, unfast
The blinds; again lay down, longing for dreams
And sweet slumber that came not. till at last,
Just as across the hills the daybreak crept
And the redbreasts sang of morning, I slept.

Rhymes of the Farm
AD Aug. 21, 1891

Read at the Old Settlers Picnic

No wonder one grows old so fast,
The hours unreckoned run;
A day flies like a shuttle thrown
Across from sun to sun.
Unceasingly the seasons glide

Within their courses ranged;
The world keeps spinning round and round.
And we alone are changed.

Aye, changed, though scarce because of years
That swiftly come and go;
The white flecks sprinkled in our beards
Are not all winter's snow;
'Tis not the weight of time alone
That leaves us bent and lame,
But burthens early borne beyond
The strength of mortal frame.

God help the shoulders that grow round
From toil because of need,
But not the back that bends beneath
A load of selfish greed;
God wipe the sweat from honest brows
That faint before the noon;
God pity us, it is not strange
We all grow old so soon.

The slow, dull drag behind the plow,
From twilight in the morn,
Till evening falls and darkens out
The long rows of the corn;
The broiling sun of harvest fields,
The stifling heat of mows,
The endless chores about the barns,
The drudge of milking cows —

Especially when days are bad,
And "Brindle" sends her tail
Kerslap across a fellow's face,
And over-kicks the pail!
It's pleasant too, to race a hog
Around and 'round a lot
Some twenty times right past the hole
Wherein the critter got!

To have a calf you're weaning ram
Its head — in wanton sport —
Into the milk above the eyes,
And then to give a snort!
To set a hen on fancy eggs
That cost a fancy price,
And have them hatch only to die
From cholera and lice!

To bet your money on a colt
You've trained to trot, to find
Him breaking down the homeward stretch
A half a mile behind;
To pet a lamb and have it butt
Your breath out when it grows;
To proffer seed of good intent
And reap a crop of woes.

All tend to shorten and to pull
The pucker-string of time,
And set the wrinkles round the eyes
Before a body's prime.

Work, work from early morn to night
Or weeds will surely grow,
There is no use to drop the seed
Unless you use the hoe.

The farm is not a playing ground,
The soil will only yield
The sheaf and cluster to the hand
That tills aright the field.
And though the plow-share never rusts
The furrows have no end,
Ere long the brow will cease to sweat
The back will cease to bend.

As after toil comes recompense,
And bliss comes after pain,
It is the darkest cloud that pours
The fullest founts of rain.
'Tis but the story as of old,
Work, only trusting Him,
Hold out the empty cup and God
Will fill it to the brim.

So with the years come younger hands
To lift the burthen down;
And give the dear old folks a rest
By moving them to town,
Where every week they visit them
With cheer and kindly words,
And baskets filled with goodly things,
The best the farm affords.

Beneath the maples tilted back,
Adrowse in easy chairs —
Their silver-threaded temples fanned
With soft autumnal airs —
They turn in fondness to the past —
Forgetful of its ills —
The distance seems not half so long
Nor half so rough the hills.

For lo, the great green goodly land
Of yore comes into view;
Again the distant groves are robed
Like isles in purple hue;
Once more the grand old prairies sweep,
And roll, and flash and change,
As rolls a sapphire sea, till lost
Beyond the boundless range.

Once more the cattle graze at will,
The deer in tandem run;
The uncovered quail in coveys flock
Unscared of net or gun;
And as in morns of early spring,
When dews the grasses pearled,
Again the prairie chickens belt
With mellow beams the world.

Earth held no land so beautiful,
No clime so sweet with song;
No wonder memory backward strays
And loves to cling so long.

And yet one forward glance in faith,
One look with steadfast eyes
And lo, amid the purple hills
The vale of Beulah lies:

A land that joins just this side heaven,
Of one perpetual spring,
And, aye, so near the golden gates
You hear the angels sing;
A land wherein your hurts are healed
Of earth that so oppressed —
A claim of everlasting love
And everlasting rest.

INDEX

Items marked * appear with additional context and historical information in *Beyond the Gray Leaf: The Life and Poems of J.P. Irvine*.

Items marked + were published with an inverted pyramid symbol and not Irvine's name. See the note on page 18.

POEMS

36th Ill. Volunteers	75
A Hymn	171
A Kiss	200
Address to Religion	9
April Morning	374
Arlington / Death's Encampment	166
At the Golden Gates She'll Meet Us	148
* At the Pasture Bars	265
* August Afternoon On the Farm	376
Beau Hickman	219

Beautiful Land of Beulah	83
Before Harvest	377
Before the Rain	371
* Bells of Kirkwood / "Peace, Be Still"	242
Bob White	45
Boys in Blue	139
* Brace of Canary Birds	231
Burial in the Snowstorm	42
Concerning Washington and His Monument	243
David	92
Death's Encampment / Arlington	166
Defunctus Niger	161
Doorstep Society	176
* Drums	383
Easy Chair, For Dr. A. W. Armstrong	394
Evening of the Year	349
* Farmer	33
Fever	356
Fond Heart's Benediction	306
* For the Back of a Photograph	366
Fort Donelson	43
* Franklin, Tenn.	386
Freedom's Excelsior	36
* From The Album of Miss Ina Allen	397
From The Album of Miss Libbie Hamshire	398
* Golden Wedding	389
Grandpa in the Cottage of Death	39
* Halt	385
Heaven	30
How are the Mighty Fallen	94
Hymn for the Battle Year	48

Hymn of Thanksgiving	190
* Ichabod	230
In Memoriam	130
* Indian Summer	250
Ink Droppings	77
Jemima Jackson	188
* Jo Leeper	396
Johanus Leonidus Murpheus, Esq.	141
Josie	399
Judgment Morning	361
June Morning	371
* Lightning Express	346
Loss of the Lady Elgin	38
+ Maniac's Grave	18
* May Thirtieth	282
Mayflower	364
Mother-in-Law	198
Mustered Out	260
My Angel Visitant	169
+ My Homestead	13
* My Little Girl Under the Snow	150
My Soul and I	88
My Two White Doves	365
Myrrh and Frankincense	368
* New Year	99
New Year's Dawn	158
November Quatrains	378
+ Office Calendar	23
Old Umbrella Man	227
Old Year and The New	62
One Hundred Thousand Slain	78

Organic Remains	159
* Our Dead Caesars	90
Our Pilot	81
Pair of Dainty Gaiters	178
* "Peace, Be Still" / The Bells of Kirkwood	242
Planting Corn	84
Plow, the Anvil, and Loom	16
Powers that Be	53
Prelude	351
Psalm of Trust	367
Razor Grinder	220
Resignation	146
* Rest	359
Resurrection Morning	272
* Rhymes of the Farm	400
Shining One	354
* Slave's Lamentation	27
Smith Sanderson	236
Something Rotten In Denmark	164
Song of Thanksgiving	235
Storm of Ellison	14
Sultry Night	372
* Summer Drought	270
Thanksgiving	360
Thine and Mine	233
Three Cities	55
Tossings	400
Tulkinghorn's Offense	222
Twelve Hundred A Year	205
Twilight	11
Two Kids	357

* Two Taverns	104
* Two Towns	251
* Unknown	208
Untitled	382
Washington Monument	201
Window-Pane Tinker	225
Winter	10
* Winter Morning Still Life	373
* Wooden Leg	172
Ye Umbrella Mann	196

LETTERS AND ESSAYS

Atlantic Monthly	96
Change Baggage	212
Dime Novel	254
Farewell	155
"Free-Lunch" Clerk	191
Going West I	106
Going West II	110
Going West III	115
Going West IV	120
Going West V	124
Going West VI	128
Jewel in the Casket	144
Moses W. Allen	266
Niagara Falls	68
Reunion Address	330
+ Special from Kirkwood	288
To The Author of "Life in Death"	179

Voice from Kirkwood: Drought	308
Voice from Kirkwood: Hangings	302
Voice from Kirkwood: Humbuggery	285
Voice from Kirkwood: Illinois Tax Law I	312
Voice from Kirkwood: Illinois Tax Law II	317
Voice from Kirkwood: Illinois Tax Law III	322
Voice from Kirkwood: Illinois Tax Law IV	326
Voice from Kirkwood: Patent Medicine	290
Voice from Kirkwood: Quack Doctors I	293
Voice from Kirkwood: Quack Doctors II	296
Voice from Kirkwood: Quack Doctors III	299

GOODIES

ABOUT THE TITLE
J.P. Irvine published most of his poetry and essays in newspapers. In the mid 1800s, *The Monmouth Atlas* posted a feature in its weekly issues called The Poet's Corner, predictably located in one of the upper corners of the sheet. The tagline for the section: "Poetry moves the pen, the cannon and the plow."

COLOPHON
This book uses Alegreya, a family of fonts designed by Juan Pablo del Peral.

FIVE THINGS THAT HELPED FINISH THIS BOOK
podcasts: *99% Invisible, The Allusionist, Radiolab*
free admission into the Figge Art Museum
outdoor wi-fi
November Project Summit 4.0
from-scratch pie dough

ABOUT THE AUTHOR

Dustin Renwick fills his life with writing and competing in any sports events he can find. Usually, this choice involves running, but options like pickleball and the occasional limbo contest have made the list. His work has appeared in publications such as *The Washington Post* and *USA Triathlon*. Plus, *National Geographic* once selected his photo as an editor's pick. Check out more of his work at www.dustinrenwick.com.

Twitter: @drenwick110

Instagram: @swimbikerungram

www.ingramcontent.com/pod-product-compliance
Lightning Source LLC
LaVergne TN
LVHW041537070426
835507LV00011B/810